Principles of Database Management

Principles of Database Management

Gabrielle Reid

MURPHY & MOORE
www.murphy-moorepublishing.com

Murphy & Moore Publishing,
1 Rockefeller Plaza,
New York City, NY 10020, USA

ISBN: 978-1-63987-456-9

Cataloging-in-Publication Data

Principles of database management / Gabrielle Reid.
p. cm.
Includes bibliographical references and index.
ISBN 978-1-63987-456-9
1. Database management. 2. Databases. 3. Electronic data processing.
I. Reid, Gabrielle.
QA76.9.D3 P75 2022
005.756 5--dc23

For information on all Murphy & Moore Publications
visit our website at www.murphy-moorepublishing.com

Contents

Preface

A database is defined as a collection of inter-related data which is used to insert, retrieve and delete the data efficiently. Such data is often stored and accessed electronically from a computer system. Several design and modeling such as relationship model, object model, array model, etc. are often used to create complex databases. The softwares which are used to analyze and capture the data are called database management softwares or DBMS. They are also responsible for interacting with the end-user. A few different types of databases are cloud database, distributed database, embedded database and in-memory database. Advantages of a database management system include data sharing, controllable data redundancy, easy maintenance and ability to share data between different users. A database management system provides user access to database on three different levels-conceptual level, internal level and external level. The topics included in this book on database management systems are of utmost significance and bound to provide incredible insights to readers. The book studies, analyses and uphold the pillars of database management systems and its utmost significance in modern times. It will serve as a valuable source of reference for those interested in this field.

To facilitate a deeper understanding of the contents of this book a short introduction of every chapter is written below:

Chapter 1- A collection of data that is organized and generally stored and accessed electronically from a computer system is known as a database and a software system that enables users to create, maintain and control access to the database is known as database management system. This chapter delves into the topic of database management system.

Chapter 2- Data mining is a process of extracting usable data from a large set of raw data using one or more software. There are various types of data mining such as pictorial data mining, text mining, social media mining, web mining and audio and video mining. The topics elaborated in this chapter will help in gaining a better perspective about data mining and its types.

Chapter 3- A database model defines the logical structure of a database and also determines how data will be stored, accessed and updated in a database management system. Hierarchical database model is a database model which contains data that is organized in a tree-like structure. Many database models like network model, hierarchical model, entity-attribute-value model, etc. are explained in this chapter.

Chapter 4- Organizing data according to a database model is known as database design. Any change to a database schema which improves the design of the database while holding on to its behavioral and informational semantics is known as database refactoring. This chapter discusses in detail the theories and methodologies related to database design.

Chapter 5- The computer languages which are used to make queries in information systems and databases are known as query languages. A data control language is a computer programming language which is used to control access to data stored in a database. This chapter closely examines the key concepts of database designing languages to provide an extensive understanding of the subject.

Chapter 6- ACID is atomicity, consistency, isolation, durability. It is a set of properties of database transactions that can ensure database transactions can be processed reliably. There are four basic functions of persistent storage; create, read, update and delete. The diverse tools and techniques of database management in the current scenario have been thoroughly discussed in this chapter.

I would like to share the credit of this book with my editorial team who worked tirelessly on this book. I owe the completion of this book to the never-ending support of my family, who supported me throughout the project.

Gabrielle Reid

Understanding Database Management System

A collection of data that is organized and generally stored and accessed electronically from a computer system is known as a database and a software system that enables users to create, maintain and control access to the database is known as database management system. This chapter delves into the topic of database management system.

Database

Database, also called electronic database is the any collection of data, or information, that is specially organized for rapid search and retrieved by a computer. Databases are structured to facilitate the storage, retrieval, modification, and deletion of data in conjunction with various data-processing operations.

A database is stored as a file or a set of files. The information in these files may be broken down into records, each of which consists of one or more fields. Fields are the basic units of data storage, and each field typically contains information pertaining to one aspect or attribute of the entity described by the database. Records are also organized into tables that include information about relationships between its various fields. Although *database* is applied loosely to any collection of information in computer files, a database in the strict sense provides cross-referencing capabilities. Using keywords and various sorting commands, users can rapidly search, rearrange, group, and select the fields in many records to retrieve or create reports on particular aggregates of data.

Database records and files must be organized to allow retrieval of the information. Queries are the main way users retrieve database information. The power of a DBMS comes from its ability to define new relationships from the basic ones given by the tables and to use them to get responses to queries. Typically, the user provides a string of characters, and the computer searches the database for a corresponding sequence and provides the source materials in which those characters appear; a user can request, for example, all records in which the contents of the field for a person's last name is the word *Smith*.

The many users of a large database must be able to manipulate the information within it quickly at any given time. Moreover, large business and other organizations tend to build up many independent files containing related and even overlapping data, and their data-processing activities often require the linking of data from several files. Several different types of DBMS have been developed to support these requirements: flat, hierarchical, network, relational, and object-oriented.

Early systems were arranged sequentially (i.e., alphabetically, numerically, or chronologically); the development of direct-access storage devices made possible random access to data via indexes. In flat databases, records are organized according to a simple list of entities; many simple databases for personal computers are flat in structure. The records in hierarchical databases are organized in a treelike structure, with each level of records branching off into a set of smaller categories. Unlike hierarchical databases, which provide single links between sets of records at different levels, network databases create multiple linkages between sets by placing links, or pointers, to one set of records in another; the speed and versatility of network databases have led to their wide use within businesses and in e-commerce. Relational databases are used where associations between files or records cannot be expressed by links; a simple flat list becomes one row of a table, or "relation," and multiple relations can be mathematically associated to yield desired information. Various iterations of SQL (Structured Query Language) are widely employed in DBMS for relational databases. Object-oriented databases store and manipulate more complex data structures, called "objects," which are organized into hierarchical classes that may inherit properties from classes higher in the chain; this database structure is the most flexible and adaptable.

The information in many databases consists of natural-language texts of documents; number-oriented databases primarily contain information such as statistics, tables, financial data, and raw scientific and technical data. Small databases can be maintained on personal-computer systems and used by individuals at home. These and larger databases have become increasingly important in business life, in part because they are now commonly designed to be integrated with other office software, including spreadsheet programs.

Typical commercial database applications include airline reservations, production management functions, medical records in hospitals, and legal records of insurance companies. The largest databases are usually maintained by governmental agencies, business organizations, and universities. These databases may contain texts of such materials as abstracts, reports, legal statutes, wire services, newspapers and journals, encyclopaedias, and catalogs of various kinds. Reference databases contain bibliographies or indexes that serve as guides to the location of information in books, periodicals, and other published literature. Thousands of these publicly accessible databases now exist, covering topics ranging from law, medicine, and engineering to news and current events, games, classified advertisements, and instructional courses.

Increasingly, formerly separate databases are being combined electronically into larger collections known as data warehouses. Businesses and government agencies then employ "data mining" software to analyze multiple aspects of the data for various patterns. For example, a government agency might flag for human investigation a company or individual that purchased a suspicious quantity of certain equipment or materials, even though the purchases were spread around the country or through various subsidiaries.

Types of Database

There are various types of databases used for storing different varieties of data.

Centralized Database

It is the type of database that stores data at a centralized database system. It comforts the users to access the stored data from different locations through several applications. These applications contain the authentication process to let user access data securely. An example of a Centralized database can be Central Library that carries a central database of each library in a college/university.

Advantages of Centralized Database:

- It has decreased the risk of data management, i.e., manipulation of data will not affect the core data.

- Data consistency is maintained as it manages data in a central repository.

- It provides better data quality, which enables organizations to establish data standards.

- It is less costly because fewer vendors are required to handle the data sets.

Disadvantages of Centralized Database:

- The size of the centralized database is large, which increases the response time for fetching the data.

- It is not easy to update such an extensive database system.

- If any server failure occurs, entire data will be lost, which could be a huge loss.

Relational Database

This database is based on the relational data model, which stores data in the form of rows(tuple) and columns(attributes), and together forms a table(relation). A relational database uses SQL for storing, manipulating, as well as maintaining the data. E.F. Codd invented the database in 1970. Each table in the database carries a key that makes the data unique from others. Examples of Relational databases are MySQL, Microsoft SQL Server, Oracle, etc.

Properties of Relational Database

There are following four commonly known properties of a relational model known as ACID properties, where:

- A means Atomicity: This ensures the data operation will complete either with success or with failure. It follows the 'all or nothing' strategy. For example, a transaction will either be committed or will abort.

- C means Consistency: If we perform any operation over the data, its value before and after the operation should be preserved. For example, the account balances before and after the transaction should be correct, i.e., it should remain conserved.

- I mean Isolation: There can be concurrent users for accessing data at the same time from the database. Thus, isolation between the data should remain isolated. For example, when multiple transactions occur at the same time, one transaction effects should not be visible to the other transactions in the database.

- D means Durability: It ensures that once it completes the operation and commits the data, data changes should remain permanent.

NoSQL Database

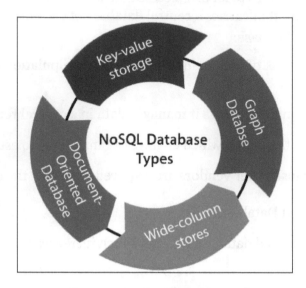

Non-SQL/Not Only SQL is a type of database that is used for storing a wide range of data sets. It is not a relational database as it stores data not only in tabular form but in several different ways. It came into existence when the demand for building modern applications increased. Thus, NoSQL presented a wide variety of database technologies in response to the demands. We can further divide a NoSQL database into the following four types:

- Key-value storage: It is the simplest type of database storage where it stores every single item as a key (or attribute name) holding its value, together.

- Document-oriented Database: A type of database used to store data as JSON-like document. It helps developers in storing data by using the same document-model format as used in the application code.

- Graph Databases: It is used for storing vast amounts of data in a graph-like structure. Most commonly, social networking websites use the graph database.

- Wide-column stores: It is similar to the data represented in relational databases. Here, data is stored in large columns together, instead of storing in rows.

Advantages of NoSQL Database:

- It enables good productivity in the application development as it is not required to store data in a structured format.

- It is a better option for managing and handling large data sets.

- It provides high scalability.

- Users can quickly access data from the database through key-value.

Cloud Database

A type of database where data is stored in a virtual environment and executes over the cloud computing platform is called Cloud database. It provides users with various cloud computing services (SaaS, PaaS, IaaS, etc.) for accessing the database. There are numerous cloud platforms, but the best options are:

- Amazon Web Services (AWS),

- Microsoft Azure,

- Kamatera,

- PhonixNAP,

- ScienceSoft,

- Google Cloud SQL, etc.

Object-oriented Databases

The type of database that uses the object-based data model approach for storing data in the database system is called Object-oriented databases. The data is represented and stored as objects which are similar to the objects used in the object-oriented programming language.

Hierarchical Databases

It is the type of database that stores data in the form of parent-children relationship nodes. Here, it organizes data in a tree-like structure.

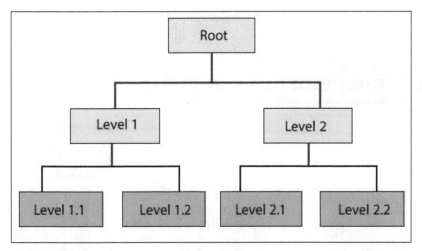

Data get stored in the form of records that are connected via links. Each child record in the tree will contain only one parent. On the other hand, each parent record can have multiple child records.

Network Databases

It is the database that typically follows the network data model. Here, the representation of data is in the form of nodes connected via links between them. Unlike the hierarchical database, it allows each record to have multiple children and parent nodes to form a generalized graph structure.

Personal Database

Collecting and storing data on the user's system defines a Personal Database. This database is basically designed for a single user.

Advantages of Personal Database:

- It is simple and easy to handle.

- It occupies less storage space as it is small in size.

Operational Database

The type of database which creates and updates the database in real-time is called Operational Database. It is basically designed for executing and handling the daily data operations in several businesses. For example, An organization uses operational databases for managing per day transactions.

Enterprise Database

Large organizations or enterprises use this database for managing a massive amount of data. It helps organizations to increase and improve their efficiency. Such a database allows simultaneous access to users.

Advantages of Enterprise Database:

- Multi processes are supportable over the Enterprise database.

- It allows executing parallel queries on the system.

Database Management System

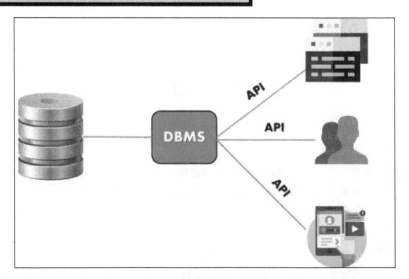

DBMS or Database Management System is a software application used to access, create, and manage databases. With the help of DBMS, you can easily create, retrieve and update data in databases.

A DBMS consists of a group of commands to manipulate the database and acts as an interface between the end-users and the database. Database Management Systems also aims to facilitate an overview of the databases, by providing a variety of administrative operations such as tuning, performance monitoring, and backup recovery. Database Management Systems allows users to do the following:

- Define Data: Allows the users to create, modify and delete the definitions which define the organization of the database.

- Update Data: Provides access to the users to insert, modify and delete data from the database.

- Retrieve Data: Allows the users to retrieve data from the database based on the requirement.

- Administration of users: Registers the users and monitors their action, enforces data security, maintains data integrity, monitors performance and deals with concurrency control.

Characteristics of DBMS

The following are a few characteristics of DBMS:

- To limit the permissions of the users.

- Provide multiple views of the single database schema.

- Facilitates security and removes data redundancy.

- Allows multi-user transaction processing and sharing of data.

- Follows the ACID property.

- Offers both physical and logical data independence.

Advantages of DBMS

Few of the advantages of the database management system are as follows:

- It offers a variety of methods to store and retrieve various formats of data using the query language.

- It can be *easily maintained* because of its nature of a centralized database system.

- Facilitates *multiple applications* using the same data with less development and maintenance time.

- Provides data security and integrity with minimal data duplicity and redundancy.

- It allows seamless integration into the application programming languages like Java and Python to enable the users to connect a database with any application or website.

- It has *automatic backup and recovery* systems to create an automatic backup of data.

- Authorizes users who can view share and access data.

Disadvantages of DBMS

- Databases Management Systems are often complex systems.

- Few of the DBMS available in the market are licensed. So, you have to pay to us that DBMS in your organization.

- Most leading companies store their data in a single database. Hence, if that database is damaged due to any reason, the complete data would be lost.

- DBMS that you wish to use might not be compatible with an organization's operational requirements.

- DBMS are large in size and need time to setup.

Applications of DBMS

A database management system stores data in such a way that it becomes easier to retrieve, manipulate, and produce information. Following are the important characteristics and applications of DBMS:

- ACID Properties: DBMS follows the concepts of Atomicity, Consistency, Isolation, and Durability (normally shortened as ACID). These concepts are applied on transactions, which manipulate data in a database. ACID properties help the database stay healthy in multi-transactional environments and in case of failure.

- Multiuser and Concurrent Access: DBMS supports multi-user environment and allows them to access and manipulate data in parallel. Though there are restrictions on transactions when users attempt to handle the same data item, but users are always unaware of them.

- Multiple views: DBMS offers multiple views for different users. A user who is in the Sales department will have a different view of database than a person working in the Production department. This feature enables the users to have a concentrate view of the database according to their requirements.

- Security: Features like multiple views offer security to some extent where users are unable to access data of other users and departments. DBMS offers methods to impose constraints while entering data into the database and retrieving the same at a later stage. DBMS offers many different levels of security features, which enables multiple users to have different views with different features. For example, a user in the Sales department cannot see the data that belongs to the Purchase department. Additionally, it can also be managed how much data of the Sales department should be displayed to the user. Since a DBMS is not saved on the disk as traditional file systems, it is very hard for miscreants to break the code.

Database System Architecture

Database architecture uses programming languages to design a particular type of software for businesses or organizations. Database architecture focuses on the design, development, implementation and maintenance of computer programs that store and organize information for businesses, agencies and institutions. A database architect develops and implements software to meet the needs of users.

The design of a DBMS depends on its architecture. It can be centralized or decentralized or hierarchical. The architecture of a DBMS can be seen as either single tier or multi-tier. The tiers are classified as follows:

- 1-tier architecture,
- 2-tier architecture,
- 3-tier architecture,
- N-tier architecture.

1-tier Architecture

One-tier architecture involves putting all of the required components for a software application or technology on a single server or platform.

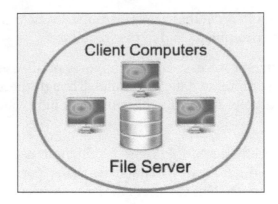

Basically, one-tier architecture keeps all of the elements of an application, including the interface, Middleware and back-end data, in one place. Developers see these types of systems as the simplest and most direct way.

2-tier Architecture

The two-tier is based on Client Server architecture. The two-tier architecture is like client server application. The direct communication takes place between client and server. There is no intermediate between client and server.

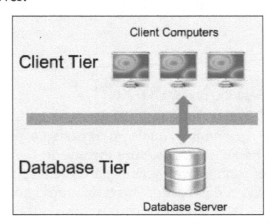

3-tier architecture

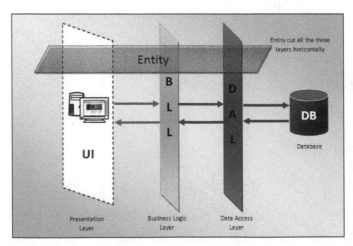

3-tier architecture separates its tiers from each other based on the complexity of the users and how they use the data present in the database. It is the most widely used architecture to design a DBMS. This architecture has different usages with different applications. It can be used in web applications and distributed applications. The strength in particular is when using this architecture over distributed systems.

- Database (Data) Tier: At this tier, the database resides along with its query processing languages. We also have the relations that define the data and their constraints at this level.

- Application (Middle) Tier: At this tier reside the application server and the programs that access the database. For a user, this application tier presents an abstracted view of the database. End-users are unaware of any existence of the database beyond the application. At the other end, the database tier is not aware of any other user beyond the application tier. Hence, the application layer sits in the middle and acts as a mediator between the end-user and the database.

- User (Presentation) Tier: End-users operate on this tier and they know nothing about any existence of the database beyond this layer. At this layer, multiple views of the database can be provided by the application. All views are generated by applications that reside in the application tier.

N-tier Architecture

N-tier architecture would involve dividing an application into three different tiers. These would be the:

- Logic tier,

- The presentation tier,

- The data tier.

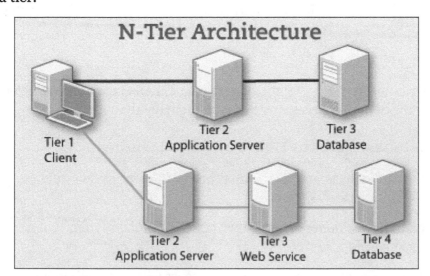

It is the physical separation of the different parts of the application as opposed to the usually conceptual or logical separation of the elements in the model-view-controller (MVC) framework.

Another difference from the MVC framework is that n-tier layers are connected linearly, meaning all communication must go through the middle layer, which is the logic tier. In MVC, there is no actual middle layer because the interaction is triangular; the control layer has access to both the view and model layers and the model also accesses the view; the controller also creates a model based on the requirements and pushes this to the view. However, they are not mutually exclusive, as the MVC framework can be used in conjunction with the n-tier architecture, with the n-tier being the overall architecture used and MVC used as the framework for the presentation tier.

Distributed Database System

A distributed database system allows applications to access data from local and remote databases. In a homogenous distributed database system, each database is an Oracle database. In a heterogeneous distributed database system, at least one of the databases is a non-Oracle database. Distributed databases use client/server architecture to process information requests.

Homogenous Distributed Database Systems

A homogenous distributed database system is a network of two or more Oracle databases that reside on one or more machines. An application can simultaneously access or modify the data in several databases in a single distributed environment. For example, a single query from a Manufacturing client on local database mfg can retrieve joined data from the products table on the local database and the dept table on the remote hq database.

For a client application, the location and platform of the databases are transparent. You can also create synonyms for remote objects in the distributed system so that users can access them with the same syntax as local objects. For example, if you are connected to database mfg but want to access data on database hq, creating a synonym on mfg for the remote dept table enables you to issue this query:

```
SELECT * FROM dept;
```

In this way, a distributed system gives the appearance of native data access. Users on mfg do not have to know that the data they access resides on remote databases.

Distributed Databases versus Distributed Processing

The terms distributed database and distributed processing are closely related, yet have distinct meanings. There definitions are as follows:

- Distributed database: A set of databases in a distributed system that can appear to applications as a single data source.

- Distributed processing: The operation that occurs when an application distributes its tasks among different computers in a network. For example, a database application typically distributes front-end presentation tasks to client computers and allows a back-end database server to manage shared access to a database. Consequently, a distributed database application processing system is more commonly referred to as a client/server database application system.

Oracle distributed database systems employ a distributed processing architecture. For example, an Oracle database server acts as a client when it requests data that another Oracle database server manages.

The terms distributed database system and database replication are related, yet distinct. In a pure (that is, not replicated) distributed database, the system manages a single copy of all data and supporting database objects. Typically, distributed database applications use distributed transactions to access both local and remote data and modify the global database in real-time.

The term replication refers to the operation of copying and maintaining database objects in multiple databases belonging to a distributed system. While replication relies on distributed database technology, database replication offers applications benefits that are not possible within a pure distributed database environment.

Most commonly, replication is used to improve local database performance and protect the availability of applications because alternate data access options exist. For example, an application may normally access a local database rather than a remote server to minimize network traffic and achieve maximum performance. Furthermore, the application can continue to function if the local server experiences a failure, but other servers with replicated data remain accessible.

In a heterogeneous distributed database system, at least one of the databases is a non-Oracle system. To the application, the heterogeneous distributed database system appears as a single, local, Oracle database. The local Oracle database server hides the distribution and heterogeneity of the data.

The Oracle database server accesses the non-Oracle system using Oracle Heterogeneous Services in conjunction with an agent. If you access the non-Oracle data store using an Oracle Transparent Gateway, then the agent is a system-specific application. For example, if you include a Sybase database in an Oracle distributed system, and then you need to obtain a Sybase-specific transparent gateway so that the Oracle databases in the system can communicate with it. Alternatively, you can use generic connectivity to access non-Oracle data stores so long as the non-Oracle system supports the ODBC or OLE DB protocols.

Heterogeneous Services

Heterogeneous Services (HS) is an integrated component within the Oracle database server and the enabling technology for the current suite of Oracle Transparent Gateway products. HS provides the common architecture and administration mechanisms for Oracle gateway products and other heterogeneous access facilities. Also, it provides upwardly compatible functionality for users of most of the earlier Oracle Transparent Gateway releases.

Transparent Gateway Agents

For each non-Oracle system that you access, Heterogeneous Services can use a transparent gateway agent to interface with the specified non-Oracle system. The agent is specific to the non-Oracle system, so each type of system requires a different agent.

The transparent gateway agent facilitates communication between Oracle and non-Oracle databases and uses the Heterogeneous Services component in the Oracle database server. The agent executes SQL and transactional requests at the non-Oracle system on behalf of the Oracle database server.

Schema Objects and Naming in a Distributed Database

A schema object (for example, a table) is accessible from all nodes that form a distributed database. Therefore, just as a non-distributed local DBMS architecture must provide an unambiguous naming scheme to distinctly reference objects within the local database, a distributed DBMS must use a naming scheme that ensures that objects throughout the distributed database can be uniquely identified and referenced.

To resolve references to objects (a process called name resolution) within a single database, the DBMS usually forms object names using a hierarchical approach. For example, within a single database, a DBMS guarantees that each schema has a unique name, and that within a schema, each object has a unique name. Because uniqueness is enforced at each level of the hierarchical structure, an object's local name is guaranteed to be unique within the database and references to the object's local name can be easily resolved.

Distributed database management systems simply extend the hierarchical naming model by enforcing unique database names within a network. As a result, an object's global object name is guaranteed to be unique within the distributed database, and references to the object's global object name can be resolved among the nodes of the system.

Transparency in a Distributed Database System

The functionality of a distributed database system must be provided in such a manner that the complexities of the distributed database are transparent to both the database users and the database administrators.

For example, a distributed database system should provide methods to hide the physical location of objects throughout the system from applications and users. Location transparency exists if a user can refer to the same table the same way, regardless of the node to which the user connects. Location transparency is beneficial for the following reasons:

- Access to remote data is simplified, because the database users do not need to know the location of objects.

- Objects can be moved with no impact on end-users or database applications.

A distributed database system should also provide query, update, and transaction transparency. For example, standard SQL commands, such as SELECT, INSERT, UPDATE, and DELETE, should allow users to access remote data without the requirement for any programming. Transaction transparency occurs when the DBMS provides the functionality described below using standard

SQL COMMIT, SAVEPOINT, and ROLLBACK commands, without requiring complex programming or other special operations to provide distributed transaction control.

- The statements in a single transaction can reference any number of local or remote tables.

- The DBMS guarantees that all nodes involved in a distributed transaction take the same action: they either all commit or all roll back the transaction.

- If a network or system failure occurs during the commit of a distributed transaction, the transaction is automatically and transparently resolved globally; that is, when the network or system is restored, the nodes either all commit or all roll back the transaction.

A distributed DBMS architecture should also provide facilities to transparently replicate data among the nodes of the system. Maintaining copies of a table across the databases in a distributed database is often desired so that:

- Tables that have high query and low update activity can be accessed faster by local user sessions because no network communication is necessary.

- If a database that contains a critical table experiences a prolonged failure, replicates of the table in other databases can still be accessed.

A DBMS that manages a distributed database should make table replication transparent to users working with the replicated tables.

Finally, the functional transparencies explained above are not sufficient alone. The distributed database must also perform with acceptable speed.

Traditionally in many organizations, the control of data resources has been centralized due to the origin of data management within the mainframe environment. However, with the emergence of client-server technology and the blending of data and process in the object-oriented methodologies, many organizations are questioning the need to retain the centralized data and database management functions. These organizations are experimenting with the concept of decentralized data and database management, where application developers/programmers/integrators perform many, if not all, the functions of a data analyst and/or database analyst. There are numerous risks associated with such a decision and few benefits.

Data analysis, database administration and application development/integration are very separate functions and require separate skill sets. A data analyst, who is responsible for the conceptual and logical gathering and organization of information facts, is a person with broad-based analytical talents, is a good and discerning listener, and has excellent oral and written communications skills. These talents serve the role of data analyst by allowing the analyst to determine the relevant facts (data) in a business user's description of the information needed to perform a function.

Frequently, this description flows in a "stream-of-consciousness" manner and the listening and analytical skills help the data analyst focus on the real entities and attributes instead of the inconsequential information. This skill is developed through training and practice and is essential to the proper collection and organization of relevant data.

As the area responsible for the establishment and reusability of data, a data analyst is expected to understand the uses of each entity and its role in the corporate data management scheme. This duty requires the data analyst to provide flexible yet solid definitions and usage of the logical entities and attributes found in all the organization's data and file structures. In advocating and participating in the planning and coordination of the information resource across related applications and business areas, the amount of data sharing can be maximized, and the amount of design and data redundancy can be minimized. Data analysts are also concerned with the metadata (definitions, standard names, formats, common code sets, etc.) of an object and its accessibility and central storage.

Perhaps more than any other of the discrete disciplines within IS, Data Administration requires a concrete grasp of the real business the company is in, not just the technical aspects of interaction with a computer. Database administrators and application developers/integrators are not required to possess this level of business understanding.

The database administrator, a function separate from a data analyst, is a person with special skills relating to the DBMS under their control. This physical data management function requires intimate knowledge of the DBMS, the platform it operates upon, and the performance and technical usage requirements of the application under construction or enhancement. Proper database analysis and database structure and design can prevent the problems of poor performance and high maintenance databases, and the creation of unsharable data.

Defining proper access to the database, providing appropriate storage parameters and executing regular and robust maintenance routines (backup and recovery, performance monitoring, etc.) are all the responsibility of a database administrator. These functions require the talents of technical expertise and tenacious problem solving. It also requires detailed training in the DBMS' operations, acquired through courses and practice. Database administrators are usually less concerned with the business content of the data under their control than are data analysts, but they must understand the expected usage to design and enhance optimally performing databases. The enhancement of database structures (adding or deleting columns, renaming columns or tables, etc.) must be done judiciously and by a technician skilled in the nuances of the database. For example, Oracle does not provide a facility for dropping and renaming columns; a point known to Oracle DBA's but not by many other IS professionals.

Application developers/integrators are expected to code and design the applications that provide data to the databases and present that data to the users. Application developers are usually trained in the languages and interfaces of their applications, but are not usually concerned with the analysis of that data from a business perspective. Since they work with data after the database has been structured, they frequently do not understand fully the need for normalized logical design. This lack of understanding can result in incorrect normalizing of data if application developers perform database design or enhancement. This improper normalizing can cause a database to perform poorly and require users to re-enter rather than reuse data in the application. Also, application developers concentrate on a single application at a time. Frequently, they do not have the broad, enterprise perspective necessary for the reduction or elimination of redundancy that is essential if data is to be used as a corporate resource. The development of many stovepipe applications in the past is a result of data structure design by application specialists who were not considering the broader implications of sharing data and reducing data redundancy.

Many organizations considering the combination of data management and application development cite the need for swifter implementation of databases and more rapid enhancements to existing databases. Sensitivity to deadline pressures in a constant throughout all development projects. Decentralizing data management (logical and/or physical) appears to offer some slight advantages in faster application development. However, the actual exposure to poorly defined data and poorly structured databases, incorrect enhancement procedures and unsharable data far outweigh the small saving in time resulting from application developers performing data management functions. Industry studies have consistently shown high costs for redesign and re-enhancement when the logical and physical data management functions are not performed by data management specialists (data analysts and database administrators). Effective project management practices suggest the division of labor into discrete tasks and each of those tasks to be performed by a specialist in that area. Employing this management practice in the area of data management in a system-development or enhancement project will enable an organization to adequately maintain the costs of that project. Simply stated, faster application development is not the objective. The correct objective is the development and enhancement of high quality and high integrity applications as efficiently as possible.

Data is rapidly growing in stature as a recognized corporate resource. A centralized approach to logical and physical data management will promote the development and use of integrated, sharable data throughout applications, preserve the quality of that data and serve the needs of the business more effectively.

Distribution transparency is the property of distributed databases by the virtue of which the internal details of the distribution are hidden from the users. The DDBMS designer may choose to fragment tables, replicate the fragments and store them at different sites. However, since users are oblivious of these details, they find the distributed database easy to use like any centralized database.

The three dimensions of distribution transparency are:

- Location transparency,
- Fragmentation transparency,
- Replication transparency.

Location Transparency

Location transparency ensures that the user can query on any table(s) or fragment(s) of a table as if they were stored locally in the user's site. The fact that the table or its fragments are stored at remote site in the distributed database system should be completely oblivious to the end user. The address of the remote site(s) and the access mechanisms are completely hidden. In order to incorporate location transparency, DDBMS should have access to updated and accurate data dictionary and DDBMS directory which contains the details of locations of data.

Fragmentation Transparency

Fragmentation transparency enables users to query upon any table as if it were unfragmented. Thus, it hides the fact that the table the user is querying on is actually a fragment or union of some fragments. It also conceals the fact that the fragments are located at diverse sites. This is somewhat similar to users of SQL views, where the user may not know that they are using a view of a table instead of the table itself.

Replication Transparency

Replication transparency ensures that replication of databases are hidden from the users. It enables users to query upon a table as if only a single copy of the table exists. Replication transparency is associated with concurrency transparency and failure transparency. Whenever a user updates a data item, the update is reflected in all the copies of the table. However, this operation should not be known to the user. This is concurrency transparency. Also, in case of failure of a site, the user can still proceed with his queries using replicated copies without any knowledge of failure. This is failure transparency.

Combination of Transparencies

In any distributed database system, the designer should ensure that all the stated transparencies are maintained to a considerable extent. The designer may choose to fragment tables, replicate them and store them at different sites; all oblivious to the end user. However, complete distribution transparency is a tough task and requires considerable design efforts.

In synchronous replication approach, the database is synchronized so that all the replications always have the same value. A transaction requesting a data item will have access to the same value in all the sites. To ensure this uniformity, a transaction that updates a data item is expanded so that it makes the update in all the copies of the data item. Generally, two-phase commit protocol is used for the purpose.

In asynchronous replication approach, the replicas do not always maintain the same value. One or more replicas may store an outdated value, and a transaction can see the different values. The process of bringing all the replicas to the current value is called synchronization.

XML Database System

XML database is a data persistence software system used for storing the huge amount of information in XML format. It provides a secure place to store XML documents. You can query your stored data by using XQuery, export and serialize into desired format. XML databases are usually associated with document-oriented databases.

Types of XML Databases

There are two types of XML databases:

- XML-enabled database,

- Native XML database (NXD).

XML-enabled Database

XML-enabled database works just like a relational database. It is like an extension provided for the conversion of XML documents. In this database, data is stored in table, in the form of rows and columns.

Native XML Database

Native XML database is used to store large amount of data. Instead of table format, Native XML database is based on container format. You can query data by XPath expressions. It is database is preferred over XML-enable database because it is highly capable to store, maintain and query XML documents.

Let's take an example of XML database:

```
1.   <?xml version="1.0"?>
2.   <contact-info>
3.      <contact1>
4.         <name>Vimal Jaiswal</name>
5.         <company>SSSIT.org</company>
6.         <phone>(0120) 4256464</phone>
7.      </contact1>
8.      <contact2>
9.         <name>Mahesh Sharma </name>
10.        <company>SSSIT.org</company>
11.        <phone>09990449935</phone>
12.     </contact2>
13.  </contact-info>
```

In the above example, a table named contacts is created and holds the contacts (contact1 and contact2). Each one contains 3 entities name, company and phone.

Multimedia Database System

A multimedia database system is comprised of a multimedia database management system (MM-DBMS) that manages a multimedia database, which is a database containing multimedia data. Multimedia data may include structured data as well as semi structured and unstructured data such as voice, video, text, and images. That is, an MM-DBMS provides support for storing, manipulating, and retrieving multimedia data from a multimedia database. In a certain sense, a multimedia database system is a type of heterogeneous database system because it manages heterogeneous data types.

An MM-DBMS must provide support for typical database management system functions. These include query processing; update processing, transaction management, storage management, metadata management, security, and integrity. In addition, in many cases, the various types of data such as voice and video have to be synchronized for display, and, therefore, real-time processing is also a major issue in an MM-DBMS. MM-DBMSs are becoming popular for various applications including C4I, CAD/CAM, air traffic control, and, particularly, entertainment. While the terms multimedia and hypermedia are often used interchangeably, we differentiate between the two. While an MM-DBMS manages a multimedia database, a hypermedia DBMS not only manages a multimedia database, but also provides support for browsing the database by following links. That is, a hypermedia DBMS contains an MM-DBMS. Recently, there has been much research on designing and developing MMDBMSs. Research on developing an appropriate data model to support data types such as video is needed. Some experts have proposed object-oriented database management systems (OODBMS) for storing and managing multimedia data because they have been found to be more suitable for handling large objects and multimedia data such as sound and video which consume considerable storage space.139 Although such systems show some promise, they are not sufficient to capture all of the requirements of multimedia applications. For example, in many cases, voice and video data which may be stored in objects have to be synchronized when displayed. The constraints for synchronization are not specified in the object models. Another area that needs research is the development of efficient techniques for indexing. Data manipulation operations such as video editing are still in the early stages. Furthermore, the multimedia databases need to be integrated for many applications as they are distributed.

Media Types and Multimedia

Media refer to the types of information or types of information representation, such as alphanumeric data, images, audio, and video. There are many ways to classify media. Common classifications are based on physical formats and media relationships with time.

Static media do not have a time dimension, and their contents and meanings do not depend on the presentation time. Static media include alphanumeric data, graphics, and still images. Dynamic media have time dimensions, and their meanings and correctness depend on the rate at which they are presented.

Dynamic media include animation, audio, and video. These media have their intrinsic unit intervals or rates. For example, to convey a perceptually smooth movement, video must be played back at 25 frames per second (or 30 frames, depending on the video system used).

Multimedia refers to a collection of media types used together. It is implied that at least one media type is not alphanumeric data (i.e., at least one media type is image, audio, or video). Here, "multimedia" is used as an adjective—so we will specifically say multimedia information, multimedia data, multimedia system, multimedia communications, multimedia applications, and so forth. Multimedia data refers to the computer readable representation of multiple media types.

Multimedia information refers to the information conveyed by multiple media types. Sometimes, multimedia information and multimedia data are used interchangeably. We sometimes use multimedia or media item and object to refer to any autonomous entity in an MIRS that can be queried, retrieved, and presented. The term "object" may not be properly defined in the technical object-oriented (OO) sense. The context should make it clear whether it is used in a general sense or refers to a properly defined object in an OO approach.

Multimedia Indexing and Retrieval

DBMSs retrieve items based on structured data using exact matching. IR is also called text-based retrieval. Content-based retrieval refers to retrieval based on actual media features such as color and shape, instead of text annotation of the media item. Content-based retrieval is normally based on similarity instead of an exact match between a query and a set of database items. MIRS refers to a basic system providing multimedia information retrieval using a combination of DBMS, IR, and content-based retrieval techniques. In MIRS, some issues such as versioning and security control may not be fully implemented. Fully fledged MIRS is called a multimedia DBMS (MMDBMS).

Feature Extraction, Content Representation and Indexing

In MIRSs, one of the most important issues is feature extraction or content representation (what are the main features or contents in a multimedia item). Feature extraction may be an automatic or semiautomatic process. In some of the content based retrieval literature, feature extraction is also called indexing. When the term "index" is used as a noun, it refers to a data structure or to the organization of extracted features for efficient search and retrieval.

DBMSs and their Role in Handling Multimedia Data

DBMSs are now well developed and used widely for structured data. The dominant DBMSs are relational database management systems (RDBMSs). In RDBMSs, information is organized in tables or relations. The rows of the table correspond to information item or records, while the columns correspond to attributes. The structured query language (SQL) is used to create such tables and to insert and retrieve information from them. We use a simple example to show how to use SQL to create a table and insert and retrieve information from it. Suppose we want to create a table containing student records consisting of the student number, name, and address. The following statement is used:

Create table STUDENT (stu# integer, name char(20), address char(100));

When we want to insert student records into the table, we use the SQL insert command as follows:

Insert into STUDENT values (10, "Kannan, Arputharaj", "2 Main St., Quarters", "Chennai");

Information in the table is retrieved using the SQL select command. For example, if we want to retrieve the name of a student with student number 32, we use the following query statement:

Select name from STUDENT where stu#=32

Attributes in a RDBMS have fixed types with fixed widths. In the above example, the attribute stu#

is an integer type of fixed length of 32 bits. Thus RDBMSs are well suited for handling numeric data and short alphanumeric strings.

To support large variable fields in a RDBMS, a concept called binary large objects (BLOBs) was introduced. A BLOB is a large bit string of variable length. For example, if we want to store students' pictures in the above student record example, we can create a table using the following statement:

Create table STUDENT (stu# integer, name char(20), address char(100) picture BLOB);

BLOBs are normally just bit strings and operations such as comparison cannot be carried out on them. That is, a RDBMS does not know the contents or semantics of a BLOB. All it knows is a block of data.

The main difference between the BLOB and the object is that the object is properly defined, including its properties and allowed operations on the properties, while the BLOB is not.

The concepts of BLOBs and objects are a step toward handling multimedia data. But BLOBs are used just to store large data. While objects contain some simple attributes, mANY more capabilities should be developed to handle content based multimedia retrieval. Some of the required capabilities are as follows:

- Tools, to automatically, or semi automatically extract contents and features contained in multimedia data.

- Multidimensional indexing structures, to handle multimedia feature vectors.

- Similarity metrics, for multimedia retrieval instead of exact match.

- Storage subsystems, redesigned to cope with the requirements of large size and high bandwidth and meet real-time requirements.

- The user interface, designed to allow flexible queries in different media types and provide multimedia presentations.

Integrated Approach to Multimedia Information Indexing and Retrieval

From the above discussion we see that DBMSs and IR cannot fully meet the requirements of multimedia indexing and retrieval, so new techniques to handle special characteristics of multimedia data are required. Nevertheless, we recognize that DBMSs and IR can play important roles in MMDBMSs. Parts of multimedia data, such as the creation date and author of a multimedia document, are structured. This structured data can be handled with DBMS techniques. Text annotation is still a powerful method for capturing the contents of multimedia data, so IR techniques have an important role to play. To summarize, an integrated approach combining DBMSs, IR, and specific techniques for handling multimedia data is required to develop an efficient and effective MIRS.

In the loose coupling approach, the multimedia data is managed by the file system, while the database system manages the metadata. In the tight coupling approach, the multimedia data is managed by the database system. Another type of architecture is schema architecture. For example, does the three-schema architecture apply for a multimedia database system? A third type of architecture is functional architecture, describing the functions of a multimedia database system. A fourth type of architecture is whether a multimedia database system extends a traditional database system. This is what we call system architecture. A fifth type of architecture is a distributed architecture, where a multimedia database is distributed. Finally, multimedia databases may be heterogeneous in nature and need to be integrated. The architecture for integrating heterogeneous databases is known as interoperable architecture.

Loose Coupling versus Tight Coupling

Here we see the loose coupling versus tight coupling approaches to designing a multimedia database system. In the loose coupling approach, the DBMS is used to manage only the metadata, and a multimedia file manager is used to manage the multimedia data. Then there is a module for integrating the DBMS and the multimedia file manager. Metadata, the multimedia file manager, and the module for integrating the two. The advantage of the loose coupling approach is that one can use various multimedia file systems to manage the multimedia data.

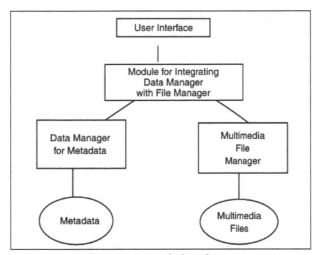

Figure: Loose Coupled Architecture.

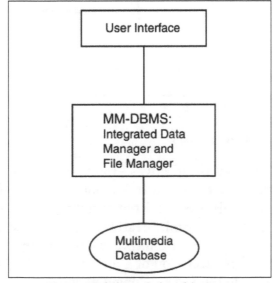

Figure: Tight Coupled Architecture.

In tight coupling architecture, the DBMS manages both the multimedia database and the metadata. That is, the DBMS is an MM-DBMS. Tight coupling architecture is advantageous because all DBMS functions can be applied on the multimedia database. This includes query management, transaction processing, metadata management, storage management, and security and integrity management.

Note that with the loose coupling approach, unless the file manager performs the DBMS functions, the DBMS only manages the metadata for the multimedia data. Much of the discussion in this book assumes a tight coupling design. That is, the MM-DBMS manages the multimedia database and performs various functions such as query processing and storage management.

Schema Architecture

Schema architectures can be described in various ways with respect to different characteristics. Schema is essentially the metadata that describes the multimedia data. Here, the external schema will define the views that users have of the database, such as video or audio views. The logical schema is based on the data model for the multimedia database. One can also look at schema from another point of view. Instead of multimedia data, assume that individual data types are stored in separate databases. For example, video schema will describe the video database and audio schema will describe the audio database.

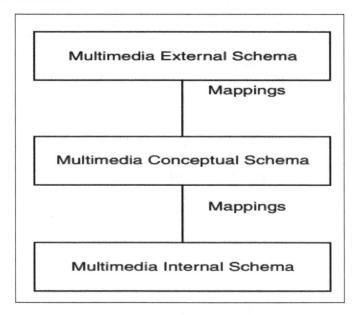

Modeling Multimedia Collections

Media objects are modeled from two perspectives - the first describing the *context* of the object, the second giving its *semantic meaning*. Context data includes such characteristics as the media object's origin/creator, the materials used, and the current location can be modeled as is done for the structured objects in traditional administrative systems. Describing or modeling semantic meaning is more difficult, since meaning or interpretation can vary from one observer/reader to another. Typically the semantic interpretation of a media object is given as a set of keyword descriptors or as a free text description stored as a long data type.

Owners of large collections of media objects, such as libraries, museums and archives, have long had electronic versions of their catalog data on-line. These organizations have also been working on standardizing their object descriptions in order to facilitate data exchange. In this effort several *metadata* standards have been proposed and are being adopted by an increasing number of institutions.

Users of media objects frequently search by their *semantic content*, for example, by asking for texts on *information and data management*. Different approaches for modeling text and image media are presented.

Finally, administrators of electronic media data collections need to be able to store and utilize both context and semantic media descriptors to the functions provided by the local data management system. Vendors of object-relational software claim that or-dbm systems can be used to manage media collections. If this is correct, then it should be possible to model media data using an extended ER model type.

Metadata

Metadata can be defined simply as *data about data*. Such a broad definition has given rise to multiple "perspective" definitions of, and different names for, *metadata* that suit particular application types, such as the original statistical metadata, *catalog* and *data dictionary* for traditional database applications, *metadata* for document (text, image, video) management, data mining, data warehousing, and more. Note that the metadata recorded in a library catalog came in use "with the first librarian".

Metadata have 2 primary uses:

- Specification and interpretation of user requests – queries.

- Determining storage, indexing, and retrieval of the data to/from the database.

Metadata for electronic data collections are specified during:

- Database design: Often using a semantic data model for description of user requirements, data structures, and constraints, and then expanded during.

- DB implementation: Using a data definition language, DDL, to add metadata describing DB storage structures, control functions, and access criteria.

Metadata can be stored in the DB schema, the indexes and/or as attribute values in the DB itself, Figure below. For example, semantic content description can be contained in the *report.summary* attribute.

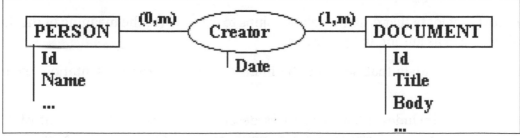

Figure: A data model of an example DB.

For *relational DB* systems, metadata include the table, attribute, constraint, trigger, and index names and definitions. These metadata provide some semantics, in the name set and relationships used, in addition to structural and implementation-oriented metadata. RDB metadata are modeled as the elements of a data model as shown in Figure above, and compiled into the RDB schema. The user uses table and attribute names for specification of an information/data request. For example, the SQL query in table below includes both DB table and column names to specify the DB region where data relevant to the query can be found. The SQL query processor uses the metadata in the DB schema to first interpret the query and then to locate and retrieve the requested data.

In *text document databases*, semantic content metadata, represented by the concepts/terms in the document collection, are stored in the DB indexes. Execution of the user query shown in below table, involves a search in these indexes for a match between the query search terms and documents containing them.

Query language examples	
List the titles of database texts written by Joan Nordbotten.	Find texts on database management using SLQ3 or MSQL or MSQL+.
SELECT D.Title	Search statement (within Document.body):
FROM PERSON P, AUTHOR A, DOCUMENT D	Database ADJ Management
WHERE P.Name ='Joan Nordbotten'	AND (SQL3 OR MSQL %)
AND P.Id = A.PId	
AND A.DId = D.Id	
AND D.Body like '%database%';	
Result: a list of titles	Result: a set of documents

Metadata for Multimedia

Numerous authors, particularly those working on cultural heritage (digital library, virtual museum), video/film on demand and *semantic web* projects, have noted the importance of metadata for managing collections (databases) of multimedia data. Media data are intrinsically unstructured and cannot be easily described as tables with meaningful column/attribute names, thereby making the metadata structures designed for relational DBs less useful. Metadata types required for multimedia data collections can be classified into 3 categories:

- Semantic metadata that characterize the subject matter of the document.

- Context metadata that describe relationships to external (to the meaning of the document) objects, such as author and publisher.

- Structural metadata that describe the internal structure and presentation layout for the media object.

Semantic metadata includes a list of features describing the semantic content of the media object. For text documents, features are commonly represented by *index terms* or *keywords* selected from the document. Index terms can be selected from the title, abstract, summary, and/ or body of a text document, or from the title and description of other media types. Index terms can also be assigned manually, by the author or librarian/curator, from controlled vocabularies or domain ontologies.

Techniques for search and retrieval of text documents utilize the index terms to match user queries (given as a search term list) to documents containing these terms. Some authors refer to such queries as *text-based queries*. In general, queries for media objects that refer to their semantic content can be termed *content-based queries*. Note though, that in image processing the term *content-based retrieval* is used to refer to image retrieval using implementation-level features such as color, texture and shape, which do not necessarily confer semantic meaning.

For example, the information need given in the query in table above is represented as a request for those documents that contain the concepts/terms "database management" and ("SLQ3" or "MySQL" or "MySQL+"). Assuming that the semantic metadata for the DB includes a term list extracted from the documents, the query processor can use this list, rather than searching each document, to locate the documents that contain matching terms and thus satisfy the query. This is the principle strategy used in current search engines such as *Google*.

The attributes: Title, Summary, and Topics, for the multimedia object *Report* can be used to store and retrieve terms that describe the semantic content of the report. The values of these attributes thus contain *semantic metadata*.

Context metadata for media objects include the author/creator, publisher, the date of creation/ purchase/publication, and the current location of the object. This type of data can be modeled as objects, attributes and/or relationships in a traditional data model and stored in a tabular DB for later retrieval. Queries that use context metadata for specification of the required media data are frequently referred to as *attribute-based* or *exact-match queries*.

For example the Name and Address attributes of Person also describe the context for Person.Picture and can be used for search & retrieval of the image. In addition, the relationship "WrittenBy" functions as the context for a report by identifying its author(s).

Structural metadata describe presentation style and layout, for example; spatial and temporal placement of objects within a document. Typical structural attributes would include length, language, and type of media object, placement, and presentation speed. Attributes for image color and texture, supported in the multimedia extensions of many Object-Relational data management systems, also describe structural characteristics of media objects.

Structural attributes can describe both the media object itself and the relationship between media objects and their parent document. Most of the tags of mark-up languages, such as HTML, are used to specify structural metadata. Structural characteristics can be included as selection criteria in queries, but are more frequently used by the data management system for result presentation.

Standards for Metadata Specification

The objective of standardizing metadata is to facilitate information retrieval and data exchange between organizations. Work on standardizing on-line metadata for media objects began in the mid-1960s with the development of on-line medical and judicial journals and with automation of the library catalogs. This work has been intensified with the advent of the Internet and done in parallel in the major organizations for libraries, the film industry, museums and archives. In addition, standards have been proposed by the W3C for use in the *semantic web*.

All this has led to multiple, overlapping standards for metadata frameworks/specification tools, developed initially for specific application areas that can be used for the specification of metadata for multimedia data. In the following, we will focus on 3 standards:

- Dublin Core originally developed for on-line library 'catalogs'.

- Mpeg-7 developed for streamed multimedia such as film.

- CIDOC/CRM developed for museum artifacts.

Dublin Core

In the mid-1990s, the Dublin Core Working Group convened to address the needs of the digital library community for management of digital text-documents (books, articles, and letters). The resulting Dublin Core (DC) standard proposes an explicit metadata element set to catalog whole, *static* documents using a manual process aided by *controlled vocabularies* also called *domain ontologies*.

The metadata elements included in the Dublin Core (DC) standard have been compiled from work initiated in the library science field. The core DC attribute set consists of 15 elements that can be organized according to the type of metadata captured, as shown below:

Metadata Type	DC element
Semantic	Title, Subject, Description, Type, Coverage, Relation
Context	Creator, Contributor, Publisher, Date, Rights, Source
Structural	Type, Format, Language, Identifier

Note that the element "type" has 2 meanings: Semantic.type can be used to indicate the category, function or genres of the object, while the Structural.type can be used to indicate the media type, such as text, image, sound, video or simulation.

Other elements include: abstract, accessRights, accrualMethod, alternative, audience valid (about 40 elements). DC elements may be qualified by attributes that reduce the scope of the core element. For example the *date* element may be qualified as DateSubmitted, DateAccepted, DateCopywritted. Each of the DC elements can be repeated as necessary making for a rich framework for describing media objects.

Each of the core DC elements can be defined as an attribute of media objects or as a relationship to other objects within the database. This allows semantic data modeling of metadata, for example using the SSM syntax.

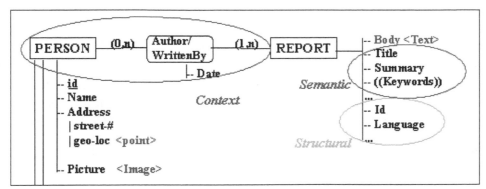

Figure: Metadata types.

DC users claim that the DC elements are applicable and sufficient for description of all types of multimedia objects based on the observation that a *document* can be presented in any media form such as photographs of a person or event, a film, or speech. The standard has also been adopted in a wide variety of organizations for both text and image object description.

MPEG-7

The Dublin Core standard has focused on (has most of its elements describing) *context* metadata as is customary for library documentation. However, these characteristics, while essential for cataloging, do not describe basic characteristics of moving pictures (streamed data), such as the temporal and sequencing requirements or the object identification and inter-relationships depicted in the film media.

In the late 90s, the Moving Picture Experts Group was created with the purpose of establishing standards for transmitting digital films and videos on the Internet. The standards Mpeg-1, 2, and 4 all focus on representation standards for streamed media - audio, video, including image objects and include descriptors of the structural aspects of the media, such as coding and compression format, length and speed of transmission, synchronization, etc. The Mpeg-7 standard adds description of the semantic and inter-relationship content of multimedia objects.

Unlike Dublin Core, no specific elements are specified, rather Mpeg-7 - the "Multimedia Content Description Interface" standard consists of a framework of descriptors and description schemes that can be used to describe any characteristic deemed relevant for the application. In addition, the Mpeg-7 standard includes recommendations as to the type of metadata that should be included for description of multimedia data.

Mpeg-7 *descriptors* are used to describe the basic characteristics of the media object. They can be used to encode the DC element set, but, in the Mpeg-7 recommendations, are focused on describing the semantic and structural content of multimedia. Descriptors are recommended used for describing such "low level" structural features as the color, texture, shape, and location of features within an object that can be automatically generated from the digital version of a document/image. They can also be used to describe semantic metadata that must be manually annotated.

Mpeg-7 *Description schemes* are used to describe relationships between descriptors and thus the structural and semantic features, such as temporal and spatial characteristics between objects in the media, as well as production and presentation of the media objects.

CIDOC-CRM

The International Committee for Documentation, CIDOC, of international council of museums, ICOM has developed CIDOC-CRM for describing cultural heritage objects, particularly those found in museum collections. CIDOC/CRM descriptions include the spatial, temporal and event aspects of museum objects, in addition to the semantic, context and structural aspects emphasized in the Dublin Core standard. In fact, the intended scope of the CIDOC CRM has been defined as:

> "All information required for the scientific documentation of cultural heritage collections, with a view to enabling wide area information exchange and integration of heterogeneous sources."

CIDOC/CRM is envisioned as ontology for the museum domain that incorporates 'all' of the currently existing metadata standards. An interesting application of CIDOC/CRM as the basis for a system to support integrated information retrieval from multiple sources is described by researchers in "New Ways to Search, Navigate and Use Multimedia Museum Collections over the Web".

RDF

Both Dublin Core and Mpeg-7 have been developed to describe 'real' media objects, i.e. texts and film respectively. The World-Wide Web (W3) Consortium has been developing a standard, the *Resource Description Framework - RDF* - for description of Web material with the goal of providing a standard for interoperability between Web applications.

If the database consists of a set of Web pages, the HTML, XML, or other mark-up language tag set can be used to specify both structural metadata such as existence and placement of imbedded media-objects, and semantic metadata such as the title and classification terms. Standard descriptions for a set of documents can be given by providing an RDF (Resource Description Framework) specification.

Modeling Multimedia Objects

Increasingly, organizations need to extend their administrative (relational) databases with media data to represent text documents, images, charts, audio, or video (as streamed images). The resulting database becomes a multimedia database consisting of a combination of media data types and 'traditional' structured data. Examples include:

- A report, containing text, images, as well as structural data for title, author, date.

- A map, containing points, lines, areas or regions, as well as title, place names, facts (distances, heights), and icons.

- A film, containing image stream, and (multiple) audio streams as well as a title, actor list, producer.

Modeling these databases poses a challenge for our traditional data modeling methods. Extended ER (EER) modeling approaches, such as SSM, were originally developed to add 'semantic' descriptions, principally hierarchic or role information, to the *structured data* supported by the relational model. The objective was to provide a more complete description of the application and a more robust system when new applications required data from the database.

Modeling Text Documents

As noted above, a text document can be described from 3 perspectives:

- Semantic content of the document, i.e. representation of its meaning.

- Context of the document, e.g. its author, publisher.

- Structure of the document, e.g. its language, style, length.

Context and structure descriptors are commonly given as regular attributes of the document and can be modeled using any structural data model. Modeling the semantic content may be done manually, traditionally by the author and/or a librarian, by assigning keyword descriptors from a controlled vocabulary and by creating a free text description field. However, there exist algorithms that can provide a semantic descriptor, or *signature* automatically using techniques developed for text-based Information Retrieval systems.

Automatic modeling of the semantic content of a document collection is based on two laws that describe the distribution of the words used in the document and within a document collection:

- Heaps' law of vocabulary growth.

- Zipf's law of term distribution.

Heaps' law indicates that there will be a near finite vocabulary for a set of documents that can be used to describe the semantic content of the documents in a document collection. Zipf's law illustrates that the vocabulary is unequally distributed. Studies of vocabulary distribution, confirm the 'obvious' that the most frequent words; articles, prepositions, adjectives, adverbs and some verbs, "a, the, one, to, he, she, not, is ", do not carry independent meaning and therefore are not good descriptors of the semantic content of a document. Further, the most infrequent words are frequently alternative or misspellings of other terms in the vocabulary. These observations lead to the use of the medium frequency terms as semantic descriptors for a document collection. Good semantic descriptors can be found in the title, keywords (if present), the abstract/summary, and in the main body of the document.

The semantic content of a document can be represented by a *document signature*, consisting of a list of weighted terms, called index terms that are selected from the document and possibly weighted to reflect their descriptive strength in characterization of the document. Alternatively, the index terms can be selected from a domain taxonomy or ontology.

Modeling Images

In Image Retrieval systems, the semantic content of a document is represented by *features* that are commonly recorded as descriptive text attributes, such as title/caption, keywords and/or text descriptions. Image descriptors/features can be classified according to the level of abstraction, or distance from the actual physical content of the image.

Level	Descriptor	Examples
1	Structural	Color, texture, shape region, location
2	Objects in image	Building, plants, person relationships between objects
3	Identification of objects in image	The White House, roses, George W. Bush
4	Event representation	Press conference, flight to camp david
5	Emotion represented	Urgency, anger, joy

Structural features, also called *low level features*, such as color, texture and shape can be used to compose an *image signature*. The advantage of using these features is that they can be extracted automatically. The problem with them is that they seldom represent the semantic content of the image, which is commonly the focus of a user query. This phenomenon is known as the *semantic gap* between the image descriptor and the user search criteria.

Identification of objects in an image, level 2, can be automated to a certain extent, commonly restrained to a particular domain, for example: medical, security, logo identification. General object identification is still very difficult, though there are a number of research projects addressing this descriptor level.

The remaining levels, #3-5, need to be specified manually as *text annotations*. The advantages with text annotations are that they can be used to provide a very rich interpretation of the image and can be searched using traditional exact match on attribute content or using similarity measures from text retrieval algorithms. The disadvantage of manual annotation of images is that it is time consuming and subjective. The latter can again cause a form for *semantic gap* if the language used and content seen by the indexer differs from that of the user/requestor.

Modeling Multimedia Collections in SSM

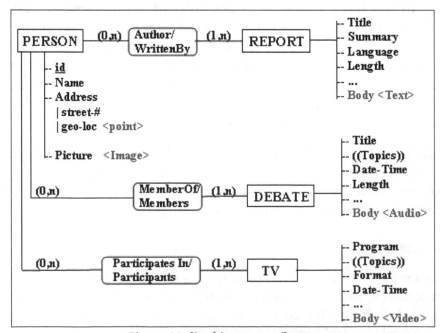

Figure: Media objects as attributes.

Multimedia objects can be modeled in SSM in several ways depending on the complexity and independence of the media objects and on the level of detail required by the application. For example, media objects can be modeled as:

- An attribute of an entity-type: ex. Person. Picture or Person. geographic_location.

- An entity-type: ex. Report with such attributes as {id, title, keywords, summary, content}.

- A set of related entity-types: ex. Report consists of Media Objects of text and image type.

Figure above presents a data model of a multimedia database in which 5 media objects of various types are embedded as attributes in a traditional database application. In SSM, the data-type name reflects the source media object type:

SSM Attribute	Media data type
Person.geo_loc	point - a location on a geographic map
Person.Picture	image
Report.Body	text
Debate.Body	audio stream
TV.Body	video (image + audio) stream

By the above definition of multimedia, all of the entity types (Person, Report, Debate, and TV) in above figure represent multimedia objects; though popular use of the term would probably only cover the video data type. None the less, the variety and complexity of these multimedia data requires additional concepts in the data modeling language and additional functionality in the data management system.

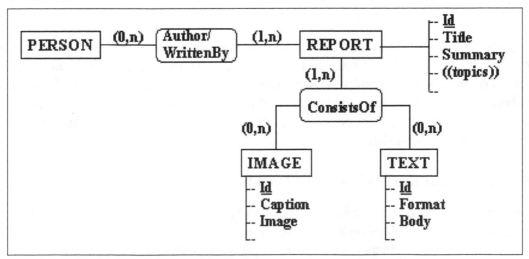

Figure: Complex media object - as a ternary-relationship.

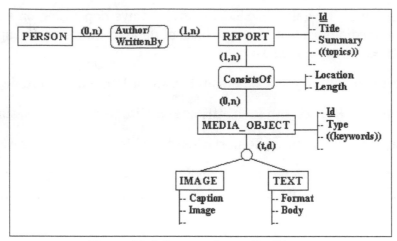

Figure: Modeling complex media objects.

Figure above presents 2 additional ways to model a complex multimedia object type. In this example, the entity type *Report* is modeled using:

- A *ternary relationship* between the report components; image, text, and the report header.

- A *classification hierarchy* "Media object" with subclasses *image* and *text*, which is related to Report through a binary relationship.

In both models, the collections of images and texts may contain elements that are not used or that are used more than once. The consists of relationship is vital for specification of the spatial and temporal relationships between the media objects and within the multimedia object.

The *n-ary relationship* model of multimedia objects, illustrated is useful when a balanced set of related media objects occur in the 'parent' multimedia object. This structure is good when the media objects are related to each other in space and/or time. Examples include images with descriptive text in a document or the audio and image streams in video/film. The relationship itself should include attributes describing the spatial and temporal relationships used for presentation of the component parts. These attributes will be multi-valued, one set for each media object in the relationship, making the relationship complex.

The *classification hierarchy* model is useful when the sets of media objects are relatively independent and used in multiple multimedia objects, as is the case in image reuse in news articles and advertising. The binary relationship between the multimedia object and each of its components allows a straight forward location for spatial and temporal relationships defining the placement of each media object in the multimedia object. SSM is primarily a structural model, representing the static structure of inter-related data.

Data Manipulation for Multimedia Databases

While query processing is the major focus of this chapter, data manipulation, which is much broader than query processing and includes editing as well as transaction management, is discussed here. Data manipulation involves various aspects. Support for querying, browsing, and filtering the data is essential for multimedia databases. In addition to querying the data, one may also want to edit the data.

1. Object Editing: Consider editing multimedia objects. For example, two objects may be merged to form a third object. One can project an object to form a smaller object. As an example, objects may be merged based on time intervals, and an object may be projected based on time intervals. Objects may also be updated in whole or in part.

2. Browsing: Browsing multimedia data is essentially carried out by a hypermedia database management system. The multimedia data is presented in terms of nodes and links. One traverses the links to reach the nodes and clicks on the links to get the relevant multimedia data.

3. Filtering: Filtering is the process of removing unnecessary material from data. This occurs quite often in video data where material inappropriate for children may be removed from a video clip. This means that the video clips have to be filtered and the filtered data displayed to the users.

4. Transaction Management: This function is also an aspect of data manipulation as it involves querying and updating databases. There has been some discussion as to whether transaction management is needed in MM-DBMSs. We feel that this is important because, in many cases, annotations may be associated with multimedia objects. For example, if one updates an image, its annotation must also be updated. Therefore, the two operations have to be carried out as part of a transaction. Unlike query processing, transaction management in an MM-DBMS is still a new area. Associated with transaction management are concurrency control and recovery. The issue is what are the transaction models? Are there special concurrency control and recovery mechanisms? Much research is needed in this area.

5. Update Processing: Update processing is usually considered part of query processing or transaction management. Update processing is essentially updating the multimedia data and is often a single user update. An example of a request is, "update the text paragraph C in document A to paragraph B." There have been many discussions on updating video and audio data. That is, how do you update part of a video or parts of an image? Is it possible to delete part of an image and replace it with some other image? We do not have satisfactory answers to update processing for multimedia databases. This is also related to the difficulties in transactions processing in multimedia databases.

Multimedia Indexing

The storage manager is responsible for accessing the database. To improve the efficiency of query and update algorithms, appropriate access methods and index strategies have to be enforced. That is, in generating strategies for executing query and update requests, the access methods and index strategies that is used need to be taken into consideration. The access methods used to access the database depend on the indexing methods. Therefore, creating and maintaining appropriate index files is a major issue in database management systems. By using an appropriate indexing mechanism, the query processing algorithms may not have to search the entire database. Instead, the data to be retrieved could be accessed directly. Consequently, the retrieval algorithms are more efficient.

Extensive research has been performed to develop appropriate access methods and index strategies for relational database systems. Some examples of index strategies are B trees and hashing. The major issues in storage management for multimedia databases include developing special index methods and access strategies for multimedia data types. Content-based data access is important for many multimedia applications. However, efficient techniques for content-based data access are still a challenge.

One could also develop indexes for the annotations. Since the annotations describe information about the multimedia data, if one can access the annotations, one can get the multimedia data. Various indexing techniques for multimedia data have been proposed. Also, extensions to B trees and B + trees have been proposed for multimedia data.

Other storage issues include caching data. How often should data be cached? Are there any special considerations for multimedia data? Are there special algorithms? Also, storage techniques for integrating different data types are needed. For example, a multimedia database may contain video, audio, and text databases instead of just one data type. The displays of these different data types have to be synchronized. Appropriate storage mechanisms are needed so that there is continuous display of the data. It is important that the display of multimedia data is synchronized with the retrieval of the data. This is especially true in the case of video on demand (VOD). Suppose we want to look at a film and we retrieve the video through the Internet or with the VOD boxes from our television sets. If the presentation is much quicker than the retrieval, there will be periods where we will have no display, which may not be acceptable to many viewers. In other words, we need continuous presentation of the film. In some cases, we can cache the film in order to get continuous display. It is impossible to cache all the films, and, therefore, we need efficient synchronization techniques. Typically, a user may specify the quality of service primitives, and the video should be presented according to the specifications. Video streaming has been a topic of much recent research. Furthermore, we now have special devices that consumers can purchase and attach to their television sets so that quality of service video on demand is and possible.

Parallel Database System

Parallel database system improves performance of data processing using multiple resources in parallel, like multiple CPU and disks are used parallely. It also performs many parallelization operations like, data loading and query processing.

Goals of Parallel Databases

The concept of Parallel Database was built with a goal to:

- Improve performance: The performance of the system can be improved by connecting multiple CPU and disks in parallel. Many small processors can also be connected in parallel.

- Improve availability of data: Data can be copied to multiple locations to improve the availability of data. For example: if a module contains a relation (table in database) which is unavailable then it is important to make it available from another module.

- Improve reliability: Reliability of system is improved with completeness, accuracy and availability of data.

- Provide distributed access of data: Companies having many branches in multiple cities can access data with the help of parallel database system.

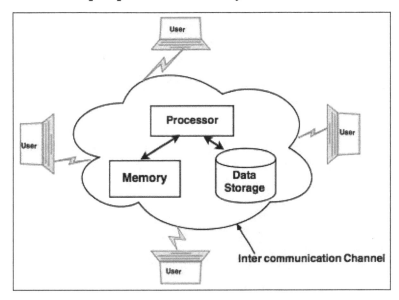

Parallel Database Architecture

We need architectures which can handle data through data distribution, parallel query execution thereby produce good throughput of queries or Transactions. Figure shows the different architecture proposed and successfully implemented in the area of Parallel Database systems. In the figures, P represents Processors, M represents Memory, and D represents Disks/Disk setups.

Shared Memory Architecture

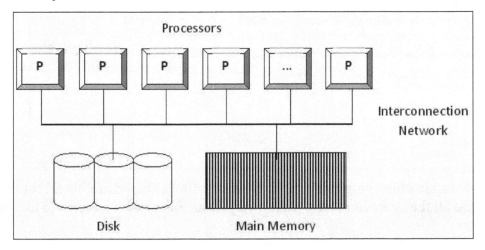

In Shared Memory architecture, single memory is shared among many processors as show in above Figure. As shown in the figure, several processors are connected through an interconnection network with Main memory and disk setup. Here interconnection network is usually a high speed network (may be Bus, Mesh, or Hypercube) which makes data sharing (transporting) easy among the various components (Processor, Memory, and Disk).

Advantages:

- Simple implementation.

- Establishes effective communication between processors through single memory addresses space.

- Above point leads to less communication overhead.

Disadvantages:

- Higher degree of parallelism (more number of concurrent operations in different processors) cannot be achieved due to the reason that all the processors share the same interconnection network to connect with memory. This causes Bottleneck in interconnection network (Interference), especially in the case of Bus interconnection network.

- Addition of processor would slow down the existing processors.

- Cache-coherency should be maintained. That is, if any processor tries to read the data used or modified by other processors, then we need to ensure that the data is of latest version.

- Degree of Parallelism is limited. More number of parallel processes might degrade the performance.

Shared Disk Architecture

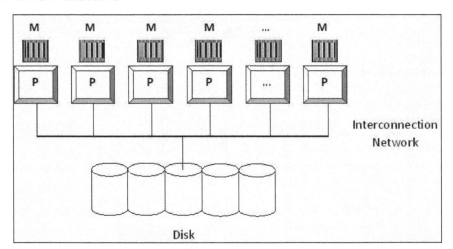

In Shared Disk architecture, single disk or single disk setup is shared among all the available processors and also all the processors have their own private memories as shown in above Figure.

Advantages:

- Failure of any processors would not stop the entire system (Fault tolerance).

- Interconnection to the memory is not a bottleneck. (It was bottleneck in Shared Memory architecture).

- Support larger number of processors (when compared to Shared Memory architecture).

Disadvantages:

- Interconnection to the disk is bottleneck as all processors share common disk setup.

- Inter-processor communication is slow. The reason is, all the processors have their own memory. Hence, the communication between processors need reading of data from other processors' memory which needs additional software support.

Example Real Time Shared Disk Implementation:

- DEC clusters (VMScluster) running Rdb.

Shared Nothing Architecture

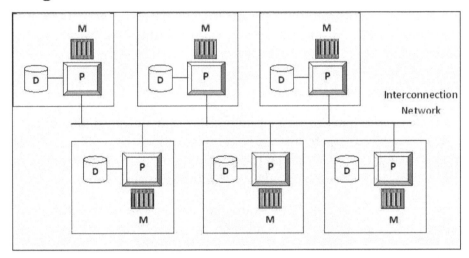

In Shared Nothing architecture, every processor has its own memory and disk setup. This setup may be considered as set of individual computers connected through high speed interconnection network using regular network protocols and switches for example to share data between computers. (This architecture is used in the Distributed Database System). In Shared Nothing parallel database system implementation, we insist the use of similar nodes that are Homogenous systems. (In distributed database System we may use Heterogeneous nodes).

Advantages:

- Number of processors used here is scalable. That is, the design is flexible to add more number of computers.

- Unlike in other two architectures, only the data request which cannot be answered by local processors need to be forwarded through interconnection network.

Disadvantages:

- Non-local disk accesses are costly. That is, if one server receives the request. If the required data not available, it must be routed to the server where the data is available. It is slightly complex.

- Communication cost involved in transporting data among computers.

Example Real Time Shared Nothing Implementation:

- Teradata,

- Tandem,

- Oracle nCUBE.

Data Warehouse

Data warehousing is the process of constructing and using a data warehouse. A data warehouse is constructed by integrating data from multiple heterogeneous sources that support analytical reporting, structured and/or ad hoc queries, and decision making. Data warehousing involves data cleaning, data integration, and data consolidations.

Using Data Warehouse Information

There are decision support technologies that help utilize the data available in a data warehouse. These technologies help executives to use the warehouse quickly and effectively. They can gather data, analyze it, and take decisions based on the information present in the warehouse. The information gathered in a warehouse can be used in any of the following domains:

- Tuning Production Strategies: The product strategies can be well tuned by repositioning the products and managing the product portfolios by comparing the sales quarterly or yearly.

- Customer Analysis: Customer analysis is done by analyzing the customer's buying preferences, buying time, budget cycles, etc.

- Operations Analysis: Data warehousing also helps in customer relationship management, and making environmental corrections. The information also allows us to analyze business operations.

Integrating Heterogeneous Databases

To integrate heterogeneous databases, we have two approaches:

- Query-driven Approach,

- Update-driven Approach.

Query-Driven Approach

This is the traditional approach to integrate heterogeneous databases. This approach was used to build wrappers and integrators on top of multiple heterogeneous databases. These integrators are also known as mediators.

Process of Query-Driven Approach

- When a query is issued to a client side, a metadata dictionary translates the query into an appropriate form for individual heterogeneous sites involved.

- Now these queries are mapped and sent to the local query processor.

- The results from heterogeneous sites are integrated into a global answer set.

Disadvantages

This approach has following disadvantages:

- Query-driven approach needs complex integration and filtering processes.

- This approach is very inefficient.

- It is very expensive for frequent queries.

- This approach is also very expensive for queries that require aggregations.

Update-Driven Approach

This is an alternative to the traditional approach. Today's data warehouse systems follow update-driven approach rather than the traditional approach. In update-driven approach, the information from multiple heterogeneous sources is integrated in advance and is stored in a warehouse. This information is available for direct querying and analysis.

Advantages:

- This approach provides high performance.

- The data is copied, processed, integrated, annotated, summarized and restructured in semantic data store in advance.

- Query processing does not require an interface to process data at local sources.

Functions of Data Warehouse Tools and Utilities:

- Data Extraction: Involves gathering data from multiple heterogeneous sources.

- Data Cleaning: Involves finding and correcting the errors in data.

- Data Transformation: Involves converting the data from legacy format to warehouse format.

- Data Loading: Involves sorting, summarizing, consolidating, checking integrity, and building indices and partitions.

- Refreshing: Involves updating from data sources to warehouse.

Data Warehouse Architecture

Architecture, in the Data warehousing world, is the concept and design of the data base and technologies that are used to load the data. A good architecture will enable scalability, high performance and easy maintenance. Data warehouse architecture consists of the following interconnected layers:

- Operational database layer: Operational database layer serves as source for the Data warehouse. This may include the Operation Data Store (ODS) and other similar sources (Ex. Flat files).

- Data access layer: The data access layer is the part which involves in extracting the data from multiple sources, cleansing and transforming the data and loading it.

- Metadata layer: The data directory. This is usually more detailed than an operational system data directory. There are dictionaries for the entire warehouse and sometimes dictionaries for the data that can be accessed by a particular reporting and analysis tool.

- Informational access layer: The data accessed for reporting and analyzing and the tools for reporting and analyzing data. Business intelligence tools fall into this layer.

Famous authors and data warehouse experts Ralph Kimball and Bill Inmon give two different design methodologies for building a data warehouse. Kimball's approach is more of a Bottom-up design where data marts are created first for specific subject/business areas and have the capability to report and analyze. Then these data marts are combined to create a data warehouse. This approach provides quicker approach to get the data ready for individual subjects/businesses. The major task in this design is maintaining the Dimensions across multiple data marts. Inmon has defined a data warehouse as a centralized repository for the entire enterprise, in which the data warehouse is designed using a normalized enterprise data model. Data at the lowest level of detail is stored in the data warehouse. Dimensional data marts containing data needed for specific business processes or specific departments are created from the data warehouse. Inmon states that the data warehouse is: Subject-oriented, Non-volatile and Integrated.

This methodology generates highly consistent dimensional views of data across data marts since all data marts are loaded from the centralized repository. Top-down design has also proven to be robust against business changes. Generating new dimensional data marts against the data stored in the data warehouse is a relatively simple task. The main disadvantage to the top-down methodology is that it represents a very large project with a very broad scope. The up-front cost for implementing a data warehouse using the top-down methodology is significant, and the duration of time from the start of project to the point that end users experience initial benefits can be substantial. In addition, the top down methodology can be inflexible and unresponsive to changing departmental needs during the implementation phases.

Now there are new methodologies commonly called as Hybrid Design, that combine these two and provide more comprehensive and robust data warehouse design. We can divide IT systems into transactional (OLTP) and analytical (OLAP). In general we can assume that OLTP systems provide source data to data warehouses, whereas OLAP systems help to analyze it.

OLTP: On-line Transaction Processing

It is characterized by a large number of short on-line transactions (INSERT, UPDATE, and

DELETE). The main emphasis for OLTP systems is put on very fast query processing, maintaining data integrity in multi-access environments and an effectiveness measured by number of transactions per second. In OLTP database there is detailed and current data, and schema used to store transactional databases is the entity model (usually 3NF).

OLAP: On-line Analytical Processing

It is characterized by relatively low volume of transactions. Queries are often very complex and involve aggregations. For OLAP systems a response time is an effectiveness measure. OLAP applications are widely used by Data Mining techniques. In OLAP database there is aggregated, historical data, stored in multi-dimensional schemas (usually star schema).

	OLTP System Online Transaction Processing (Operational System)	OLAP System Online Analytical Processing (Data Warehouse)
Source of data	Operational data; OLTPs are the original source of the data.	Consolidation data; OLAP data comes from the various OLTP Databases.
Purpose of data	To control and run fundamental business tasks.	To help with planning, problem solving, and decision support.
What the data	Reveals a snapshot of ongoing business Processes.	Multi-dimensional views of variouskinds of business activities.
Inserts and Updates	Short and fast inserts and updates initiated by end users.	Periodic long-running batch jobs refresh the data.
Queries	Relatively standardized and simple queries Returning relatively few records.	Often complex queries involving Aggregations.
Processing Speed	Typically very fast.	Depends on the amount of data involved; batch data refreshes and complex queries may take many hours; query speed can be improved by creating indexes.
Space Requirements	Can be relatively small if historical data is archived.	Larger due to the existence of aggregation structures and history data; requires more indexes than OLTP.
Database Design	Highly normalized with many tables.	Typically de-normalized with fewer tables; use of star and/or snowflake schemas.
Backup and Recovery	Backup religiously; operational data is critical to run the business; data loss is likely to entail significant monetary loss and legal liability.	Instead of regular backups, some environments may consider simply reloading the OLTP data as a recovery method.

Online Analytical Processing (OLAP) databases facilitate business-intelligence queries. OLAP is a database technology that has been optimized for querying and reporting, instead of processing transactions. The source data for OLAP is Online Transactional Processing (OLTP) databases that are commonly stored in data warehouses. OLAP data is derived from this historical data, and aggregated into structures that permit sophisticated analysis. OLAP data is also organized hierarchically and stored in cubes instead of tables. It is a sophisticated technology that uses multidimensional structures to provide rapid access to data for analysis. This organization makes it easy for a PivotTable report or PivotChart report to display high-level summaries, such as sales totals across an entire country or region, and also display the details for sites where sales are particularly strong or weak.

OLAP databases are designed to speed up the retrieval of data. Because the OLAP server, rather than Microsoft Office Excel, computes the summarized values, less data needs to be sent to Excel when you create or change a report. This approach enables you to work with much larger amounts of source data than you could if the data were organized in a traditional database, where Excel retrieves all of the individual records and then calculates the summarized values.

OLAP databases contain two basic types of data: measures, which are numeric data, the quantities and averages that you use to make informed business decisions, and dimensions, which are the categories that you use to organize these measures. OLAP databases help organize data by many levels of detail, using the same categories that you are familiar with to analyze the data.

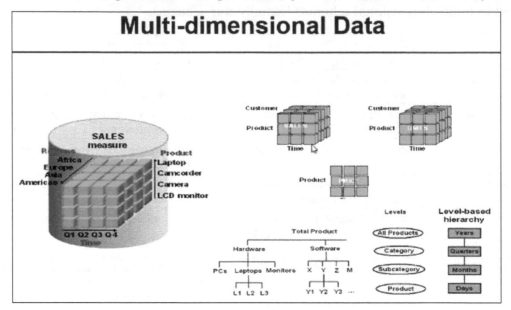

1. Cube: It is a data structure that aggregates the measures by the levels and hierarchies of each of the dimensions that you want to analyze. Cubes combine several dimensions, such as time, geography, and product lines, with summarized data, such as sales or inventory figures. Cubes are not "cubes" in the strictly mathematical sense because they do not necessarily have equal sides. However, they are an apt metaphor for a complex concept.

2. Measure: It is a set of values in a cube that are based on a column in the cube's fact table and that are usually numeric values. Measures are the central values in the cube that are preprocessed, aggregated, and analyzed. Common examples include sales, profits, revenues, and costs.

3. Member: It is an item in a hierarchy representing one or more occurrences of data. A member can be either unique or non-unique. For example, 2007 and 2008 represent unique members in the year level of a time dimension, whereas January represents non-unique members in the month level because there can be more than one January in the time dimension if it contains data for more than one year.

4. Calculated Member: It is a member of a dimension whose value is calculated at run time by using an expression is called calculated member. Calculated member values may be derived from other members' values. For example, a calculated member, Profit, can be determined by subtracting the value of the member, Costs, from the value of the member, Sales.

5. Dimension: It is a set of one or more organized hierarchies of levels in a cube that a user understands and uses as the base for data analysis. For example, a geography dimension might include levels for Country/Region, State/Province, and City. Or, a time dimension might include a hierarchy with levels for year, quarter, month, and day. In a PivotTable report or PivotChart report, each hierarchy becomes a set of fields that you can expand and collapse to reveal lower or higher levels.

6. Hierarchy: It is a logical tree structure that organizes the members of a dimension such that each member has one parent member and zero or more child members. A child is a member in the next lower level in a hierarchy that is directly related to the current member. For example, in a Time hierarchy containing the levels Quarter, Month, and Day, January is a child of Qtr1. A parent is a member in the next higher level in a hierarchy that is directly related to the current member. The parent value is usually a consolidation of the values of all of its children. For example, in a Time hierarchy that contains the levels Quarter, Month, and Day, Qtr1 is the parent of January.

Level

Within a hierarchy, data can be organized into lower and higher levels of detail, such as Year, Quarter, Month, and Day levels in a Time hierarchy.

Star Schema

The star schema architecture is the simplest data warehouse schema. It is called a star schema because the diagram resembles a star, with points radiating from a center. The center of the star consists of fact table and the points of the star are the dimension tables. Usually the fact tables in a star schema are in third normal form (3NF) whereas dimensional tables are de-normalized. Despite the fact that the star schema is the simplest architecture, it is most commonly used nowadays and is recommended by Oracle.

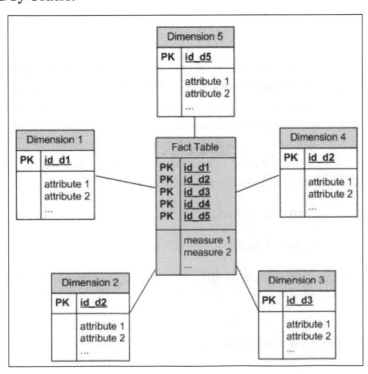

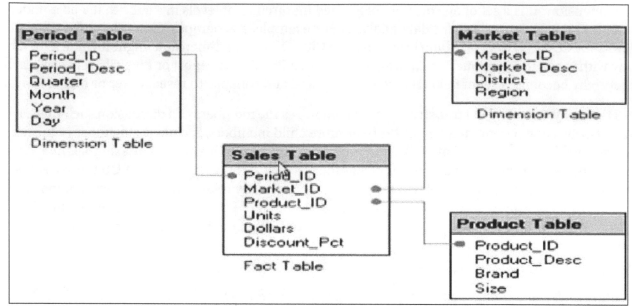

Figure: Star Schema.

There is a single fact table for each dimension one dimension table. It does not capture hierarchies directly.

Fact Tables

A fact table typically has two types of columns: foreign keys to dimension tables and measures those that contain numeric facts. A fact table can contain fact's data on detail or aggregated level.

Dimension Tables

A dimension is a structure usually composed of one or more hierarchies that categorizes data. If a dimension hasn't got a hierarchies and levels it is called flat dimension or list. The primary keys of each of the dimension tables are part of the composite primary key of the fact table. Dimensional attributes help to describe the dimensional value. They are normally descriptive, textual values. Dimension tables are generally small in size then fact table. Typical fact tables store data about sales while dimension tables data about geographic region (markets, cities), clients, products, times, channels. The main characteristics of star schema:

- Simple structure: Easy to understand schema.

- Great query effectives: Small number of tables to join.

- Relatively long time of loading data into dimension tables: De-normalization, redundancy data caused that size of the table could be large.

- The most commonly used in the data warehouse implementations: Widely supported by a large number of business intelligence tools.

Snowflake Schema

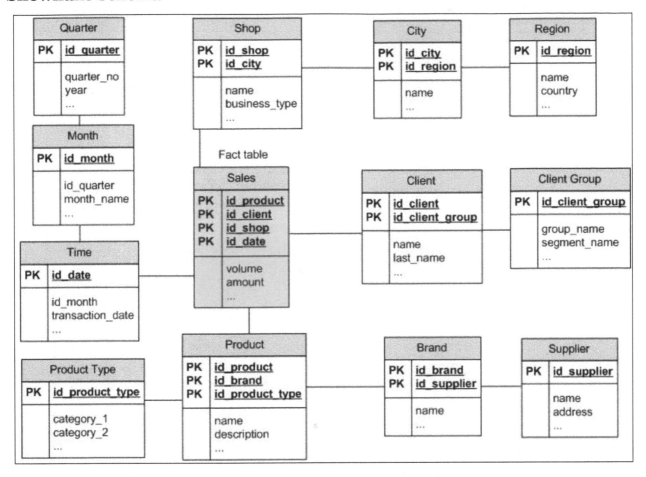

A snowflake schema is a logical arrangement of tables in a relational database such that the entity relationship diagram resembles a snowflake in shape. Closely related to the star schema, the snowflake schema is represented by centralized fact tables which are connected to multiple dimensions. In the snowflake schema, however, dimensions are normalized into multiple related tables whereas the star schema's dimensions are denormalized with each dimension being represented by a single table. When the dimensions of a snowflake schema are elaborate, having multiple levels of relationships, and where child tables have multiple parent tables ("forks in the road"), a complex snowflake shape starts to emerge. The "snow flaking" effect only affects the dimension tables and not the fact tables.

Fact Constellation Schema

For each star schema it is possible to construct fact constellation schema (for example by splitting the original star schema into more star schemes each of them describes facts on another level of dimension hierarchies). The fact constellation architecture contains multiple fact tables that share many dimension tables.

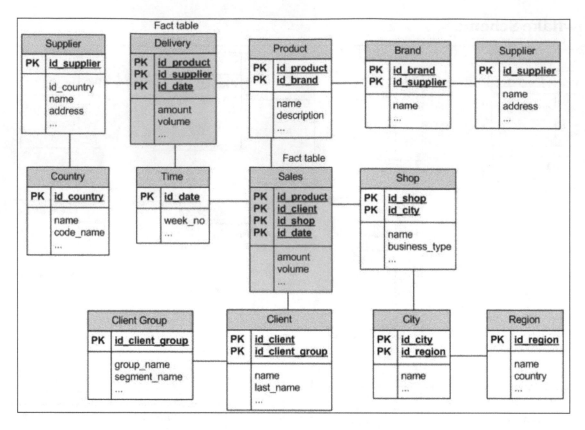

The main shortcoming of the fact constellation schema is a more complicated design because many variants for particular kinds of aggregation must be considered and selected. Moreover, dimension tables are still large.

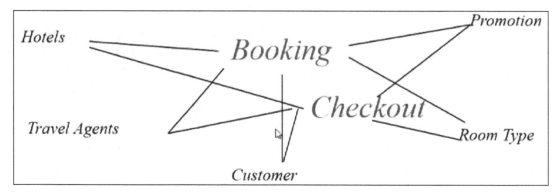

Multiple fact tables share many dimension tables. Booking and checking may share many dimension tables in the hotel industry.

Granularity

The single most important aspect and issue of the design of the data warehouse is the issue of granularity. It refers to the detail or summarization of the units of data in the data warehouse. The more detail there is, the lower the granularity level. The less detail there is, the higher the granularity level. Granularity is a major design issue in the data warehouse as it profoundly affects the volume of data. The figure below shows the issue of granularity in a data warehouse.

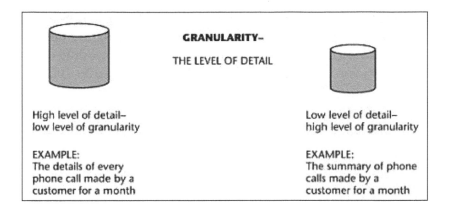

Dual Levels of Granularity

Sometimes there is a great need for efficiency in storing and accessing data and the ability to analyze the data in great data. When an organization has huge volumes of data it makes sense to consider two or more levels of granularity in the detailed portion of the data warehouse. The figure below shows two levels of granularity in a data warehouse. In the below figure we see a phone company which fits the needs of most of its shops. There is a huge amount of data in the operational level. The data up to 30 days is stored in the operational environment. Then the data shifts to the lightly and highly summarized zone.

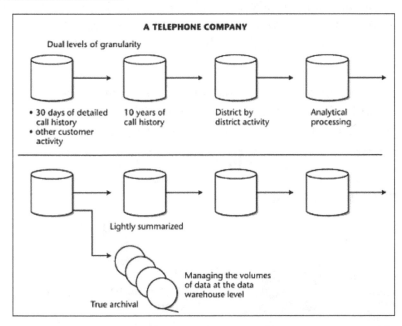

This process of granularity not only helps the data warehouse it supports more than data marts. It supports the process of exploration and data mining. Exploration and data mining takes masses of detailed historical data and examine the same to analyze and previously unknown patterns of business activity.

A multidimensional database is a computer software system designed to allow for the efficient and convenient storage and retrieval of large volumes of data that is (1) intimately related and (2) stored, viewed and analyzed from different perspectives. These perspectives are called dimensions.

Getting answers to typical business questions from raw data often requires viewing that data from various perspectives. For example, an automobile marketer wanting to improve business activity might want to examine sales data collected throughout the organization. The evaluation would entail viewing historical sales volume figures from multiple perspectives such as:

- Sales volumes by model.

- Sales volumes by color.

- Sales volumes by dealership.

- Sales volumes over time.

Analyzing the Sales Volumes data from any one or more of the above perspectives can yield answers to important questions such as: What is the trend in sales volumes over a period of time for a specific model and color across a specific group of dealerships?

Having the ability to respond to these types of inquiries in a timely fashion allows managers to formulate effective strategies, identify trends and improve their overall ability to make important business decisions. Certainly, relational databases could answer the question above, but query results must also come to the manager in a meaningful and timely way. End users needing interactive access to large volumes of data stored in a relational environment are often frustrated by poor response times and lack of flexibility offered by relational database technology and their SQL query building tools. What follow now is an explanation of the reason for their frustration and a set of examples that assist in comparing the multidimensional database to its most common alternative–the relational database.

Granularity is the most important to the data warehouse architect because it affects all the environments that depend in the data warehouse for data. The main issue of granularity is that of getting it at the right level. The level of granularity needs to be neither too high nor too low.

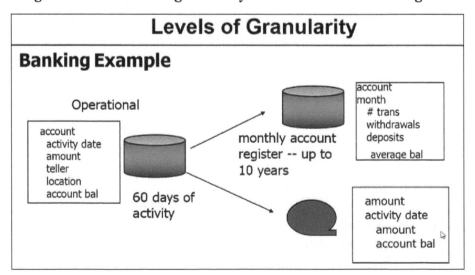

Raw Estimates

The starting point to determine the appropriate level of granularity is to do a rough estimate of the number of rows that would be there in the data warehouse. If there are very few rows in the data warehouse then any level of granularity would be fine. After these projections are made the index data space projections are calculated. In this index data projection we identify the length of the key or element of data and determine whether the key would exist for each and every entry in the primary table.

Data in the data warehouse grows in a rate never seen before. The combination of historical data and detailed data produces a growth rate which is phenomenal. It is only after data warehouse the terms terabyte and petabyte came into existence. As data keeps growing some part of the data becomes inactively used and they are sometimes called as dormant data. So it is always better to have these kinds of dormant data in external storage media.

Data which is usually stored externally are much less expensive than the data which resides on the disk storage. Some times as these data are external it becomes difficult to retrieve the data and this causes lots of performance issues and these issues cause lots of effect on the granularity. It is usually the rough estimates which tell whether the overflow storage should be considered or not.

Levels of Granularity

After simple analysis is done the next step would be to determine the level of granularity for the data which is residing on the disk storage. Determining the level of granularity requires some extent of common sense and intuition. Having a very low level of granularity also doesn't make any sense as we will have to need many resources to analyze and process the data. While if the level of granularity is very high then this means that analysis needs to done on the data which reside in the external storage. Hence this is a very tricky issue so the only way to handle this to put the data in front of the user and let he/she decide on what the type of data should be. The below figure shows the iterative loop which needs to be followed.

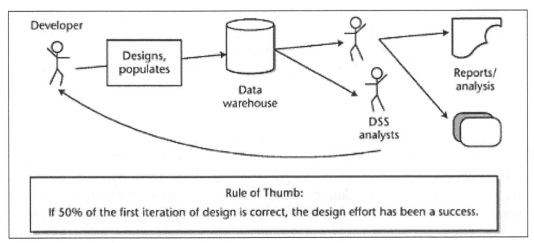

The process which needs to be followed is:

- Build a small subset quickly based on the feedback.

- Prototyping.

- Looking what other people have done.

- Working with experienced user.

- Looking at what the organization has now.

- Having sessions with the simulated output.

Database Replication

Data Replication is the process of storing data in more than one site or node. It is useful in improving the availability of data. It is simply copying data from a database from one server to another server so that all the users can share the same data without any inconsistency. The result is a distributed database in which users can access data relevant to their tasks without interfering with the work of others.

Data replication encompasses duplication of transactions on an ongoing basis, so that the replicate is in a consistently updated state and synchronized with the source. However in data replication data is available at different locations, but a particular relation has to reside at only one location.

There can be full replication, in which the whole database is stored at every site. There can also be partial replication, in which some frequently used fragment of the database are replicated and others are not replicated.

Types of Data Replication

- Transactional Replication: In Transactional replication users receive full initial copies of the database and then receive updates as data changes. Data is copied in real time from the publisher to the receiving database (subscriber) in the same order as they occur with the publisher therefore in this type of replication, transactional consistency is guaranteed. Transactional replication is typically used in server-to-server environments. It does not simply copy the data changes, but rather consistently and accurately replicates each change.

- Snapshot Replication: Snapshot replication distributes data exactly as it appears at a specific moment in time does not monitor for updates to the data. The entire snapshot is generated and sent to Users. Snapshot replication is generally used when data changes are infrequent. It is bit slower than transactional because on each attempt it moves multiple records from one end to the other end. Snapshot replication is a good way to perform initial synchronization between the publisher and the subscriber.

- Merge Replication: Data from two or more databases is combined into a single database. Merge replication is the most complex type of replication because it allows both publisher and subscriber to independently make changes to the database. Merge replication is typically used in server-to-client environments. It allows changes to be sent from one publisher to multiple subscribers.

Replication Schemes

Full Replication

The most extreme case is replication of the whole database at every site in the distributed system. This will improve the availability of the system because the system can continue to operate as long as at least one site is up.

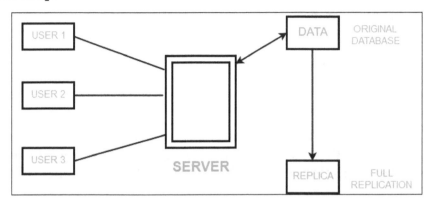

Advantages of full replication:

- High Availability of Data.

- Improves the performance for retrieval of global queries as the result can be obtained locally from any of the local site.

- Faster execution of Queries.

Disadvantages of Full Replication:

- Concurrency is difficult to achieve in full replication.

- Slow update process as a single update must be performed at different databases to keep the copies consistent.

No Replication

The other case of replication involves having No replication – that is, each fragment is stored at only one site.

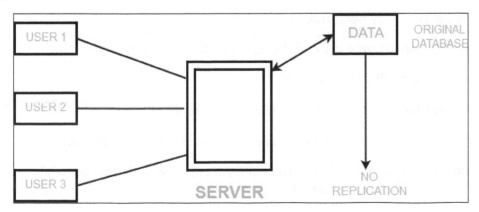

Advantages of No replication:

- The data can be easily recovered.

- Concurrency can be achieved in no replication.

Disadvantages of No replication:

- Since multiple users are accessing the same server, it may slow down the execution of queries.

- The data is not easily available as there is no replication.

Partial Replication

In this type of replication some fragments of the database may be replicated whereas others may not. The number of copies of the fragment may range from one to the total number of sites in the distributed system. The description of replication of fragments is sometimes called the replication schema.

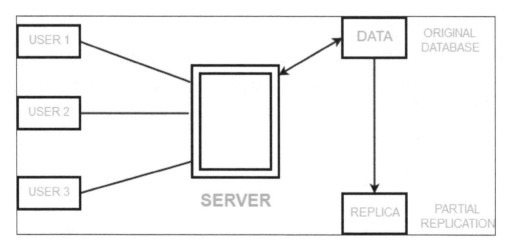

Advantages of Partial replication:

- The number of copies of the fragment depends upon the importance of data.

Advantages of Data Replication

Data Replication is generally performed to:

- To provide a consistent copy of data across all the database nodes.

- To increase the availability of data.

- The reliability of data is increased through data replication.

- Data Replication supports multiple users and gives high performance.

- To remove any data redundancy, the databases are merged and slave databases are updated with outdated or incomplete data.

- Since replicas are created there are chances that the data is found itself where the transaction is executing which reduce the data movement.

- To perform faster execution of queries.

Disadvantages of Data Replication

- More storage space is needed as storing the replicas of same data at different sites consumes more space.

- Data Replication becomes expensive when the replicas at all different sites need to be updated.

- Maintaining Data consistency at all different sites involves complex measures.

Replica Control

When a data item is updated, its physical copies need to be updated. As easy as this might sound, this task, called replica control, is not a straightforward approach as there are many possible approaches, each having its advantages and its drawbacks depending on the application and the configuration. Let us illustrate this with an example. Assume our puppet company has decided to deploy a cluster of database replicas. Each node maintains a full copy of the database. When a client request arrives, it is redirected to one of the replicas that controls its execution. In most applications, there are two major request types: update requests, such as purchase() in the figure, update at least one data item; and read-only requests, such as check-status(), only read data items. Our company employs a Read-one-write-all (ROWA) replication strategy: the update of a data item is performed at all replicas, while a read operation accesses a single replica. ROWA can be implemented in various ways. The fundamental differences between existing approaches lie in where and when copies are updated. In regard to where, our company uses a primary copy approach. There is one database replica that is considered the primary (replica). It holds the primary copy of the database. The other replicas hold secondary copies and are called secondary (replicas). All update requests are sent to the primary replica and are first executed there. An update request might read and write several data items. All writes are forwarded to the secondary's where they are also executed. Read-only requests can be executed at the primary or the secondary's. They can execute completely locally without coordination with other replicas. In regard to when copies are updated, our company uses an eager approach, also referred to as synchronous replication. The secondary's apply the changes to their own copies immediately when they receive them, and then send a confirmation to the primary. Only when the primary knows that all secondary's have the changes, it confirms to the user that the execution was successful.

1. Primary copy vs. update anywhere: The use of a primary replica forces all updates to be executed first at a single node. This simplifies the coordination of concurrent update requests. However, it has several disadvantages. For example, the primary can become a bottleneck. The alternative is to use an update anywhere approach (also called update everywhere). Each replica accepts both update and read-only requests and is responsible for their execution. While it avoids the pitfalls of the primary copy approach, it has its own problems. In particular, it is

much harder to guarantee consistency as data copies might now be updated concurrently at different replicas.

2. Eager vs. lazy: By using eager replication, the primary only returns a confirmation to the user once all secondary's have the updates executed. Thus, copies are "virtually" consistent. However, clients might experience prolonged response times due to the replication coordination.

Especially with wide area replication, this can become a serious problem. Also network connectivity can be spotty in wide area networks, and the entire service might render unavailable if one replica is not reachable due to network problems. The alternative is to use lazy replication, also called asynchronous replication. With lazy replication, an update request is completely executed at one replica, which propagates the writes to the other replicas after returning a confirmation to the client. Thus, the coordination tasks do not affect the user. However, maintaining consistency is more difficult, as the same update takes place at different times at the various replicas. Additionally, when lazy replication is combined with update anywhere, two updates concurrently submitted to two replicas can update the same data item and succeed. Later, when the updates are propagated, the system has to detect such conflict, possibly undo one of the updates despite the fact that the client was already informed that the update was successful. Transactions, although we have not yet mentioned it, but to many readers, it will probably already be obvious that many of the applications that require replication will also require transactions and their properties – in particular atomicity, isolation and durability. In fact, it is pretty straightforward to map the execution of a client request to a transaction. Each request reads and/or writes several data items. From the outside, the execution of the request should appear as one logical execution unit. That is exactly the definition of a transaction. A transaction is a user-defined sequence of read and writes operations on data items, and the system provides a set of properties for their execution. Atomicity guarantees that a transaction either executes entirely or commits, or it aborts not leaving any changes in the database.

Thus, database systems provide rollback mechanisms to abort transactions and provide distributed commit protocols for distributed transactions, i.e., for transactions that access data items residing on different nodes. Isolation provides a transaction with the impression that no other transaction is currently executing in the system. Concurrency control mechanisms such as locking are in charge of that. Durability guarantees that once the initiator of the transaction has received the confirmation of commit, the changes of the transaction are, indeed, reflected in the database (they can, of course, later be overwritten by other transactions). Sophisticated logging protocols guarantee durability despite individual node failures. Replication does not make it easier to achieve these properties. In fact, replica control, atomic commit protocols and concurrency control often work tightly together to let a replicated system appear as a single transactional system. In this book, transactions will be first-class citizens in considering and analyzing replica control algorithms.

Replication Model

A database consists of a set of data items x, y. In a replicated database, there is a set of database nodes RA, RB. each of them having copies of data items. Thus, we refer to x, y as logical data items, and each logical data item x has physical copies x^A, x^B. Where RA is the node (replica) on which x^A resides. From the perspective of the application, a transaction is a sequence of read and writes operations on the logical data items of the database. The transaction is ended with a commit or an abort request. The latter indicates that the updates executed so far need to be rolled back. One of the tasks of replica control is to map the operations on the logical data items onto operations on the physical copies. The most common execution model is to translate a logical read operation $ri(x)$ of transaction Ti to one physical read operation $ri(x^A)$ on one particular copy x^A. And a logical write operation $wi(x)$ is mapped to physical write operations $wi(x^A)$, $wi(x^B)$, ... on all copies of x. This is called a read-one-write-all (ROWA) approach. Thus, a transaction Ti can have sub-transactions on many nodes, namely on each node on which it accesses at least one physical copy. For simplicity of the discussion, we assume in this and most of the other chapters full replication where each node in the system has a full copy of the database, i.e., copies of all data items. The terms "node" and "replica" are used interchangeably. With full replication, an update transaction, i.e., a transaction that has at least one write operation has sub-transactions on all nodes, while read-only transactions typically only access the copies of a single node, albeit it is possible to distribute the reads among several nodes. ROWA works fine because in most applications reads by far outnumber writes.

Hence, it makes sense to keep the overhead for read operations as small as possible. ROWA is not suitable when failures occur, as an update transaction cannot complete anymore once a single copy becomes unavailable. Therefore, a derivation is the read-one-write-all-available, or ROWAA, approach where write operations execute only on all copies that are currently available. Performing the mapping between logical and physical operations is not sufficient. Replica control must be tightly coupled with the mechanisms that achieve the transactional ACID properties: atomicity, consistency, isolation and durability. In fact, the ultimate goal is that the replicated system provides the same semantics as the original non-replicated system. This is what is termed as 1-copy-equivalence: the replicated system behaves like a 1-copy non-replicated system. The ACID properties are all related to providing well-defined consistency in the advent of concurrent access and failures. When replicating a database, due to the distributed execution and the possibility of node failures, if no extra measures are taken, one can easily end up with transaction executions that would be disallowed in a non-replicated system. This means that designing a database replication solution implies to take care of 1-copy equivalence. In this chapter, we look at each of the ACID properties individually and discuss what it means to provide this property in a replicated environment, i.e., what does it mean to extend it with 1-copy-equivalence.

Database Recovery

Database systems, like any other computer system, are subject to failures but the data stored in it must be available as and when required. When a database fails it must possess the facilities for fast recovery. It must also have atomicity i.e. either transactions are completed successfully and committed (the effect is recorded permanently in the database) or the transaction should have no effect on the database.

There are both automatic and non-automatic ways for both, backing up of data and recovery from any failure situations. The techniques used to recover the lost data due to system crash, transaction errors, viruses; catastrophic failure, incorrect commands execution etc. are database recovery techniques. So to prevent data loss recovery techniques based on deferred update and immediate update or backing up data can be used.

Recovery techniques are heavily dependent upon the existence of a special file known as a system log. It contains information about the start and end of each transaction and any updates which occur in the transaction. The log keeps track of all transaction operations that affect the values of database items. This information is needed to recover from transaction failure.

- The log is kept on disk start_transaction(T): This log entry records that transaction T starts the execution.

- read_item(T, X): This log entry records that transaction T reads the value of database item X.

- write_item(T, X, old_value, new_value): This log entry records that transaction T changes the value of the database item X from old_value to new_value. The old value is sometimes known as a before an image of X, and the new value is known as an afterimage of X.

- commit(T): This log entry records that transaction T has completed all accesses to the database successfully and its effect can be committed (recorded permanently) to the database.

- abort(T): This records that transaction T has been aborted.

- Checkpoint: Checkpoint is a mechanism where all the previous logs are removed from the system and stored permanently in a storage disk. Checkpoint declares a point before which the DBMS was in consistent state, and all the transactions were committed.

A transaction T reaches its commit point when all its operations that access the database have been executed successfully i.e. the transaction has reached the point at which it will not abort (terminate without completing). Once committed, the transaction is permanently recorded in the database. Commitment always involves writing a commit entry to the log and writing the log to disk. At the time of a system crash, item is searched back in the log for all transactions T that have written a start_transaction(T) entry into the log but have not written a commit(T) entry yet; these transactions may have to be rolled back to undo their effect on the database during the recovery process.

- Undoing: If a transaction crashes, then the recovery manager may undo transactions i.e. reverse the operations of a transaction. This involves examining a transaction for the log entry write_item(T, x, old_value, new_value) and setting the value of item x in the database to old-value.There are two major techniques for recovery from non-catastrophic transaction failures: deferred updates and immediate updates.

- Deferred update: This technique does not physically update the database on disk until a transaction has reached its commit point. Before reaching commit, all transaction updates are recorded in the local transaction workspace. If a transaction fails before reaching its commit point, it will not have changed the database in any way so UNDO is not needed. It may be necessary to REDO the effect of the operations that are recorded in the local transaction workspace, because their effect may not yet have been written in the database. Hence, a deferred update is also known as the No-undo/redo algorithm.

- Immediate update: In the immediate update, the database may be updated by some operations of a transaction before the transaction reaches its commit point. However, these operations are recorded in a log on disk before they are applied to the database, making recovery still possible. If a transaction fails to reach its commit point, the effect of its operation must be undone i.e. the transaction must be rolled back hence we require both undo and redo. This technique is known as undo/redo algorithm.

- Caching/Buffering: In this one or more disk pages that include data items to be updated are cached into main memory buffers and then updated in memory before being written back to disk. A collection of in-memory buffers called the DBMS cache is kept under control of DBMS for holding these buffers. A directory is used to keep track of which database items are in the buffer. A dirty bit is associated with each buffer, which is 0 if the buffer is not modified else 1 if modified.

- Shadow paging: It provides atomicity and durability. A directory with n entries is constructed, where the ith entry points to the ith database page on the link. When a transaction began executing the current directory is copied into a shadow directory. When a page is to be modified, a shadow page is allocated in which changes are made and when it is ready to become durable, all pages that refer to original are updated to refer new replacement page.

Some of the backup techniques are as follows:

- Full database backup: In this full database including data and database, Meta information needed to restore the whole database, including full-text catalogs are backed up in a predefined time series.

- Differential backup: It stores only the data changes that have occurred since last full database backup. When same data has changed many times since last full database backup, a differential backup stores the most recent version of changed data. For this first, we need to restore a full database backup.

- Transaction log backup: In this, all events that have occurred in the database, like a record of every single statement executed is backed up. It is the backup of transaction log entries and contains all transaction that had happened to the database. Through this, the database can be recovered to a specific point in time. It is even possible to perform a backup from a transaction log if the data files are destroyed and not even a single committed transaction is lost.

References

- Database-recovery-techniques-in-dbms: geeksforgeeks.org, Retrieved 03, April 2020

- Dwh-data-warehousing, dwh: tutorialspoint.com, Retrieved 17, August 2020

- Parallel-database-architectures: exploredatabase.com, Retrieved 09, Feb 2020

- What-is-dbms: edureka.co, Retrieved 16, May 2020

- Types-of-databases: javatpoint.com, Retrieved 22, January 2020

- Concepts-of-database-architecture: medium.com, Retrieved 13, March 2020

Data Mining: A Comprehensive Study

Data mining is a process of extracting usable data from a large set of raw data using one or more software. There are various types of data mining such as pictorial data mining, text mining, social media mining, web mining and audio and video mining. The topics elaborated in this chapter will help in gaining a better perspective about data mining and its types.

Data mining is a process which tries to use a variety of data analysis tools to discover patterns and relationships in data that may be used to make valid predictions. The first step in data mining is to describe the data — summarize its statistical attributes (such as means and standard deviations), visually review it using charts and graphs, and look for potentially meaningful links among variables (such as values that often occur together). Data mining process include collecting, exploring and selecting the right data that are critically important. But, action plan cannot be derived from the data description alone. One must build a predictive model based on patterns determined from known results, and then test that model on results outside the original sample. We should not confuse a good model with reality (you know a road map isn't a perfect representation of the actual road), but the same be a useful guide to understanding your business. The final step of the data mining process is to empirically verify the model. For example, from a database of customers who have already responded to a particular offer, you've built a model predicting which prospects are likeliest to respond to the same offer.

Data mining is just a tool, not a magic wand. This does not reside in the database watching what happens and send you e-mail to get your attention, when it sees an interesting pattern. Further, it doesn't also try to eliminate the need to know your business, to understand your data, or to understand analytical methods. Data mining assists business analysts with finding patterns and relationships in the data — it does not project the value of the patterns to the organization. Furthermore, the patterns uncovered by data mining must be verified in the real world.

To ensure meaningful results, it's vital that you understand your data. The quality of your output is often decided by various factors and will often be sensitive to outliers (data values that are very different from the typical values in your database), irrelevant columns or columns that vary together (such as age and date of birth), the way you encode your data, and the data you leave in and the data you exclude. Algorithms vary in their sensitivity to such data issues, but it is depend on a data mining product to make all the right decisions on its own.

Data mining without proper guidance will not automatically discover solutions. Rather than setting the vague goal, "it helps improve the response to my direct mail solicitation". One might use data mining to find the characteristics of people who (1) respond to your solicitation, or (2) respond AND make a large purchase. The patterns that the data mining generate and finds for those two goals may be very different. Good data mining techniques gives intricacies of statistical techniques; it further requires understanding the workings of the tool you choose and the algorithms on which it is dependent. Data mining tool and optimization algorithms will affect the accuracy and speed of the models.

Data mining can never replace a business analyst or a manager, rather this initiates a new powerful tool to improve the job they are doing. High-payoff patterns of its employees have been observed over years, which help understanding the business and its customers.

Data Mining and Data Warehousing

Data to be mined is first extracted from an enterprise data warehouse into a data mining database or data mart. There is some real benefit if your data is already part of a data warehouse. The data mining database may be a logical rather than a physical subset of your data warehouse, provided that the data warehouse DBMS can support the additional resource demands of data mining. If it cannot, then you will be better off with a separate data mining database.

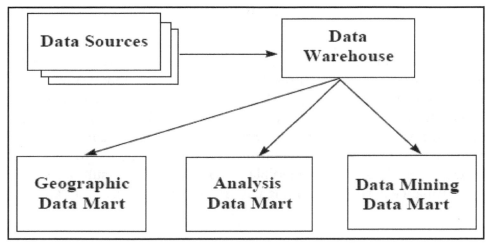

Figure: Data mart extracted from a Data Warehouse.

Data Mining, Machine Learning and Statistics

Data mining takes advantage of advances in the fields of machine learning, artificial intelligence (AI) and statistics. These disciplines have been working on problems of pattern recognition and classification. This has made great contributions to the understanding and application of neural nets and decision trees.

Data mining does not replace traditional statistical techniques rather it is an extension to statistics. The development of most statistical techniques was based on elegant theory and analytical methods that worked quite well on the modest amounts of data being analyzed. The increased power of computers and their lower cost, coupled with the need to analyze enormous data sets with millions of rows. This has allowed the development of new techniques based on a brute-force exploration of possible solutions.

New techniques include relatively recent algorithms like neural nets and decision trees, and new approaches to older algorithms such as discriminant analysis. By virtue of bringing to bear the increased computer power on the huge volumes of available data, these techniques can approximate almost any functional form or interaction on their own. Traditional statistical techniques rely on the modeler to specify the functional form and interactions.

The key point is that data mining is the application of these and other AI and statistical techniques to common business problems in a fashion that makes these techniques available to the skilled knowledge worker as well as the trained statistics professional. Data mining is a tool for increasing the productivity of people trying to build predictive models.

A key enabler of data mining is the major progress in hardware price and performance. The dramatic 99% drop in the price of computer disk storage in just the last few years has radically changed the economics of collecting and storing massive amounts of data.

The drop in the cost of computer processing has been equally dramatic. Each generation of chips greatly increases the power of the CPU, while allowing further drops on the cost curve. This is also reflected in the price of RAM (random access memory), where the cost of a megabyte has dropped from hundreds of dollars to around a dollar in just a few years. PCs routinely have 64 megabytes or more of RAM, and workstations may have 256 megabytes or more, while servers with gigabytes of main memory are not a rarity.

While the power of the individual CPU has greatly increased, the real advances in scalability stem from parallel computer architectures. Virtually all servers today support multiple CPUs using symmetric multi-processing, and clusters of these SMP servers can be created that allow hundreds of CPUs to work on finding patterns in the data. Advances in database management systems to take advantage of this hardware parallelism also benefit data mining. If you have a large or complex data mining problem requiring a great deal of access to an existing database, native DBMS access provides the best possible performance. The result of these trends is that many of the performance barriers to finding patterns in large amounts of data are being eliminated.

Data Mining Applications

Here is the list of areas where data mining is widely used:

- Financial Data Analysis,
- Retail Industry,
- Telecommunication Industry,
- Biological Data Analysis,
- Other Scientific Applications,
- Intrusion Detection.

Financial Data Analysis

The financial data in banking and financial industry is generally reliable and of high quality which facilitates systematic data analysis and data mining. Some of the typical cases are as follows:

- Design and construction of data warehouses for multidimensional data analysis and data mining.
- Loan payment prediction and customer credit policy analysis.

- Classification and clustering of customers for targeted marketing.

- Detection of money laundering and other financial crimes.

Retail Industry

Data Mining has its great application in Retail Industry because it collects large amount of data from on sales, customer purchasing history, goods transportation, consumption and services. It is natural that the quantity of data collected will continue to expand rapidly because of the increasing ease, availability and popularity of the web.

Data mining in retail industry helps in identifying customer buying patterns and trends that lead to improved quality of customer service and good customer retention and satisfaction. Here is the list of examples of data mining in the retail industry:

- Design and Construction of data warehouses based on the benefits of data mining.

- Multidimensional analysis of sales, customers, products, time and region.

- Analysis of effectiveness of sales campaigns.

- Customer Retention.

- Product recommendation and cross-referencing of items.

Telecommunication Industry

Today the telecommunication industry is one of the most emerging industries providing various services such as fax, pager, cellular phone, internet messenger, images, e-mail, web data transmission, etc. Due to the development of new computer and communication technologies, the telecommunication industry is rapidly expanding. This is the reason why data mining is become very important to help and understand the business.

Data mining in telecommunication industry helps in identifying the telecommunication patterns, catch fraudulent activities, make better use of resource, and improve quality of service. Here is the list of examples for which data mining improves telecommunication services:

- Multidimensional analysis of telecommunication data.

- Fraudulent pattern analysis.

- Identification of unusual patterns.

- Multidimensional association and sequential patterns analysis.

- Mobile telecommunication services.

- Use of visualization tools in telecommunication data analysis.

Biological Data Analysis

In recent times, we have seen a tremendous growth in the field of biology such as genomics, proteomics, functional Genomics and biomedical research. Biological data mining is a very important part of Bioinformatics. Following are the aspects in which data mining contributes for biological data analysis:

- Semantic integration of heterogeneous, distributed genomic and proteomic databases.

- Alignment, indexing, similarity search and comparative analysis multiple nucleotide sequences.

- Discovery of structural patterns and analysis of genetic networks and protein pathways.

- Association and path analysis.

- Visualization tools in genetic data analysis.

Other Scientific Applications

The applications tend to handle relatively small and homogeneous data sets for which the statistical techniques are appropriate. Huge amount of data have been collected from scientific domains such as geosciences, astronomy, etc. A large amount of data sets is being generated because of the fast numerical simulations in various fields such as climate and ecosystem modeling, chemical engineering, fluid dynamics, etc. Following are the applications of data mining in the field of Scientific Applications:

- Data Warehouses and data preprocessing.

- Graph-based mining.

- Visualization and domain specific knowledge.

Intrusion Detection

Intrusion refers to any kind of action that threatens integrity, confidentiality, or the availability of network resources. In this world of connectivity, security has become the major issue. With increased usage of internet and availability of the tools and tricks for intruding and attacking network prompted intrusion detection to become a critical component of network administration. Here is the list of areas in which data mining technology may be applied for intrusion detection:

- Development of data mining algorithm for intrusion detection.

- Association and correlation analysis, aggregation to help select and build discriminating attributes.

- Analysis of Stream data.

- Distributed data mining.

- Visualization and query tools.

Data Mining System Products

There are many data mining system products and domain specific data mining applications. The new data mining systems and applications are being added to the previous systems. Also, efforts are being made to standardize data mining languages.

Choosing a Data Mining System

The selection of a data mining system depends on the following features:

- Data Types: The data mining system may handle formatted text, record-based data, and relational data. The data could also be in ASCII text, relational database data or data warehouse data. Therefore, we should check what exact format the data mining system can handle.

- System Issues: We must consider the compatibility of a data mining system with different operating systems. One data mining system may run on only one operating system or on several. There are also data mining systems that provide web-based user interfaces and allow XML data as input.

- Data Sources: Data sources refer to the data formats in which data mining system will operate. Some data mining system may work only on ASCII text files while others on multiple relational sources. Data mining system should also support ODBC connections or OLE DB for ODBC connections.

- Data Mining functions and methodologies: There are some data mining systems that provide only one data mining function such as classification while some provides multiple data mining functions such as concept description, discovery-driven OLAP analysis, association mining, linkage analysis, statistical analysis, classification, prediction, clustering, outlier analysis, similarity search, etc.

- Coupling data mining with databases or data warehouse systems: Data mining systems need to be coupled with a database or a data warehouse system. The coupled components are integrated into a uniform information processing environment. Here are the types of coupling listed below:

  - No coupling,

  - Loose Coupling,

  - Semi tight Coupling,

  - Tight Coupling.

- Scalability: There are two scalability issues in data mining:

  - Row (Database size) Scalability: A data mining system is considered as row scalable when the number or rows are enlarged 10 times. It takes no more than 10 times to execute a query.

  - Column (Dimension) Salability: A data mining system is considered as column scalable if the mining query execution time increases linearly with the number of columns.

- Visualization Tools: Visualization in data mining can be categorized as follows:
    - Data Visualization,
    - Mining Results Visualization,
    - Mining process visualization,
    - Visual data mining.
- Data mining query language and graphical user interface: An easy-to-use graphical user interface is important to promote user-guided, interactive data mining. Unlike relational database systems, data mining systems do not share underlying data mining query language.

Trends in Data Mining

Data mining concepts are still evolving and here are the latest trends that we get to see in this field:

- Application Exploration.
- Scalable and interactive data mining methods.
- Integration of data mining with database systems, data warehouse systems and web database systems.
- Standardization of data mining query language.
- Visual data mining.
- New methods for mining complex types of data.
- Biological data mining.
- Data mining and software engineering.
- Web mining.
- Distributed data mining.
- Real time data mining.
- Multi database data mining.
- Privacy protection and information security in data mining.

Data Mining Models and Algorithms

Now let's examine some of the types of models and algorithms used to mine data. Most products use variations of algorithms that have been published in computer science or statistics journals, with their specific implementations customized to meet the individual vendor's goal. For example, many vendors sell versions of the CART or CHAID decision trees with enhancements to work on parallel computers. Some vendors have proprietary algorithms which, while not extensions or enhancements of any published approach, may work quite well. Most of the models and algorithms discussed here can be thought of as generalizations of the standard workhorse of modeling, the linear regression model. Much effort has been expended in the statistics, computer science, artificial intelligence and engineering communities to overcome the limitations of this basic model. The common characteristic of many of the newer technologies we will consider is that the pattern-finding mechanism is data-driven rather than user-driven. That is, the relationships are found inductively by the software itself based on the existing data rather than requiring the modeler to specify the functional form and interactions. Perhaps the most important thing to remember is that no one model or algorithm can or should be used exclusively. For any given problem, the nature of the data itself will affect the choice of models and algorithms you choose. There is no "best" model or algorithm. Consequently, you will need a variety of tools and technologies in order to find the best possible model.

Neural Networks

Neural networks are of particular interest because they offer a means of efficiently modeling large and complex problems in which there may be hundreds of predictor variables that have many interactions.(Actual biological neural networks are incomparably more complex.) Neural nets may be used in classification problems (where the output is a categorical variable) or for regressions (where the output variable is continuous).

A neural network starts with an input layer, where each node corresponds to a predictor variable. These input nodes are connected to a number of nodes in a hidden layer. Each input node is connected to every node in the hidden layer. The nodes in the hidden layer may be connected to nodes in another hidden layer, or to an output layer. The output layer consists of one or more response variables.

Process Models

Recognizing that a systematic approach is essential to successful data mining, many vendor and consulting organizations have specified a process model designed to guide the user (especially someone new to building predictive models) through a sequence of steps that will lead to good results.

The Two Crows Process Model

The Two Crows data mining process model described below is derived from the Two Crows process model and also takes advantage of some insights from CRISP-DM. Keep in mind that while the steps appear in a list, the data mining process is not linear — you will inevitably need to loop back to previous steps. For example, what you learn in the "explore data" step may require you to add new data to the data mining database. The initial models you build may provide insights that lead you to create new variables. The basic steps of data mining for knowledge discovery are:

- Define business problem,
- Build data mining database,

- Explore data,

- Prepare data for modeling,

- Build model,

- Evaluate model,

- Deploy model and results.

Define the Business Problem

First and foremost, the prerequisite to knowledge discovery is understanding your data and your business. Without this understanding, no algorithm, regardless of sophistication, is going to provide you with a result in which you should have confidence. Without this background you will not be able to identify the problems you're trying to solve, prepare the data for mining, or correctly interpret the results. To make the best use of data mining you must make a clear statement of your objectives. It may be that you wish to increase the response to a direct mail campaign. Depending on your specific goal, such as "increasing the response rate" or "increasing the value of a response," you will build a very different model. An effective statement of the problem will include a way of measuring the results of your knowledge discovery project. It may also include a cost justification.

Build a Data Mining Database

This step along with the next two constitutes the core of the data preparation. Together, they take more time and effort than all the other steps combined. There may be repeated iterations of the data preparation and model building steps as you learn something from the model that suggests you modify the data. These data preparation steps may take anywhere from 50% to 90% of the time and effort of the entire knowledge discovery process.

The data to be mined should be collected in a database. Note that this does not necessarily imply a database management system must be used. Depending on the amount of the data, the complexity of the data, and the uses to which it is to be put, a flat file or even a spreadsheet may be adequate. In general, it's not a good idea to use your corporate data warehouse for this. You will be better off creating a separate data mart. Mining the data will make you a very active user of the data warehouse, possibly causing resource allocation problems. You will often be joining many tables together and accessing substantial portions of the warehouse. A single trial model may require many passes through much of the warehouse. Almost certainly you will be modifying the data from the data warehouse. In addition you may want to bring in data from outside your company to overlay on the data warehouse data or you may want to add new fields computed from existing fields. You may need to gather additional data through surveys. Other people building different models from the data warehouse (some of whom will use the same data as you) may want to make similar alterations to the warehouse.

However, data warehouse administrators do not look kindly on having data changed in what is unquestionably a corporate resource. One more reason for a separate database is that the structure of the corporate data warehouse may not easily support the kinds of exploration you need to do to understand this data. This includes queries summarizing the data, multidimensional reports (sometimes called pivot tables), and many different kinds of graphs or visualizations.

Lastly, you may want to store this data in a different DBMS with a different physical design than the one you use for your corporate data warehouse. Increasingly, people are selecting special purpose DBMSs which support these data mining requirements quite well. If, however, your corporate data warehouse allows you to create logical data marts and if it can handle the resource demands of data mining, then it may also serve as a good data mining database. The tasks in building a data mining database are:

- Data collection.

- Data description.

- Selection.

- Data quality assessment and data cleansing.

- Consolidation and integration.

- Metadata construction.

- Load the data mining database.

- Maintain the data mining database.

You must remember that these tasks are not performed in strict sequence, but as the need arises. For example, you will start constructing the metadata infrastructure as you collect the data, and modify it continuously. What you learn in consolidation or data quality assessment may change your initial selection decision.

1. Data collection: Identify the sources of the data you will be mining. A data-gathering phase may be necessary because some of the data you need may never have been collected. You may need to acquire external data from public databases (such as census or weather data) or proprietary databases (such as credit bureau data).

2. Data Description: Describe the contents of each file or database table.

3. Selection: The next step in preparing the data mining database is to select the subset of data to mine. This is not the same as sampling the database or choosing predictor variables. Rather, it is a gross elimination of irrelevant or unneeded data. Other criteria for excluding data may include resource constraints, cost, restrictions on data use, or quality problems.

4. Data quality assessment and data cleansing: GIGO (Garbage In, Garbage Out) is quite applicable to data mining, so if you want good models you need to have good data. A data quality assessment identifies characteristics of the data that will affect the model quality. Essentially, you are trying to ensure not only the correctness and consistency of values but also that all the data you have is measuring the same thing in the same way. There are a number of types of data quality problems. Single fields may have an incorrect value. For example, recently a man's nine-digit Social Security identification number was accidentally entered as income when the government computed his taxes! Even when individual fields have what appear to be correct values, there may be incorrect combinations, such as pregnant males. Sometimes the value

for a field is missing. Inconsistencies must be identified and removed when consolidating data from multiple sources. Missing data can be a particularly pernicious problem. If you have to throw out every record with a field missing, you may wind up with a very small database or an inaccurate picture of the whole database. The fact that a value is missing may be significant in itself. Perhaps only wealthy customers regularly leave the "income" field blank, for instance. It can be worthwhile to create a new variable to identify missing values, build a model using it, and compare the results with those achieved by substituting for the missing value to see which leads to better predictions.

Another approach is to calculate a substitute value. Some common strategies for calculating missing values include using the modal value (for nominal variables), the median (for ordinal variables), or the mean (for continuous variables). A less common strategy is to assign a missing value based on the distribution of values for that variable. For example, if a database consisted of 40% females and 60% males, then you might assign a missing gender entry the value of "female" 40% of the time and "male" 60% of the time. Sometimes people build predictive models using data mining techniques to predict missing values. This usually gives a better result than a simple calculation, but is much more time-consuming. Recognize that you will not be able to fix all the problems, so you will need to work around them as best as possible. It is far preferable and more cost-effective to put in place procedures and checks to avoid the data quality problems — "an ounce of prevention." Usually, however, you must build the models you need with the data you now have, and avoidance is something you'll work toward for the future.

5. Integration and consolidation: The data you need may reside in a single database or in multiple databases. The source databases may be transaction databases used by the operational systems of your company. Other data may be in data warehouses or data marts built for specific purposes. Still other data may reside in a proprietary database belonging to another company such as a credit bureau. Data integration and consolidation combines data from different sources into a single mining database and requires reconciling differences in data values from the various sources. Improperly reconciled data is a major source of quality problems. There are often large differences in the way data are defined and used in different databases. Some inconsistencies may be easy to uncover, such as different addresses for the same customer. Making it more difficult to resolve these problems is that they are often subtle. For example, the same customer may have different names or — worse — multiple customer identification numbers. The same name may be used for different entities (homonyms), or different names may be used for the same entity (synonyms). There are often unit incompatibilities, especially when data sources are consolidated from different countries; for example, U.S. dollars and Canadian dollars cannot be added without conversion.

6. Metadata construction: The information in the Dataset Description and Data Description reports is the basis for the metadata infrastructure. In essence this is a database about the database itself. It provides information that will be used in the creation of the physical database as well as information that will be used by analysts in understanding the data and building the models.

7. Load the data mining database: In most cases the data should be stored in its own database. For large amounts or complex data, this will usually be a DBMS as opposed to a flat file. Having collected, integrated and cleaned the data, it is now necessary to actually load the database itself.

Depending on the DBMS and hardware being used, the amount of data, and the complexity of the database design, this may turn out to be a serious undertaking that requires the expertise of information systems professionals.

8. Maintain the data mining database: Once created, a database needs to be cared for. It needs to be backed up periodically; its performance should be monitored; and it may need occasional reorganization to reclaim disk storage or to improve performance. For a large, complex database stored in a DBMS, the maintenance may also require the services of information systems professionals.

Explore the Data

The goal is to identify the most important fields in predicting an outcome, and determine which derived values may be useful.

In a data set with hundreds or even thousands of columns, exploring the data can be as time consuming and labor-intensive as it is illuminating. A good interface and fast computer response are very important in this phase because the very nature of your exploration is changed when you have to wait even 20 minutes for some graphs, let alone a day.

Prepare Data for Modeling

This is the final data preparation step before building models. There are four main parts to this step:

- Select variables,
- Select rows,
- Construct new variables,
- Transform variables.

Select Variables

Ideally, you would take all the variables you have, feed them to the data mining tool and let it find those which are the best predictors. In practice, this doesn't work very well. One reason is that the time it takes to build a model increases with the number of variables. Another reason is that blindly including extraneous columns can lead to incorrect models. A very common error, for example, is to use as a predictor variable data that can only be known if you know the value of the response variable. People have actually used date of birth to "predict" age without realizing it.

While in principle some data mining algorithms will automatically ignore irrelevant variables and properly account for related (covariant) columns, in practice it is wise to avoid depending solely on the tool. Often your knowledge of the problem domain can let you make many of these selections correctly. For example, including ID number or Social Security number as predictor variables will at best have no benefit and at worst may reduce the weight of other important variables.

Select Rows

As in the case of selecting variables, you would like to use all the rows you have to build models. If you have a lot of data, however, this may take too long or require buying a bigger computer than you would like. Consequently it is often a good idea to sample the data when the database is large. This yields no loss of information for most business problems, although sample selection must be done carefully to ensure the sample is truly random. Given a choice of either investigating a few models built on all the data or investigating more models built on a sample, the latter approach will usually help you develop a more accurate and robust model.

You may also want to throw out data that are clearly outliers. While in some cases outliers may contain information important to your model building, often they can be ignored based on your understanding of the problem. For example, they may be the result of incorrectly entered data, or of a one-time occurrence such as a labor strike. Sometimes you may need to add new records (e.g., for customers who made no purchases).

Construct New Variables

It is often necessary to construct new predictors derived from the raw data. For example, forecasting credit risk using a debt-to-income ratio rather than just debt and income as predictor variables may yield more accurate results that are also easier to understand. Certain variables that have little effect alone may need to be combined with others, using various arithmetic or algebraic operations (e.g., addition, ratios). Some variables that extend over a wide range may be modified to construct a better predictor, such as using the log of income instead of income.

Transform Variables

The tool you choose may dictate how you represent your data, for instance, the categorical explosion required by neural nets. Variables may also be scaled to fall within a limited range, such as 0 to 1. Many decision trees used for classification require continuous data such as income to be grouped in ranges (bins) such as High, Medium, and Low. The encoding you select can influence the result of your model. For example, the cutoff points for the bins may change the outcome of a model.

Data Mining Model Building

The most important thing to remember about model building is that it is an iterative process. You will need to explore alternative models to find the one that is most useful in solving your business problem. What you learn in searching for a good model may lead you to go back and make some changes to the data you are using or even modify your problem statement.

Once you have decided on the type of prediction you want to make (e.g., classification or regression), you must choose a model type for making the prediction. This could be a decision tree, a neural net, a proprietary method, or that old standby, logistic regression. Your choice of model type will influence what data preparation you must do and how you go about it. For example, a neural net tool may require you to explode your categorical variables. Or the tool may require that the data be in a particular file format, thus requiring you to extract the data into that format. Once the data is ready, you can proceed with training your model. The process of building predictive models requires a well-defined training and validation protocol in order to insure the most accurate and robust predictions. This kind of protocol is sometimes called supervised learning. The essence of supervised learning is to train (estimate) your model on a portion of the data, then test and validate it on the remainder of the data. A model is built when the cycle of training and testing is completed. Sometimes a third data set, called the validation data set, is needed because the test data may be influencing features of the model, and the validation set acts as an independent measure of the model's accuracy.

Training and testing the data mining model requires the data to be split into at least two groups: one for model training (i.e., estimation of the model parameters) and one for model testing. If you don't use different training and test data, the accuracy of the model will be overestimated. After the model is generated using the training database, it is used to predict the test database, and the resulting accuracy rate is a good estimate of how the model will perform on future databases that are similar to the training and test databases. It does not guarantee that the model is correct. It simply says that if the same technique were used on a succession of databases with similar data to the training and test data, the average accuracy would be close to the one obtained this way.

Simple Validation

The most basic testing method is called simple validation. To carry this out, you set aside a percentage of the database as a test database, and do not use it in any way in the model building and estimation. This percentage is typically between 5% and 33%. For all the future calculations to be correct, the division of the data into two groups must be random, so that the training and test data sets both reflect the data being modeled. After building the model on the main body of the data, the model is used to predict the classes or values of the test database. Dividing the number of incorrect classifications by the total number of instances gives an error rate. Dividing the number of correct classifications by the total number of instances gives an accuracy rate (i.e., accuracy = 1 − error). For a regression model, the goodness of fit or "r-squared" is usually used as an estimate of the accuracy. In building a single model, even this simple validation may need to be performed dozens of times. For example, when using a neural net, sometimes each training pass through the net is tested against a test database. Training then stops when the accuracy rates on the test database no longer improve with additional iterations.

Cross Validation

If you have only a modest amount of data (a few thousand rows) for building the model, you can't afford to set aside a percentage of it for simple validation. Cross validation is a method that lets you use all your data. The data is randomly divided into two equal sets in order to estimate the predictive accuracy of the model. First, a model is built on the first set and used to predict the outcomes in the second set and calculate an error rate. Then a model is built on the second set and used to predict the outcomes in the first set and again calculate an error rate. Finally, a model is built using all the data. There are now two independent error estimates which can be averaged to give a better estimate of the true accuracy of the model built on all the data. Typically, the more general n-fold cross validation is used. In this method, the data is randomly divided into n disjoint groups. For example, suppose the data is divided into ten groups. The first group is set aside for testing and the other nine are lumped together for model building. The model built on the 90% group is then used to predict the group that was set aside. This process is repeated a total of 10 times as each group in turn is set aside, the model is built on the remaining 90% of the data, and then that model is used to predict the set-aside group. Finally, a model is built using all the data. The mean of the 10 independent error rate predictions is used as the error rate for this last model.

Bootstrapping

It is another technique for estimating the error of a model; it is primarily used with very small data sets. As in cross validation, the model is built on the entire dataset. Then numerous data sets called bootstrap samples are created by sampling from the original data set. After each case is sampled, it is replaced and a case is selected again until the entire bootstrap sample is created. Note that records may occur more than once in the data sets thus created. A model is built on this data set, and its error rate is calculated. This is called the re-substitution error. Many bootstrap samples (sometimes over 1,000) are created. The final error estimate for the model built on the whole data set is calculated by taking the average of the estimates from each of the bootstrap samples.

Based upon the results of your model building, you may want to build another model using the same technique but different parameters, or perhaps try other algorithms or tools. For example, another approach may increase your accuracy. No tool or technique is perfect for all data, and it is difficult if not impossible to be sure before you start which technique will work the best. It is quite common to build numerous models before finding a satisfactory one.

Evaluation and Interpretation

- Model Validation: After building a model, you must evaluate its results and interpret their significance. Remember that the accuracy rate found during testing applies only to the data on which the model was built. In practice, the accuracy may vary if the data to which the model is applied differs in important and unknowable ways from the original data. More importantly, accuracy by itself is not necessarily the right metric for selecting the best model. You need to know more about the type of errors and the costs associated with them.

- Confusion matrices: For classification problems, a confusion matrix is a very useful tool for understanding results. A confusion matrix (Figure 9) shows the counts of the actual versus predicted class values. It shows not only how well the model predicts, but also presents the details needed to see exactly where things may have gone wrong. The following table is a sample confusion matrix. The columns show the actual classes, and the rows show the predicted classes. Therefore the diagonal shows all the correct predictions. In the confusion matrix, you can see that our model predicted 38 of the 46 Class B's correctly, but misclassified 8 of them: two as Class A and six as Class C. This is much more informative than simply telling us an overall accuracy rate of 82% (123 correct classifications out of 150 cases).

Deploy the Model and Results

Once a data mining model is built and validated, it can be used in one of two main ways. The first way is for an analyst to recommend actions based on simply viewing the model and its results. For example, the analyst may look at the clusters the model has identified, the rules that define the model, or the lift and ROI charts that depict the effect of the model.

The second way is to apply the model to different data sets. The model could be used to flag records based on their classification, or assign a score such as the probability of an action (e.g., responding to a direct mail solicitation). Or the model can select some records from the database and subject these to further analyses with an OLAP tool. Often the models are part of a business process such as risk analysis, credit authorization or fraud detection. In these cases the model is incorporated into an application. For instance, a predictive model may be integrated into a mortgage loan application to aid a loan officer in evaluating the applicant. Or a model might be embedded in an application such as an inventory ordering system that automatically generates an order when the forecast inventory levels drop below a threshold.

The data mining model is often applied to one event or transaction at a time, such as scoring a loan application for risk. The amount of time to process each new transaction, and the rate at which new transactions arrive, will determine whether a parallelized algorithm is needed. Thus, while loan applications can easily be evaluated on modest-sized computers, monitoring credit card transactions or cellular telephone calls for fraud would require a parallel system to deal with the high transaction rate.

When delivering a complex application, data mining is often only a small, albeit critical, part of the final product. For example, knowledge discovered through data mining may be combined with the knowledge of domain experts and applied to data in the database and incoming transactions. In a fraud detection system, known patterns of fraud may be combined with discovered patterns. When suspected cases of fraud are passed on to fraud investigators for evaluation, the investigators may need to access database records about other claims filed by the claimant as well as other claims in which the same doctors and lawyers were involved.

Model Monitoring

You must, of course, measure how well your model has worked after you use it. However, even when you think you're finished because your model works well, you must continually monitor the performance of the model. Over time, all systems evolve. Salespeople know that purchasing patterns change over time. External variables such as inflation rate may change enough to alter the way people behave. Thus, from time to time the model will have to be retested, retrained and possibly completely rebuilt. Charts of the residual differences between forecasted and observed values are an excellent way to monitor model results. Such charts are easy to use and understand, not computationally intensive, and could be built into the software that implements the model. Thus, the system could monitor itself.

Data Mining Techniques

Data mining includes the utilization of refined data analysis tools to find previously unknown, valid patterns and relationships in huge data sets. These tools can incorporate statistical models, machine learning techniques, and mathematical algorithms, such as neural networks or decision trees. Thus, data mining incorporates analysis and prediction.

Depending on various methods and technologies from the intersection of machine learning, database management, and statistics, professionals in data mining have devoted their careers to better understanding how to process and make conclusions from the huge amount of data, but what are the methods they use to make it happen?

In recent data mining projects, various major data mining techniques have been developed and used, including association, classification, clustering, prediction, sequential patterns, and regression.

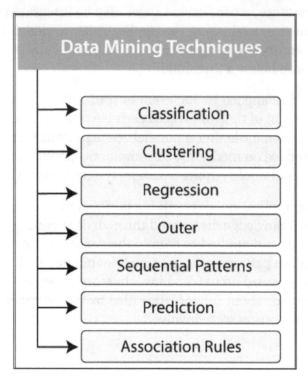

Classification

Classification is the problem of identifying to which of a set of categories (subpopulations), a new observation belongs to, on the basis of a training set of data containing observations and whose categories membership is known.

One attractive classification method involves the construction of a decision tree, a collection of decision nodes, connected by branches, extending downward from the root node until terminating in leaf nodes. Beginning at the root node, which by convention is placed at the top of the decision tree diagram, attributes are tested at the decision nodes, with each possible outcome resulting in a branch. Each branch then leads either to another decision node or to a terminating leaf node. Figure provides an example of a simple decision tree. The target variable for the decision tree in Figure is credit risk, with potential customers being classified as either good or bad credit risks. The predictor variables are savings (low, medium, and high), assets (low or not low), and income (≤$50,000 or >$50,000). Here, the root node represents a decision node, testing whether each record has a low, medium, or high savings level (as defined by the analyst or domain expert). The data set is partitioned, or split, according to the values of this attribute. Those records with low savings are sent via the leftmost branch (savings = low) to another decision node. The records with high savings are sent via the rightmost branch to a different decision node. The records with medium savings are sent via the middle branch directly to a leaf node, indicating the termination of this branch. Why a leaf node and not another decision node? Because, in the data set (not shown), all of the records with medium savings levels have been classified as good credit risks. There is no need for another decision node, because our knowledge that the customer has medium savings predicts good credit with 100% accuracy in the data set. For customers with low savings, the next decision node tests whether the customer has low assets. Those with low assets are then classified as bad credit risks; the others are classified as good credit risks. For customers with high savings, the next decision node tests whether the customer has an income of at most $30,000. Customers with incomes of $30,000 or less are then classified as bad credit risks, with the others classified as good credit risks. When no further splits can be made, the decision tree algorithm stops growing new nodes. For example, suppose that all of the branches terminate in "pure" leaf nodes, where the target variable is unary for the records in that node (e.g., each record in the leaf node is a good credit risk). Then no further splits are necessary, so no further nodes are grown. However, there are instances when a particular node contains "diverse" attributes (with nonunary values for the target attribute), and yet the decision tree cannot make a split. For example, suppose that we consider the records from figure with high savings and low income (≤$30,000). Suppose that there are five records with these values, all of which also have low assets. Finally, suppose that three of these five customers have been classified as bad credit risks and two as good credit risks, as shown in table. In the real world, one often encounters situations such as this, with varied values for the response variable, even for exactly the same values for the predictor variables.

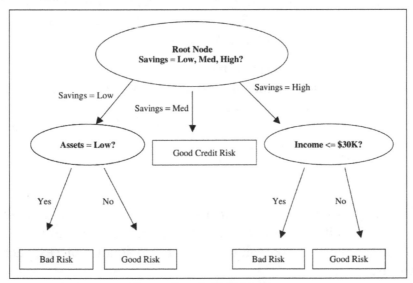

Figure: Sample Decision Tree.

Here, since all customers have the same predictor values, there is no possible way to split the records according to the predictor variables that will lead to a pure leaf node. Therefore, such nodes become diverse leaf nodes, with mixed values for the target attribute. In this case, the decision tree may report that the classification for such customers is "bad," with 60% confidence, as determined by the three-fifths of customers in this node who are bad credit risks. Note that not all attributes are tested for all records. Customers with low savings and low assets, for example, are not tested with regard to income in this example.

Table: Sample records that lead to pure leaf node.

Customer	Savings	Assets	Income	Credit risk
004	High	Low	$\leq \$30,000$	Good
009	High	Low	$\leq \$30,000$	Good
027	High	Low	$\leq \$30,000$	Bad
031	High	Low	$\leq \$30,000$	Bad
104	High	Low	$\leq \$30,000$	Bad

Certain requirements must be met before decision tree algorithms may be applied:

- Decision tree algorithms represent supervised learning, and as such require pre-classified target variables. A training data set must be supplied which provides the algorithm with the values of the target variable.

- This training data set should be rich and varied, providing the algorithm with a healthy cross section of the types of records for which classification may be needed in the future. Decision trees learn by example, and if examples are systematically lacking for a definable subset of records, classification and prediction for this subset will be problematic or impossible.

- The target attribute classes must be discrete. That is, one cannot apply decision tree analysis to a continuous target variable. Rather, the target variable must take on values that are clearly demarcated as either belonging to a particular class or not belonging.

Why in the example above, did the decision tree choose the savings attribute for the root node split? Why did it not choose assets or income instead? Decision trees seek to create a set of leaf nodes that are as "pure" as possible, that is, where each of the records in a particular leaf node has the same classification. In this way, the decision tree may provide classification assignments with the highest measure of confidence available.

Clustering

Clustering provides a way to learn about the structure of complex data, to break up the cacophony of competing signals into its components. When human beings try to make sense of complex questions, our natural tendency is to break the subject into smaller pieces, each of which can be explained more simply.

If someone were asked to describe the color of trees in the forest, the answer would probably make distinctions between deciduous trees and evergreens, and between winter, spring, summer, and fall. People know enough about woodland flora to predict that, of all the hundreds of variables associated with the forest, season and foliage type, rather than say age and height, are the best factors to use for forming clusters of trees that follow similar coloration rules. Once the proper clusters have been defined, it is often possible to find simple patterns within each cluster. "In Winter, deciduous trees have no leaves so the trees tend to be brown" or "The leaves of deciduous trees change color in the autumn, typically to oranges, reds, and yellows." In many cases, a very noisy dataset is actually composed of a number of better-behaved clusters. The question is: how can these be found? That is where techniques for automatic cluster detection come in—to help see the forest without getting lost in the trees.

Where data mining techniques are classified as directed or undirected, automatic cluster detection is described as a tool for undirected knowledge discovery. In the technical sense, that is true because the automatic cluster detection algorithms themselves are simply finding structure that exists in the data without regard to any particular target variable. Most data mining tasks start out with a pre-classified training set, which is used to develop a model capable of scoring or classifying previously unseen records.

In clustering, there is no pre-classified data and no distinction between independent and dependent variables. Instead, clustering algorithms search for groups of records—the clusters—composed of records similar to each other. The algorithms discover these similarities. It is up to the people running the analysis to determine whether similar records represent something of interest to the business—or something inexplicable and perhaps unimportant. In a broader sense, however, clustering can be a directed activity because clusters are sought for some business purpose. In marketing, clusters formed for a business purpose are usually called "segments," and customer segmentation is a popular application of clustering.

Automatic cluster detection is a data mining technique that is rarely used in isolation because finding clusters is not often an end in itself. Once clusters have been detected, other methods must be applied in order to figure out what the clusters mean. When clustering is successful, the results can be dramatic: One famous early application of cluster detection led to our current understanding of stellar evolution.

K-Means Clustering

The K-Means algorithm is one of the most commonly used clustering algorithms. The "K" in its name refers to the fact that the algorithm looks for a fixed number of clusters which are defined in terms of proximity of data points to each other. The version described here was first published by J. B. MacQueen in 1967. For ease of explaining, the technique is illustrated using two-dimensional diagrams. Bear in mind that in practice the algorithm is usually handling many more than two independent variables. This means that instead of points corresponding to two-element vectors (x_1, x_2), the points correspond to n-element vectors $(x_1, x_2, \ldots, x_n)$. The procedure itself is unchanged.

Three Steps of the K-Means Algorithm

In the first step, the algorithm randomly selects K data points to be the seeds. MacQueen's algorithm simply takes the first K records. In cases where the records have some meaningful order, it may be desirable to choose widely spaced records, or a random selection of records. Each of the seeds is an embryonic cluster with only one element. This example sets the number of clusters to 3.

The second step assigns each record to the closest seed. One way to do this is by finding the boundaries between the clusters, as shown geometrically in figure below. The boundaries between two clusters are the points that are equally close to each cluster. Recalling a lesson from high-school geometry makes this less difficult than it sounds: given any two points, A and B, all points that are equidistant from A and B fall along a line (called the perpendicular bisector) that is perpendicular to the one connecting A and B and halfway between them. In Figure below, dashed lines connect the initial seeds; the resulting cluster boundaries shown with solid lines are at right angles to the dashed lines. Using these lines as guides, it is obvious which records are closest to which seeds. In three dimensions, these boundaries would be planes and in N dimensions they would be hyper planes of dimension N – 1. Fortunately, computer algorithms easily handle these situations. Finding the actual boundaries between clusters is useful for showing the process geometrically. In practice, though, the algorithm usually measures the distance of each record to each seed and chooses the minimum distance for this step. For example, consider the record with the box drawn around it. On the basis of the initial seeds, this record is assigned to the cluster controlled by seed number 2 because it is closer to that seed than to either of the other two. At this point, every point has been assigned to exactly one of the three clusters centered around the original seeds. The third step is to calculate the centroids of the clusters; these now do a better job of characterizing the clusters than the initial seeds finding the centroids are simply a matter of taking the average value of each dimension for all the records in the cluster.

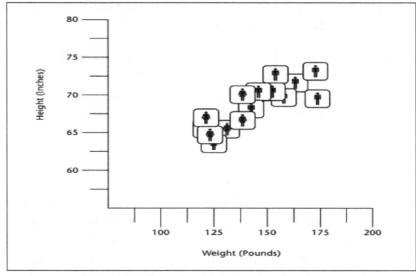

Figure: Height and weight of group of teenagers.

Similarity and Distance

Once records in a database have been mapped to points in space, automatic cluster detection is really quite simple—a little geometry, some vector means. The problem, of course, is that the databases encountered in marketing, sales, and customer support are not about points in space. They are about purchases, phone calls, airplane trips, car registrations, and a thousand other things that have no obvious connection to the dots in a cluster diagram.

Clustering records of this sort requires some notion of natural association; that is, records in a given cluster are more similar to each other than to records in another cluster. Since it is difficult to convey intuitive notions to a computer, this vague concept of association must be translated into some sort of numeric measure of the degree of similarity. The most common method, but by no means the only one, is to translate all fields into numeric values so that the records may be treated as points in space. Then, if two points are close in the geometric sense, they represent similar records in the database. There are two main problems with this approach:

- Many variable types, including all categorical variables and many numeric variables such as rankings, do not have the right behavior to properly be treated as components of a position vector.

- In geometry, the contributions of each dimension are of equal importance, but in databases, a small change in one field may be much more important than a large change in another field.

Similarity Measures and Variable Type

Geometric distance works well as a similarity measure for well-behaved numeric variables. A well-behaved numeric variable is one whose value indicates its placement along the axis that corresponds to it in our geometric model. Not all variables fall into this category. For this purpose, variables fall into four classes, listed here in increasing order of suitability for the geometric model. Categorical variables are:

- Ranks.

- Intervals.

- True measures.

Categorical variables only describe which of several unordered categories a thing belongs to. For instance, it is possible to label one ice cream pistachio and another butter pecan, but it is not possible to say that one is greater than the other or judge which one is closer to black cherry. In mathematical terms, it is possible to tell that X ≠ Y, but not whether X > Y or X < Y. Ranks put things in order, but don't say how much bigger one thing is than another. The valedictorian has better grades than the salutatorian, but we don't know by how much. If X, Y, and Z are ranked A, B, and C, we know that X > Y > Z, but we cannot define X-Y or Y-Z. Intervals measure the distance between two observations. If it is 56° in San Francisco and 78° in San Jose, then it is 22 degrees warmer at one end of the bay than the other.

True measures are interval variables that measure from a meaningful zero point. This trait is important because it means that the ratio of two values of the variable is meaningful. The Fahrenheit temperature scale used in the United States and the Celsius scale used in most of the rest of the world do not have this property. In neither system does it make sense to say that a 30° day is twice as warm as a 15° day. Similarly, a size 12 dress is not twice as large as a size 6, and gypsum is not twice as hard as talc though they are 2 and 1 on the hardness scale. It does make perfect sense, however, to say that a 50-year-old is twice as old as a 25-year-old or that a 10-pound bag of sugar is twice as heavy as a 5-pound one. Age, weight, length, customer tenure, and volume are examples of true measures.

Geometric distance metrics are well-defined for interval variables and true measures. In order to use categorical variables and rankings, it is necessary to transform them into interval variables. Unfortunately, these transformations may add spurious information. If ice cream flavors are assigned arbitrary numbers 1 through 28, it will appear that flavors 5 and 6 are closely related while flavors 1 and 28 are far apart.

Manhattan Distance

Another common distance metric gets its name from the rectangular grid pattern of streets in midtown Manhattan. It is simply the sum of the distances traveled along each axis. This measure is sometimes preferred to the Euclidean distance because given that the distances along each axis are not squared, it is less likely that a large difference in one dimension will dominate the total distance.

Number of Features in Common

When the preponderance of fields in the records is categorical variables, geometric measures are not the best choice. A better measure is based on the degree of overlap between records. As with the geometric measures, there are many variations on this idea. In all variations, the two records are compared field by field to determine the number of fields that match and the number of fields that don't match. The simplest measure is the ratio of matches to the total number of fields.

In its simplest form, this measure counts two null or empty fields as matching. This has the perhaps perverse result that everything with missing data ends up in the same cluster. A simple improvement is to not include matches of this sort in the match count. Another improvement is to weight the matches by the prevalence of each class in the general population. After all, a match on "Chevy Nomad" ought to count for more than a match on "Ford F-150 Pickup."

Scaling for Consistency

Here are three common ways of scaling variables to bring them all into comparable ranges:

- Divide each variable by the range (the difference between the lowest and highest value it takes on) after subtracting the lowest value. This maps all values to the range 0 to 1, which is useful for some data mining algorithms.

- Divide each variable by the mean of all the values it takes on. This is often called "indexing a variable."

- Subtract the mean value from each variable and then divide it by the standard deviation. This is often called standardization or "converting to z-scores." A z-score tells you how many standard deviations away from the mean a value is.

Normalizing a single variable simply changes its range. A closely related concept is vector normalization which scales all variables at once. This too has a geometric interpretation. Consider the collection of values in a single record or observation as a vector. Normalizing them scales each value so as to make the length of the vector equal one. Transforming all the vectors to unit length emphasizes the differences internal to each record rather than the differences between records.

Use Weights to Encode Outside Information

Scaling takes care of the problem that changes in one variable appear more significant than changes in another simply because of differences in the magnitudes of the values in the variable. What if we think that two families with the same income have more in common than two families on the same size plot, and we want that to be taken into consideration during clustering? That is where weighting comes in. The purpose of weighting is to encode the information that one variable is more (or less) important than others.

A good place to starts is by standardizing all variables so each has a mean of zero and a variance (and standard deviation) of one. That way, all fields contribute equally when the distance between two records is computed. We suggest going farther. The whole point of automatic cluster detection is to find clusters that make sense to you. If, for your purposes, whether people have children is much more important than the number of credit cards they carry, there is no reason not to bias the outcome of the clustering by multiplying the number of children field by a higher weight than the number of credit cards field.

After scaling to get rid of bias that is due to the units, use weights to introduce bias based on knowledge of the business context. Some clustering tools allow the user to attach weights to different dimensions, simplifying the process. Even for tools that don't have such functionality, it is possible to have weights by adjusting the scaled values. That is, first scale the values to a common range to eliminate range effects. Then multiply the resulting values by a weight to introduce bias based on the business context. Of course, if you want to evaluate the effects of different weighting strategies, you will have to add another outer loop to the clustering process.

Regression

Regression is a data mining (machine learning) technique used to fit an equation to a dataset. The simplest form of regression, linear regression, uses the formula of a straight line (y = mx + b) and determines the appropriate values for m and b to predict the value of y based upon a given value of x. Basically a Linear regression models are used to show or predict the relationship between two variables or factors. The factor that is being predicted (the factor that the equation solves for) is called the dependent variable. The factors that are used to predict the value of the dependent variable are called the independent variables.

Simple Linear Regression Model

The simple linear regression model is represented by the equation:

$$y = \alpha + \beta X$$

By mathematical convention, the two factors that are involved in a simple linear regression analysis are designated X and y. The equation that describes how y is related to x is known as the regression model. Here in the equation α is the y intercept of the regression line and β is the slope.

A regression line can show a positive linear relationship, a negative linear relationship, or no relationship. If the graphed line in a simple linear regression is flat (not sloped), there is no relationship between the two variables. If the regression line slopes upward with the lower end of the line at the y intercept (axis) of the graph, and the upper end of line extending upward into the graph field, away from the x intercept (axis) a positive linear relationship exists. If the regression line slopes downward with the upper end of the line at the y intercept (axis) of the graph, and the lower end of line extending downward into the graph field, toward the x intercept (axis) a negative linear relationship exists.

Formulation of Linear Regression Technique

Linear Regression model consist of random variable Y (called as a response variable) as a linear function of another random variable X (called as a predictor variable) that is represented by the equation:

$$Y = \alpha + \beta X$$

α & β are regression coefficients specifying the Y intercept and slope of the line respectively.

The regression coefficient α & β are solved by the method of least squares, which minimize the error between the actual data & the estimate of the line .Given s sample of data or data points of the form (x1,y1),(x2,y2)...(xs, ys) than the regression coefficients α & β are given by:

$$\beta = \Sigma(x_i - x) (y_i - y)/ \Sigma(x_i - x)$$

$$\alpha = y - \beta x$$

These values of regression coefficients α and β calculated in above equations are substituted in equation $Y = \alpha + \beta X$ so as to obtain the relationship between the response variable X and the target variable Y.

Algorithm of Linear Regression Technique

The linear regression technique works on the following algorithm:

Step 1: Take the values of variable Xi and Yi.

Step 2: Calculate the average for variable Xi such that average is x= (X1 +X2 +........+ Xi)/ Xi.

Step 3: Calculate the average for variable Yi such that average is y= (Y1 +Y2 +........+ Yi)/ Yi.

Step4: Calculate the value of regression coefficient β by substituting the values of Xi , Yi average of Xi and average of Yi in the equation $\beta = \Sigma(x_i - x) (y_i - y)/ \Sigma(x_i - x)$.

Step 5: Calculate the value of another regression coefficients α by substituting the values of β (calculated in step 4), average of Xi and average of Yi in the equation $\alpha = y - \beta x$.

Step 6: Finally substitute the value of regression coefficients α and β in the equation $Y= \alpha + \beta X$.

Test Data for Linear Regression

In order to analyze the working and result of linear regression technique we have taken a different test data. We put these data values in the regression equations and then analyze the result that has been obtained.

Table: The test data for linear regression.

X(years of experience)	Y(Salary)(in K)
3	30
8	57
9	64
13	72
3	36
6	43
11	59
21	90
1	20
156	83

Here X is the number of years of work experience and Y is the corresponding salary. We model a relationship that the salary must be related to the number of years of experience with the equation $Y = \alpha + \beta X$.

1) Given the above test data we first compute the average of x and y such that average of x is 9.1 and average of y is 55.4.

2) Next we compute the value of regression coefficients α and β Such that $\beta = \sum (x_i - x)(y_i - y)/\sum (x_i - x)$ and $\alpha = y - \beta x$.

We now have,

$$\beta = (3-9.1)(30-55.4)+(8-9.1)(57-55.4)+...+(16-9.1)(83-55.4)/(3-9.1)+(8-9.1)+....+(16-9.1) = 3.5$$

$$\alpha = 55.4 - (3.5)(9.1) = 23.6.$$

and now finally the equation of the least square line is estimated by,

$$Y = 23.6 + 3.5X$$

Using this equation we can predict the salary of college graduate with say 10 years of experience.

So now if we want to know the salary of a person whose experience is 10 years we can get the result

$$Y = 23.6 + 3.5(10)$$
$$= 58.6$$

So, a person with 10 years of experience has a salary of 58.6K. Thus the above test data can be used to verify that the linear relationship exist between the variables X and Y.

Association Rules

Association rule mining finds interesting associations and relationships among large sets of data items. This rule shows how frequently a itemset occurs in a transaction. A typical example is Market Based Analysis.

Market Based Analysis is one of the key techniques used by large relations to show associations between items. It allows retailers to identify relationships between the items that people buy together frequently. Given a set of transactions, we can find rules that will predict the occurrence of an item based on the occurrences of other items in the transaction.

TID	Items
1	Bread, Milk
2	Bread, Diaper, Beer, Eggs
3	Milk, Diaper, Beer, Coke
4	Bread, Milk, Diaper, Beer
5	Bread, Milk, Diaper, Coke

- Support Count (σ): Support count is the Frequency of occurrence of an itemset. Here: ({Milk, Bread, Diaper}) =2.

- Frequent Itemset: Frequent itemset is an itemset whose support is greater than or equal to minsup threshold.

- Association Rule: Association rule is an implication expression of the form X -> Y, where X and Y are any 2 itemsets.

Example: {Milk, Diaper} -> {Beer}.

Rule Evaluation Metrics

- Support(s): The number of transactions that include items in the {X} and {Y} parts of the rule as a percentage of the total number of transaction. It is a measure of how frequently the collection of items occurs together as a percentage of all transactions.

- Support = σ(X+Y) ÷ total: It is interpreted as fraction of transactions that contain both X and Y.

- Confidence(c): It is the ratio of the no of transactions that includes all items in {B} as well as the no of transactions that includes all items in {A} to the no of transactions that includes all items in {A}.

- Conf(X=>Y) = Supp(X $\cup$ Y) ÷ Supp(X): It measures how often each item in Y appears in transactions that contains items in X also.

- Lift(l): The lift of the rule X=>Y is the confidence of the rule divided by the expected confidence, assuming that the itemsets X and Y are independent of each other. The expected confidence is the confidence divided by the frequency of {Y}.

- Lift(X=>Y) = Conf(X=>Y) ÷ Supp(Y): Lift value near 1 indicates X and Y almost often appear together as expected, greater than 1 means they appear together more than expected and less than 1 means they appear less than expected. Greater lift values indicate stronger association.

Example: From the above table, {Milk, Diaper}=>{Beer}

s= σ({Milk, Diaper, Beer}) ÷|T|

= 2/5

= 0.4

c= σ(Milk, Diaper, Beer) ÷ σ(Milk, Diaper)

= 2/3

= 0.67

l= Supp({Milk, Diaper, Beer}) ÷Supp({Milk, Diaper})*Supp({Beer})

= 0.4/ (0.6*0.6)

= 1.11

The Association rule is very useful in analyzing datasets. The data is collected using bar-code scanners in supermarkets. Such databases consist of a large number of transaction records which list all items bought by a customer on a single purchase. So the manager could know if certain groups of items are consistently purchased together and use this data for adjusting store layouts, cross-selling, promotions based on statistics.

Sequential Patterns

Data mining consists of extracting information from data stored in databases to understand the data and/or take decisions. Some of the most fundamental data mining tasks are clustering, classification, outlier analysis, and pattern mining. Pattern mining consists of discovering interesting, useful, and unexpected patterns in databases various types of patterns can be discovered in databases such as frequent itemsets, associations, sub graphs, sequential rules, and periodic patterns.

The task of sequential pattern mining is a data mining task specialized for analyzing sequential data, to discover sequential patterns. More precisely, it consists of discovering interesting subsequences in a set of sequences, where the interestingness of a subsequence can be measured in terms of various criteria such as its occurrence frequency, length, and profit. Sequential pattern mining has numerous real-life applications due to the fact that data is naturally encoded as sequences of symbols in many fields such as bioinformatics, eLearning, market basket analysis, texts, and webpage click-stream analysis.

Here we will now explain the task of sequential pattern mining with an example. Consider the following sequence database, representing the purchases made by customers in a retail store.

SID	Sequence
1	$\langle\{a,b\},\{c\},\{f,g\},\{g\},\{e\}\rangle$
2	$\langle\{a,d\},\{c\},\{b\},\{a,b,e,f\}\rangle$
3	$\langle\{a\},\{b\},\{f,g\},\{e\}\rangle$
4	$\langle\{b\},\{f,g\}\rangle$

This database contains four sequences. Each sequence represents the items purchased by a customer at different times. A sequence is an ordered list of itemsets (sets of items bought together). For example, in this database, the first sequence (SID 1) indicates that a customer bought some items a and b together, then purchased an item c, then purchased items f and g together, then purchased an item g, and then finally purchased an item e.

Traditionally, sequential pattern mining is being used to find subsequences that appear often in a sequence database, i.e. that are common to several sequences. Those subsequences are called the frequent sequential patterns. For example, in the context of our example, sequential pattern mining can be used to find the sequences of items frequently bought by customers. This can be useful to understand the behavior of customers to take marketing decisions.

To do sequential pattern mining, a user must provide a sequence database and specify a parameter called the minimum support threshold. This parameter indicates a minimum number of sequences in which a pattern must appear to be considered frequent, and be shown to the user. For example, if a user sets the minimum support threshold to 2 sequences, the task of sequential pattern mining consists of finding all subsequences appearing in at least 2 sequences of the input database. In the example database, 29 subsequences met this requirement. These sequential patterns are shown in the table below, where the number of sequences containing each pattern (called the support) is indicated in the right column of the table.

Pattern	Sup.
$\langle\{a\}\rangle$	3
$\langle\{a\},\{g\}\rangle$	2
$\langle\{a\},\{g\},\{e\}\rangle$	2
$\langle\{a\},\{f\}\rangle$	3
$\langle\{a\},\{f\},\{e\}\rangle$	2
$\langle\{a\},\{c\}\rangle$	2
$\langle\{a\},\{c\},\{f\}\rangle$	2
$\langle\{a\},\{c\},\{e\}\rangle$	2
$\langle\{a\},\{b\}\rangle$	2

$\langle\{a\},\{b\},\{f\}\rangle$	2
$\langle\{a\},\{b\},\{e\}\rangle$	2
$\langle\{a\},\{e\}\rangle$	3
$\langle\{a,b\}\rangle$	2
$\langle\{b\}\rangle$	4
$\langle\{b\},\{g\}\rangle$	3
$\langle\{b\},\{g\},\{e\}\rangle$	2
$\langle\{b\},\{f\}\rangle$	3
$\langle\{b\},\{f,g\}\rangle$	2
$\langle\{b\},\{f\},\{e\}\rangle$	2
$\langle\{b\},\{e\}\rangle$	2
$\langle\{c\}\rangle$	3
$\langle\{c\},\{f\}\rangle$	2
$\langle\{c\},\{e\}\rangle$	2
$\langle\{e\}\rangle$	2
$\langle\{f\}\rangle$	3
$\langle\{f,g\}\rangle$	4
$\langle\{f\},\{e\}\rangle$	3
$\langle\{g\}\rangle$	2
	3
$\langle\{g\},\{e\}\rangle$	2

For example, the patterns and are frequent and have a support of 3 and 2 sequences, respectively. In other words, these patterns appear in 3 and 2 sequences of the input database, respectively. The pattern appears in the sequences 1, 2 and 3, while the pattern appears in sequences 1 and 3. These patterns are interesting as they represent some behavior common to several customers. Of course, this is a toy example. Sequential pattern mining can actually be applied on database containing hundreds of thousands of sequences.

Another example of application of sequential pattern mining is text analysis. In this context, a set of sentences from a text can be viewed as sequence database, and the goal of sequential pattern mining is then to find subsequences of words frequently used in the text. If such sequences are contiguous, they are called "ngrams" in this context.

Can Sequential Pattern Mining be Applied to Time Series?

Besides sequences, sequential pattern mining can also be applied to time series (e.g. stock data), when discretization is performed as a pre-processing step. For example, the figure below shows a time series (an ordered list of numbers) on the left. On the right, a sequence (a sequence of symbols) is shown representing the same data, after applying a transformation. Various transformations can be done to transform a time series to a sequence such as the popular SAX transformation. After performing the transformation, any sequential pattern mining algorithm can be applied.

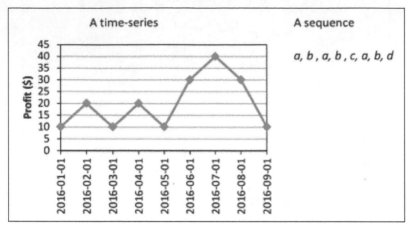

Figure: A time-series (left) and a sequence (right).

How can we get Sequential Pattern Mining Implementations?

To try sequential pattern mining with your datasets, you may try the open source SPMF data mining software, which provides implementations of numerous sequential pattern mining algorithms. It provides implementations of several algorithms for sequential pattern mining, as well as several variations of the problem such as discovering maximal sequential patterns, closed sequential patterns and sequential rules. Sequential rules are especially useful for the purpose of performing predictions, as they also include the concept of confidence.

Sequential Pattern Mining Algorithms

Apriori-like Algorithms

Let be a transaction database including customer sequences. This database is composed by three attributes (customer-id, transaction time and purchased-item). The mining process was decomposed with five steps:

- Sort step: Which sort the transactional database according the custom-id.

- L-itemset step: The objective is to obtain the large 1- itemsets from the sorted database, based on the support threshold.

- Transformation step: This step replaces the sequences by those large itemsets they contain. For efficient mining, all the large itemsets are mapped into an integer series. Finally, the original database will be transformed into set of customer sequences represented by those large itemsets.

- Sequence step: From the transformed sequential database, this step generates all frequent sequential patterns.

- Maximal step: This step prunes the sequential patterns that are contained in other super sequential patterns, because we are only concerned with maximum sequential patterns.

Even though the Apriori algorithm is the basis of many efficient algorithms developed later, it is not efficient enough. Study has detected an interesting downward closure property, studied by Apriori, among frequent kitemsets: A k-itemset is frequent only if all of its sub-itemsets are frequent. This property means that frequent itemsets can be mined by identifying frequent 1-itemsets (first scan of the database), then the frequent 1- itemsets would be used to generate candidate frequent 2- itemsets, this process will be repeated again to obtain the frequent 2-itemsets. This process iterates until any frequent k-itemsets can be generated for some k.

There have been widespread studies on the improvements of Apriori, e.g. sampling approach, dynamic itemset counting, and incremental mining, parallel and distributed mining. The work in, the number of candidate patterns that can be generated at the level-wise mining approach can be derived with a rigid upper bound. The obtained result reduces effectively the number of database scans.

In some cases, the size of candidate sets using the Apriori principle is significantly reduced. This situation can cause two problems:

- Huge number of candidate sets should be generated.

- Uses of pattern matching to constantly scan the database and discovers the candidates.

To encompass this problem, the work in proposed an FP-growth method aiming to mine the complete set of frequent itemsets without candidate generation. FP-growth compresses the database into a frequent-pattern tree, or FP-tree based on the frequency-descending list. The concatenation of the suffix pattern with the frequent patterns generated from a conditional FP-tree achieves the pattern growth. Instead to find long frequent patterns, the FP-growth algorithm searches recursively for shorter suffixes and then concatenating them. This method considerably reduces search time, according performance studies. Some extensions of the FP-growth approach, including H-Mine proposed by researchers. In 2001 which investigate a hyper-structure mining of frequent patterns; discovering the prefix-tree-structure with array-based implementation for efficient pattern growth mining by researchers in 2003 and a pattern-growth mining with top-down and bottom-up traversal of such trees proposed in the work of researchers.

BFS-based Algorithms

Breath-first (level-wise) search algorithms describe the Apriori-based algorithms because all k-sequences are constructed together in each k_{th} iteration of the algorithm as they traverse the search space. Several algorithms developed using the principle of BFS algorithms. Among them we enumerate some of them in the following sections.

GSP Algorithm

The GSP algorithm proposed in, do the same work of Apriori All algorithm, but it doesn't require finding all the frequent itemsets first. This algorithm allows a) placing bounds on the time separation between adjacent elements in a pattern, b) allowing the items included in the pattern element to span a transaction set within a time window specified by user, c) permitting the pattern discovery in different level of a taxonomy defined by user. Additionally, GSP is designed for discovering generalized sequential patterns. The GSP algorithm makes multiple passes over sequence database as follows: 1) in the first pass, it finds the frequent sequences that have the minimum support. 2) At each pass, every data sequence is examined in order to update the occurrence number of the candidates contained in this sequence. The pseudo code of GSP algorithm is as follows:

- Obtain a sequences in form of <x> as length-1 candidates.

- Find F_1 (the set of length-1 sequential patterns), after a unique scan of database.

- Let k=1.

While F_k is not empty do:

- Form C_{k+1}, the set of length-(k+1) candidates from F_k.

- If C_{k+1} is not empty, unique database scan, find F_{k+1} (the set of length-(k+1) sequential patterns).

   Let k=k+1.

   End While.

This algorithm has the following drawbacks:

- The generation if a huge set of candidate sequences, which needs a multiple scans of the database.

- The expensive number of short patterns for the mined pattern length and for that reason this algorithm is inefficient for mining long sequential patterns.

Consequently, it is important to review the sequential pattern mining problem to discover more efficient and scalable methods which may reduce the expensive candidate generation.

MFS

It is a modified version of GSP, proposed in with the aim to reduce the I/O cost needed by GSP. MFS computes as a first step the rough estimate of all the frequent sequences set as a suggested frequent sequence set and to maintain the set of maximal frequent sequences known previously it uses the candidate generation function of GSP. The results obtained in show that MFS saves I/O cost significantly in comparison with GSP.

DFS-based Algorithms

The algorithms adopting this feature show only an ineffective pruning method and engender a great number of candidate sequences, which requires consuming a lot of memory in the early stages of mining. Several algorithms developed using the principle of DFS algorithms.

Spade

This includes the features of a search space partitioning where the search space includes vertical database layout. The search space in SPADE is represented as a lattice structure and it use the notion of equivalence classes to partition it. It decomposes the original lattice into slighter sub-lattices, so that each sub-lattice can be entirely processed using either a breadth-first or depth-first search method (SPADE is also DFS based method). The SPADE support counting of the candidate sequence method includes bitwise or logical operations. A conducted experimental results shows, that SPADE is about twice as fast as GSP. The reason behind this is that SPADE uses a more efficient support counting method based on the idlest structure. Additionally, SPADE shows a linear scalability with respect to the number of sequences. The Pseudo code of SPADE algorithm is as follows:

Input:

D //ID-Lists of sequences

S //support

Output:

F //Frequent sequences

Begin:

- Determine frequent items, F_1.

- Determine frequent 2-sequences, F_2.

- Find equivalence classes for all 1- Sequences$[S]_{\theta 1}$.

- For each $[S] \in \in$ do.

  Find frequent sequences F.

End

As an example, let be the ID-List for sequences of length 1 illustrated in the Figure below. The support count for the item {A} is 3, but the support count for the element is 2. The equivalent classes θ_1 are presented in the Figure below.

A		B		C		D	
Customer	Time	Customer	Time	Customer	Time	Customer	Time
C_1	10	C_1	10	C_1	20	C_1	30
C_2	15	C_1	20	C_2	15	C_2	20
C_3	15	C_2	15	C_3	15	C_3	15

Figure: ID-List as an example of SPADE Algorithm.

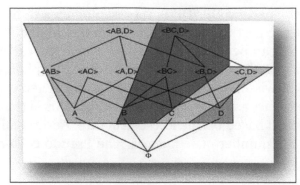

Figure: The equivalent classes generated by SPADE Algorithm.

FreeSpan

FreeSpan is an algorithm proposed by Pei et al. in 2001 with the aim to reduce the generation of candidate subsequences. It uses projected databases to generate database annotations in order to guide the mining process to rapidly find frequent patterns. The general idea of FreeSpan is to use frequent items to project sequence databases into a set of smaller projected databases recursively using the currently mined frequent sets, and subsequence fragments in each projected database are generated, respectively. Two alternatives of database projections can be used Level-by-level projection or Alternative-level projection. The method used by FreeSpan divide the data and the set of frequent patterns to be tested, and limits each test being conducted to the corresponding smaller projected database. FreeSpan scan the original database only three times, whatever the maximal length of the sequence. Experimental results show that FreeSpan is efficient and mines the complete set of patterns and it is considerably faster than the GSP algorithm. The major cost of FreeSpan is to deal with projected databases.

PrefixSpan

This algorithm is another form projection based algorithm. The general idea is to check only the prefix subsequences and only their corresponding postfix subsequences are projected into projected databases, rather than projecting sequence database. PrefixSpan uses a direct application of the Apriori property in order to reduce candidate sequences alongside projected databases. Additionally, PrefixSpan is efficient because it mines the complete set of patterns and has a significantly faster running than both GSP algorithm and FreeSpan. The major cost of PrefixSpan, similarly to FreeSpan, is the construction of projected databases. At worst, for every sequential database, PrefixSpan needs to construct a projected database. After the database projection is done, the use of bi-level projection represented in FreeSpan and PrefixSpan by the SMatrix is an additional faster way to mine. The main idea of PrefixSpan algorithm (presented in the following paragraph) is to use frequent prefixes to divide the search space and to project sequence databases. Its aim is to search the relevant sequences.

PrefixSpan $(\alpha, i, S|\alpha)$

Begin

1. Scan $S|\alpha$ once, find the set of frequent items b such that:

   • b can be assembled to the last element of a to form a sequential pattern; or.

- <b> can be appended to α to form a sequential pattern.

2. for each frequent item b, appended it to α to form a sequential pattern', and output α'.

3. For each α', construct α'-projected database $S|\alpha$', and call PrefixSpan $(\alpha', i+1, S|\alpha')$.

End

Represents a sequential pattern; b) l is the length of α; and c) $S|\alpha$ is the α-projected database if $\alpha \neq$ < >, otherwise, it is the sequence database S.

SPAM

This algorithm uses a depth-first traversal method combined with a vertical bitmap representation to store each sequence allowing a significant bitmap compression as well as an efficient support counting. SPAM uses a vertical bitmap representation of the data which are created for each item in the dataset. Each bitmap contains a bit representing each transaction in the dataset, if item i appears in transaction j, then the bit relative to transaction j of the bitmap for item i is set to 1; otherwise it is set to 0. An efficient counting and candidate generation can be enabled if the bitmap should be partitioned aiming to make sure all transaction sequences in the database appear together in the bitmap. The bitmap representation idea of SPAM requires quite a lot of memory, so it is very efficient for those databases which have very long sequential patterns. Additionally, a significant feature of this algorithm is the outputs of new frequent itemsets in an online and incremental fashion. Experimental results show that this algorithm is more efficient compared to SPADE and PrefixSpan on large datasets, but it consumes more space compared to SPADE and PrefixSpan.

DFS-Pruning (node n = $(s_1, ..., s_k)$, S_n, I_n)

Begin

(1) $S_{temp} = \varphi$.

(2) $I_{temp} = \varphi$.

(3) For each ($i \in S_n$)

(4) if ((s_1, ..., s_k, {i}) is frequent)

(5) $S_{temp} = S_{temp}$ {i}

(6) For each ($i \in S_{temp}$)

(7) DFS-Pruning ((s_1,...,s_k,{i}),S_{temp}, all elements in S_{temp} greater than i)

(8) For each ($I \in I_n$)

(9) If ((s_1... s_k » {i}) is frequent)

(10) Itemp = Itemp $\cup$ {i}

(11) For each (i $\in I_{temp}$)

(12) DFS-Pruning ((s_1, ..., $s_k \cup \{i\}$), S_{temp}, all elements in I_{temp} greater than i)

End

Algorithms based on closed sequential pattern the algorithms of sequential pattern mining presented earlier mine the full set of frequent subsequences satisfying a minimum support threshold. Nevertheless, because a frequent long sequence contains a combined number of frequent subsequences, the mining process will generate a large number of frequent subsequences for long patterns, which is expensive in both time and space. The frequent pattern mining (itemsets and sequences) needs not mine all frequent patterns but the closed ones since it leads to a better efficiency, which can really reduce the number of frequent subsequences.

CloSpan

This algorithm is used to reduce the time and space cost when generating explosive numbers of frequent sequence patterns. CloSpan mines only frequent closed subsequences (the sequences containing no super sequence with the same support), instead of mining the complete set of frequent subsequences. The mining process used by CloSpan is divided into two stages. A candidate set is generated in the first stage which is larger than the final closed sequence set. This set is called suspicious closed sequence set (the superset of the closed sequence set). A pruning method is called in the second stage to eliminate non-closed sequences. The main difference between CloSpan and PrefixSpan is the implementation of CloSpan which are an early termination mechanism that avoids the unnecessary traversing of search space. The use of backward sub-pattern and backward super pattern methods, some patterns will be absorbed or merged which, indeedly reduce the search space growth.

CloSpan (s, D_s, minsupp, L)

Input: sequence s, a projected database D_s, and minimum support

Output: the prefix search lattice L.

Begin

(1) Check whether a discovered sequence s' exists such that either $s \subseteq s'$ or $s' \subseteq s$ and database size $L(D_s) = L(D_s')$

(2) If such super-pattern or sub-pattern exists then

(3) Modify the link in L; Return

(4) else insert s in L;

(5) scan D_s once, find the set of frequent itemset α such that α can be appended to form a sequential pattern s α.

(6) If no valid α available then

(7) Return

(8) For each valid α do

Call CloSpan(s α, D_s α, minsupp, L)

(9) Return

BIDE

This algorithm, proposed by Wang and Han which mines closed sequential patterns without candidate maintenance by adopting a closure checking scheme, called Bi-Directional Extension. BIDE avoids the problem of the candidate maintenance-and-test paradigm used by CloSpan. It prunes totally the search space and checks efficiently the pattern closure which consumes a much less memory in contrast to the previously developed closed pattern mining algorithms. BIDE has a linear scalability with regards to the number of sequences in the database. Nevertheless, it will lose some all frequent-sequence mining algorithms with a high support threshold, like other closed sequence mining algorithms. Experimental results show that BIDE is more efficient than CloSpan.

Incremental-based Algorithms

In sequential pattern mining, incremental algorithm can be used for the mining of frequent and incremental database updates (insertions and deletions). We distinguish two cases to develop an incremental algorithm: (a) The complete sequences (sequence model) are inserted into and/or removed from the original database; (b) The original database contains a sequence which is updated by appending new transactions at the end.

SuffixTree

SuffixTree techniques deal with incremental sequential pattern updating. SuffixTree has only to maintain the data reading after the update, for this reason it is a very appropriate method for incremental sequence extraction. But, this algorithm presents the complexity in space which depends on the size of the database, which presents the main limitations of this method. Additionally, the sensitivity of the position to the update operation makes SuffixTree very expensive for dynamic strings.

Fastup

This algorithm presents an improvement of the candidate generation and support counting of GSP algorithm. This algorithm uses the generating pruning method to generate and validate candidates based on the previous mining result. Performance study shows that the performance of this algorithm is better than previous algorithms for the maintenance of sequential patterns in term of speediness. Nevertheless FASTUP includes the same limitations as GSP.

ISM

This algorithm deals with incremental sequence mining for vertical database based on the SPADE approach of sequential pattern mining. ISM assumes the availability of all the frequent sequences with their support counts and those sequences in the negative border and their support (contained in the old database) in a lattice. Additionally, ISM prunes the search space for potential new sequences based on the construction of Incremental Sequence Lattice (ISL) and the exploration of its properties. Performance study shows that ISM is an improvement in execution time by up to several orders of magnitude in practice, both for handling increments of the database, in addition to the handling interactive queries, compared with SPADE.

ISE

ISE considers both the appending of sequences and inserting of new sequences, in contrast to ISM which only considers sequence appending. If sequence appending is considered, all the previous frequent sequences are still frequent, but if we insert new sequences, some of them may become infrequent with the same minimum support. The incremental sequential mining is defined as following: Let S be the original database, s is considered as incremental database where new customer sequences and transactions are inserted. [L.sup.S] indicates the set of frequent sequences in S, the incremental sequential pattern mining problem is to find the frequent sequences in U =[S.sup.s] with respect to the same minimum support. We expect that the length of maximal frequent sequence in the old database is l, ISE algorithm decomposes the mining into two sub problems, for those candidate sequences having a length greater than l, the GSP algorithm is used directly. An empirical evaluation indicates that ISE was so efficient that it was quicker to extract an increment and to mine sequential patterns from the original database than to use the GSP algorithm.

GSP+ and MFS+

GSP+ and MF+ are two algorithms, used to mine incremental sequential patterns based on the inserted or deleted sequences from the original database: the first are based on GSP and the second are based on MFS. Based on the set of frequent sequences obtained from mining the old database, GSP+ and MFS+ can be used to efficiently compute the updated set of frequent sequences. Performance studies show the effectiveness of GSP+ and MFS+ in term of CPU costs reduction with only a small or even negative expense on I/O cost.

IncSP

As an efficient incremental updating algorithm used for sequential patterns maintenance after a nontrivial number of data sequences are added to the sequence database. IncSP uses the previously computed frequent sequences as knowledge, prunes candidates early after a process of data sequences merging, and counts supports of the sequences in to the original database and the newly appended database separately. To support again the increment database in order to accelerate the whole process, InsSP uses the candidate pruning after updating pattern. Additionally, it uses correctly combined data sequences while preserving previous knowledge useful for incremental updating based on implicit merging. Experimental results, shows that IncSP outperforms GSP based on different ratios of the increment database to the original database excluding the situation when the increment database becomes larger than the original database.

IncSpan

IncSpan is an algorithm used for incremental mining over multiple database increments. Inspan algorithm development is based on two novel ideas. The first idea which presents a several good properties and lead to efficient practices is the use of a set of "almost frequent" sequences as the candidates in the updated database. The second idea is constituted by two optimization techniques designed to improve the performance, which are reverse pattern matching and shared projection. The first technique is used for matching a sequential pattern in a sequence. Reverse pattern matching can prune additional search space, while the appended transactions are at the end of a sequence. Shared projection is intended to reduce the number of database projections for some sequences having a common prefix. Empirical study shows that IncSpan is better than ISM and PrefixSpan on incrementally updated databases by a wide scope.

IncSpan⁺

IncSpan⁺ proposed to improve IncSpan. The authors agree that the algorithm IncSpan cannot find the complete set of frequent sequential patterns in the updated database D', i.e., it violates the correctness condition. The proposed algorithm ensures the correctness of mining result in the updated database. IncSpan+ ensures two important tasks: 1) the discovery of the complete FS', which guarantees the correctness of the mining result and 2) the discovery of the complete SFS', which is helpful in incrementally maintaining the frequent patterns for further database updates.

MILE

MILE is an efficient algorithm to facilitate the mining process in multiple sequences. It uses recursively the knowledge of existing patterns to avoid redundant data scanning which can effectively speedup the process of new pattern's discovery. Additionally, to improve the performance of the mining process, MILE has the unique feature that can incorporate prior knowledge of the data distribution in time sequence. Empirical experiments show that MILE is significantly faster than PrefixSpan.

Decision Support System

A decision support system (DSS) is a computer-based application that collects, organizes and analyzes business data to facilitate quality business decision-making for management, operations and planning. A well-designed DSS aids decision makers in compiling a variety of data from many sources: raw data, documents, personal knowledge from employees, management, executives and business models. DSS analysis helps companies to identify and solve problems, and make decisions.

The purpose of this session is to discuss how characteristics of a decision support system (DSS) interact with characteristics of a task to affect DSS use and decision performance. This discussion is based on the motivational framework developed by Chan and the studies conducted by researchers. The key constructs in the motivational framework include task motivation, user perception of DSS, motivation to use a DSS, DSS use, and decision performance. This framework highlights the significant role of the motivation factor, an important psychological construct, in explaining DSS use and decision performance.

While DSS use is an event where users place a high value on decision performance, the Technology Acceptance Model (TAM) and the Unified Theory of Acceptance and Use of Technology (UTAUT) do not explicitly establish a connection between system use and decision performance. Thus, Chan includes decision performance as a construct in the motivational framework rather than rely on the assumption that DSS use will necessarily result in positive outcomes.

This is an important facet of the framework because the ultimate purpose of DSS use is enhanced decision performance. Chan tests some of the constructs in the motivational framework. Specifically, the author examines how task motivation interacts with DSS effectiveness and efficiency to affect DSS use. As predicted, the findings indicate that individuals using a more effective DSS to work on a high motivation task increase usage of the DSS, while DSS use does not differ between individuals using either a more or less effective DSS to complete a low motivation task. The results also show significant differences for individuals using either a more or less efficient DSS to complete a low motivation task, but no significant differences between individuals using either a more or less efficient DSS to perform a high motivation task only when the extent of DSS use is measured dichotomously (i.e., use versus non-use).

These findings suggest the importance of task motivation and corroborate the findings of prior research in the context of objective (i.e., computer recorded) rather than subjective (self-reported) DSS use. A contribution of Chan's study is use of a rich measure of DSS use based on Burton-Jones and Straub's definition of DSS use as an activity that includes a user, a DSS, and a task. Chan et al. extends the motivational framework by investigating the alternative paths among the constructs proposed in the framework. Specifically, the authors test the direct effects of feedback (a DSS characteristic) and reward (a decision environment factor), and examine these effects on decision performance. The results indicate that individuals using a DSS with the feedback characteristic perform better than those using a DSS without the feedback characteristic. The findings also show that individuals receiving positive feedback, regardless of the nature (i.e., informational or controlling) of its administration perform better than the no-feedback group. These results provide some evidence supporting the call by Johnson et al. for designers to incorporate positive feedback in their design of DSS. Positive feedback is posited to lead to favorable user perception of a DSS which in turn leads to improved decision performance. The findings also suggest that task-contingent reward undermine decision performance compared to the no reward condition, and performance contingent reward enhance decision performance relative to the task-contingent reward group. The study by Chan et al. demonstrates the need for designers to be cognizant of the types of feedback and reward structures that exist in a DSS environment and their impact on decision performance.

DSS Characteristics

The characteristics of a DSS include ease of use, presentation format, system restrictiveness, decisional guidance, feedback, and interaction support.

Ease of Use

DSS use is expected to occur if users perceive a DSS to be easy to use and that using it enhances their performance and productivity. Less cognitive effort is needed to use a DSS that is easy to use, operate, or interact with. The extent of ease of use of a DSS is dependent on features in the DSS that support the dimensions of speed, memory, effort, and comfort. A DSS is easy to use if it reduces user performance time (i.e., the DSS is efficient), decreases memory load with the nature of assistance provided (memory), reduces mental effort with simple operations (effort), and promotes user comfort (comfort). An objective of developers is to reduce the effort that users need to expend on a task by incorporating the ease of use characteristic into a DSS so that more effort can be allocated to other activities to improve decision performance. DSS use may decline if increased cognitive effort is needed to use a DSS because of lack of ease of use.

System Restrictiveness and Decisional Guidance

Two DSS attributes, system restrictiveness and decisional guidance, have been examined to show what users can and will do with a DSS. System restrictiveness refers to the degree to which a DSS limits the options available to the users, and decisional guidance refers to a DSS assisting the users to select and use its features during the decision-making process. If a decision making process encompasses the execution of a sequence of information processing activities to reach a decision, then both the structure and execution of the process can be restricted by a DSS. The structure of the process can be restricted in two ways: limit the set of information processing activities by providing only a particular subset of all possible capabilities, and restrict the order of activities by imposing constraints on the sequence in which the permitted information processing activities can be carried out. User involvement is often essential during the execution of information processing activities after the structure of the process has been determined. The structure in the decision-making process is also promoted with the use of a restrictive DSS; in this respect, users are not overwhelmed with choices among many competing DSS. In certain cases, additional structure may actually enhance DSS use when ease of use is facilitated. However, lesser system restrictiveness may be preferred to enhance learning and creativity. Users may not use a DSS that is too restrictive because they may consider DSS use to be discretionary.

References

- Data-mining: tutorialspoint.com, Retrieved 02, August 2020

- Data-mining-techniques: javatpoint.com, Retrieved 27, February 2020

- Association-rule: geeksforgeeks.org, Retrieved 10, June 2020

- An-Introduction-to-Sequential-Pattern-Mining, graph-analysis: ccs.neu.edu, Retrieved 19, January 2020

3

Varied Types of Database Models

A database model defines the logical structure of a database and also determines how data will be stored, accessed and updated in a database management system. Hierarchical database model is a database model which contains data that is organized in a tree-like structure. Many database models like network model, hierarchical model, entity-attribute-value model, etc. are explained in this chapter.

A database model shows the logical structure of a database, including the relationships and constraints that determine how data can be stored and accessed. Individual database models are designed based on the rules and concepts of whichever broader data model the designers adopt. Most data models can be represented by an accompanying database diagram.

Types

There are many kinds of data models. Some of the most common ones include:

- Hierarchical database model.
- Relational model.
- Network model.
- Object-oriented database model.
- Entity-relationship model.
- Document model.
- Entity-attribute-value model.
- Star schema.
- The object-relational model, which combines the two that make up its name.

You may choose to describe a database with any one of these depending on several factors. The biggest factor is whether the database management system you are using supports a particular model. Most database management systems are built with a particular data model in mind and require their users to adopt that model, although some do support multiple models.

In addition, different models apply to different stages of the database design process. High-level conceptual data models are best for mapping out relationships between data in ways that people perceive that data. Record-based logical models, on the other hand, more closely reflect ways that the data is stored on the server.

Selecting a data model is also a matter of aligning your priorities for the database with the strengths of a particular model, whether those priorities include speed, cost reduction, usability, or something else.

Relational Model

The most common model, the relational model sorts data into tables, also known as relations, each of which consists of columns and rows. Each column lists an attribute of the entity in question, such as price, zip code, or birth date. Together, the attributes in a relation are called a domain. A particular attribute or combination of attributes is chosen as a primary key that can be referred to in other tables, when it's called a foreign key.

Each row, also called a tuple, includes data about a specific instance of the entity in question, such as a particular employee.

The model also accounts for the types of relationships between those tables, including one-to-one, one-to-many, and many-to-many relationships. Here's an example:

Student ID	First name	Last name
52-743965	Charles	Peters
48-209689	Anthony	Sondrup
14-204968	Rebecca	Phillips

ProviderID	Provider name
156-983	UnitedHealth
146-823	Blue Shield
447-784	Carefirst Inc.

Student ID	ProviderID	Type of plan	Start date
52-743965	156-983	HSA	04/01/2016
48-209689	146-823	HMO	12/01/2015
14-204968	447-784	HSA	03/14/2016

Within the database, tables can be normalized, or brought to comply with normalization rules that make the database flexible, adaptable, and scalable. When normalized, each piece of data is atomic, or broken into the smallest useful pieces.

Relational databases are typically written in Structured Query Language (SQL).

Hierarchical Model

The hierarchical model organizes data into a tree-like structure, where each record has a single parent or root. Sibling records are sorted in a particular order. That order is used as the physical order for storing the database. This model is good for describing many real-world relationships.

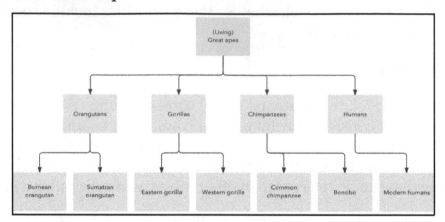

This model was primarily used by IBM's Information Management Systems in the 60s and 70s, but they are rarely seen today due to certain operational inefficiencies.

Network Model

The network model builds on the hierarchical model by allowing many-to-many relationships between linked records, implying multiple parent records. Based on mathematical set theory, the model is constructed with sets of related records. Each set consists of one owner or parent record and one or more member or child records. A record can be a member or child in multiple sets, allowing this model to convey complex relationships.

It was most popular in the 70s after it was formally defined by the Conference on Data Systems Languages (CODASYL).

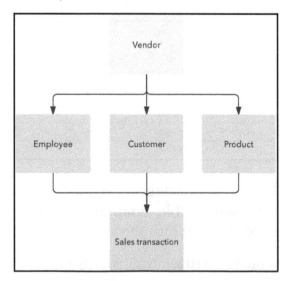

Object-oriented Database Model

This model defines a database as a collection of objects, or reusable software elements, with associated features and methods. There are several kinds of object-oriented databases:

- A multimedia database incorporates media, such as images, that could not be stored in a relational database.

- A hypertext database allows any object to link to any other object. It's useful for organizing lots of disparate data, but it's not ideal for numerical analysis.

- The object-oriented database model is the best known post-relational database model, since it incorporates tables, but isn't limited to tables. Such models are also known as hybrid database models.

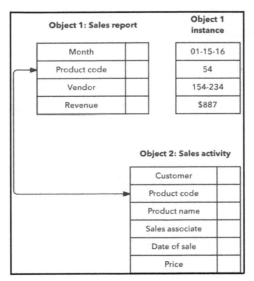

Object-relational Model

This hybrid database model combines the simplicity of the relational model with some of the advanced functionality of the object-oriented database model. In essence, it allows designers to incorporate objects into the familiar table structure.

Languages and call interfaces include SQL3, vendor languages, ODBC, JDBC, and proprietary call interfaces that are extensions of the languages and interfaces used by the relational model.

Entity-relationship Model

This model captures the relationships between real-world entities much like the network model, but it isn't as directly tied to the physical structure of the database. Instead, it's often used for designing a database conceptually.

Here, the people, places, and things about which data points are stored are referred to as entities, each of which has certain attributes that together make up their domain. The cardinality, or relationships between entities are mapped as well.

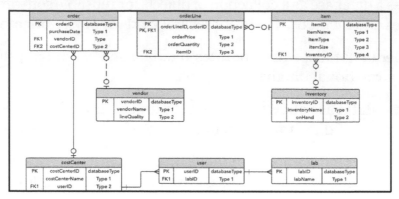

A common form of the ER diagram is the star schema, in which a central fact table connects to multiple dimensional tables.

Other Database Models

A variety of other database models have been or are still used today.

Inverted File Model

A database built with the inverted file structure is designed to facilitate fast full text searches. In this model, data content is indexed as a series of keys in a lookup table, with the values pointing to the location of the associated files. This structure can provide nearly instantaneous reporting in big data and analytics, for instance.

This model has been used by the ADABAS database management system of Software AG since 1970, and it is still supported today.

Flat Model

The flat model is the earliest, simplest data model. It simply lists all the data in a single table, consisting of columns and rows. In order to access or manipulate the data, the computer has to read the entire flat file into memory, which makes this model inefficient for all but the smallest data sets.

Multidimensional Model

This is a variation of the relational model designed to facilitate improved analytical processing. While the relational model is optimized for online transaction processing (OLTP), this model is designed for online analytical processing (OLAP).

Each cell in a dimensional database contains data about the dimensions tracked by the database. Visually, it's like a collection of cubes, rather than two-dimensional tables.

Semi Structured Model

In this model, the structural data usually contained in the database schema is embedded with the data itself. Here the distinction between data and schema is vague at best. This model is useful for describing systems, such as certain Web-based data sources, which we treat as databases but cannot constrain with a schema. It's also useful for describing interactions between databases that don't adhere to the same schema.

Context Model

This model can incorporate elements from other database models as needed. It cobbles together elements from object-oriented, semi structured, and network models.

Associative Model

This model divides all the data points based on whether they describe an entity or an association. In this model, an entity is anything that exists independently, whereas an association is something that only exists in relation to something else.

The associative model structures the data into two sets:

- A set of items, each with a unique identifier, a name and a type.

- A set of links, each with a unique identifier and the unique identifiers of a source, verb, and target. The stored fact has to do with the source, and each of the three identifiers may refer either to a link or an item.

Other, less common database models include:

- Semantic model, which includes information about how the stored data relates to the real world.

- XML database, which allows data to be specified and even stored in XML format;

- Named graph.

- Triple-store.

No-SQL Database Models

In addition to the object database model, other non-SQL models have emerged in contrast to the relational model:

- The graph database model, which is even more flexible than a network model, allowing any node to connect with any other.

- The multi value model, which breaks from the relational model by allowing attributes to contain a list of data rather than a single data point.

- The document model, which is designed for storing and managing documents or semi-structured data, rather than atomic data.

Databases on the Web

Most websites rely on some kind of database to organize and present data to users. Whenever someone uses the search functions on these sites, their search terms are converted into queries for a database server to process. Typically, middleware connects the web server with the database.

The broad presence of databases allows them to be used in almost any field, from online shopping to micro-targeting a voter segment as part of a political campaign. Various industries have developed their own norms for database design, from air transport to vehicle manufacturing.

Hierarchical Database Model

A hierarchical database consists of a collection of records that are connected to each other through links. A record is similar to a record in the network model. Each record is a collection of fields (attributes), each of which contains only one data value. A link is an association between precisely two records. Thus, a link here is similar to a link in the network model.

Consider a database that represents a customer-account relationship in a banking system. There are two record types: customer and account. It consists of three fields: customer name, customer street and customer city. Similarly, the account record consists of two fields: account number and balance.

A sample database appears in figure. It shows that customer Hayes has account A-102, customer Johnson has accounts A-101 and A-201, and customer Turner has account A-305.

Note that the set of all customer and account records is organized in the form of a rooted tree, where the root of the tree is a dummy node. As we shall see, a hierarchical database is a collection of such rooted trees, and hence forms a forest. We shall refer to each such rooted tree as a database tree.

The content of a particular record may have to be replicated in several different locations. For example, in our customer-account banking system, an account may belong to several customers. The information pertaining to that account, or the information pertaining to the various customers to which that account may belong, will have to be replicated. This replication may occur either in the same database tree or in several different trees. Record replication has two major drawbacks.

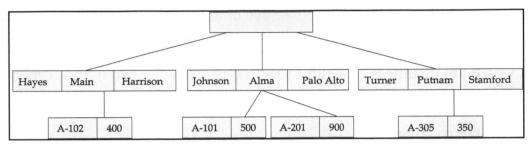

Figure: Sample database.

1. Data inconsistency may result when updating takes place.

2. Waste of space is unavoidable.

Tree-structure Diagrams

A tree-structure diagram is the schema for a hierarchical database. Such a diagram consists of two basic components:

1. Boxes, which correspond to record types.

2. Lines, which correspond to links.

A tree-structure diagram serves the same purpose as an entity–relationship (E-R) diagram; namely, it specifies the overall logical structure of the database. A tree structure diagram is similar to a data-structure diagram in the network model. The main difference is that, in the latter, record types are organized in the form of an arbitrary graph, whereas in the former, record types are organized in the form of a rooted tree.

We have to be more precise about what a rooted tree is. First, there can be no cycles in the underlying graph. Second, there is a record type that is designated as the root of the tree. The relationships formed in the tree-structure diagram must be such that only one-to-many or one-to-one relationships exist between a parent and a child. The general form of a tree-structure diagram appears in Figure below Note that the arrows are pointing from children to parents. A parent may have an arrow pointing to a child, but a child must have an arrow pointing to its parent.

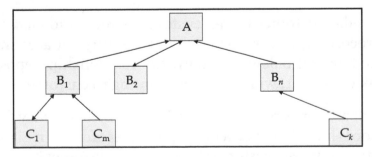

Figure: General structure of a tree-structure diagram.

The database schema is represented as a collection of tree-structure diagrams. For each such diagram, there exists one single instance of a database tree. The root of this tree is a dummy node. The children of the dummy node are instances of the root record type in the tree-structure diagram. Each record instance may, in turn, have several children, which are instances of various record types, as specified in the corresponding tree-structure diagram.

Single Relationships

Consider the E-R diagram of figure (a); it consists of the two entity sets customer and account related through a binary, one-to-many relationship depositor, with no descriptive attributes. This diagram specifies that a customer can have several accounts, but an account can belong to only one customer. The corresponding tree structure diagram appears in figure below. The record type customer corresponds to the entity set customer.

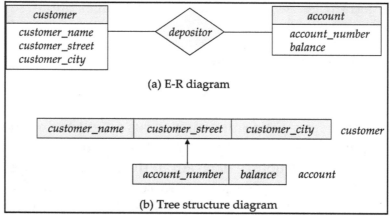

Figure: E-R diagram and its corresponding tree-structure

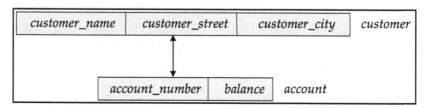

Figure: Tree-structure diagram with one-to-one relationship.

It includes three fields: customer name, customer street, and customer city. Similarly, account is the record type corresponding to the entity set account. It includes two fields: account number and balance. Finally, the relationship depositor has been replaced with the link depositor, with an arrow pointing to customer record type.

An instance of a database corresponding to the described schema may thus contain a number of customer records linked to a number of account records, as in Figure below Since the relationship is one to many from customer to account, a customer can have more than one account, as does Johnson, who has both accounts A-101 and A-201. An account, however, cannot belong to more than one customer; none do in the sample database.

If the relationship depositor is one to one, then the link depositor has two arrows: one pointing to account record type, and one pointing to customer record type. A sample database corresponding to this schema appears in figure below Since the relationship is one to one, an account can be owned by precisely one customer, and a customer can have only one account, as is indeed the case in the sample database.

If the relationship depositor is many to many then the trans- formation from an E-R diagram to a tree-structure diagram is more complicated. Only one-to-many and one-to-one relationships can be directly represented in the hierarchical model.

There are many different ways to transform this E-R diagram to a tree-structure dia- gram. All these diagrams, however, share the property that the underlying database tree (or trees) will have replicated records.

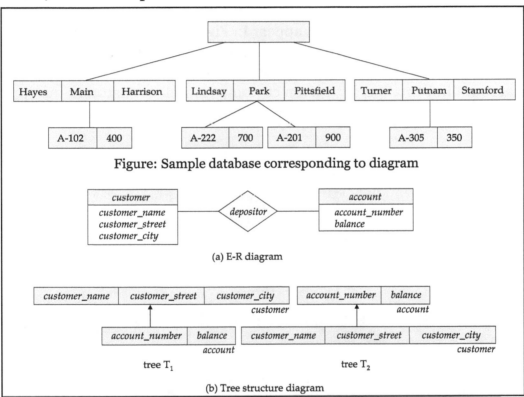

Figure: Sample database corresponding to diagram

(a) E-R diagram

(b) Tree structure diagram

Figure: E-R diagram and its corresponding tree-structure diagrams.

The decision regarding which transformation should be used depends on many factors, including:

- The type of queries expected on the database.

- The degree to which the overall database schema being modeled fits the given.

- E-R diagram.

We shall present a transformation that is as general as possible. That is, all other possi- ble transformations are a special case of this one transformation.

To transform the E-R diagram of Figure E.6a into a tree-structure diagram, we take these steps:

- Create two separate tree-structure diagrams, T1 and T2, each of which has the customer and account record types. In tree T1, customer is the root; in tree T2, account is the root.

- Create the following two links:

  ◦ Depositor, a many-to-one link from account record type to customer record type, in T1.

  ◦ Account customer, a many-to-one link from customer record type to account record type, in T2.

The resulting tree-structure diagrams appear in Figure above The presence of two diagrams permits customers who do not participate in the depositor relation- ship as well as accounts that do not participate in the depositor relationship and permits efficient access to account information for a given customer as well as customer information for a given account.

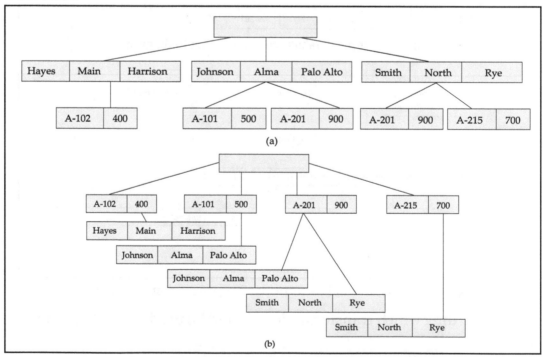

Figure: Sample database corresponding to diagram.

A sample database corresponding to the tree-structure diagram of figure (b) appears in figure. There are two database trees. The first tree corresponds to the tree-structure diagram T1; the second tree corresponds to the tree-structure diagram T2. As we can see, all customer and account records are replicated in both database trees. In addition, account record A-201 appears twice in the first tree, whereas customer records Johnson and Smith appear twice in the second tree.

If a relationship also includes a descriptive attribute, the transformation from an E-R diagram to a tree-structure diagram is more complicated. A link cannot contain any data value. In this case, a new record type needs to be created, and the appropriate links need to be established. The manner in which links are formed depends on the way the relationship depositor is defined.

Consider the above E-R diagram suppose that we add the attribute access date to the relationship depositor, to denote the most recent date on which a customer accessed the account. This newly derived E-R diagram appears in figure (a). To transform this diagram into a tree-structure diagram, we must;

- Create a new record type access date with a single field.

- Create the following two links:

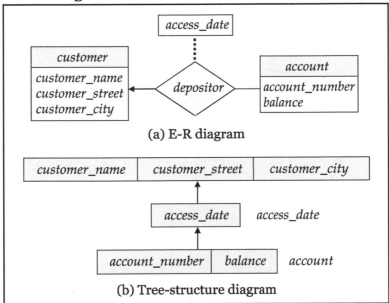

(a) E-R diagram

(b) Tree-structure diagram

Figure: E-R diagram and its corresponding tree-structure diagram.

- ○ Customer date, a many-to-one link from access date record type to customer

- Record type;

- ○ Date account, a many-to-one link from account record type to access date-record type.

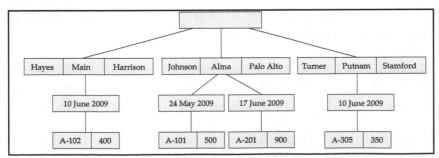

Figure: Sample database corresponding to diagram.

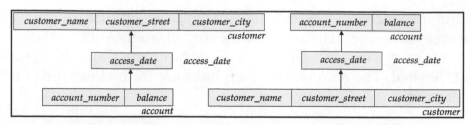

Figure: Tree-structure diagram with many-to-many relationships.

The resulting tree-structure diagram is illustrated in figure (b).

An instance corresponding to the described schema appears in figure. It shows that:

- Hayes has account A-102, which was last accessed on 10 June 2009.

- Johnson has two accounts: A-101, which was last accessed on 24 May 2009, and A-201, which was last accessed on 17 June 2009.

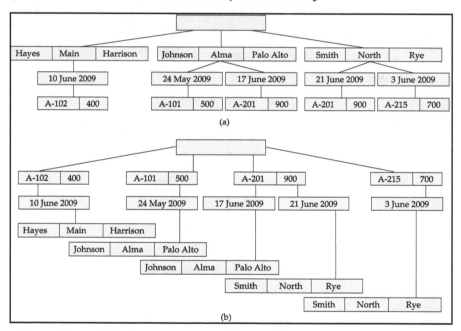

Figure: Sample database corresponding to diagram of Figure just above.

Turner has account A-305, which was last accessed on 10 June 2009.

Note that two different accounts can be accessed on the same date, as were accounts A-102 and A-305. These accounts belong to two different customers, so the access date record must be replicated to preserve the hierarchy.

If the relationship depositor were one to one with the attribute date, then the transformation algorithm would be similar to the one described. The only difference would be that the two links customer date and date account would be one-to-one links.

Assume that the relationship depositor is many to many with the attribute access date; here again, we can choose among a number of alternative transformations.

We shall use the most general transformation; it is similar to the one applied to the case where the relationship depositor has no descriptive attribute. The record type customer, account, and access date need to be replicated, and two separate tree-structure diagrams must be created, as in sample database corresponding to this schema is in Figure above.

Until now, we have considered only binary relationships. We shift our attention here to general relationships. The transformation of E-R diagrams corresponding to general relationships into tree-structure diagrams is complicated.

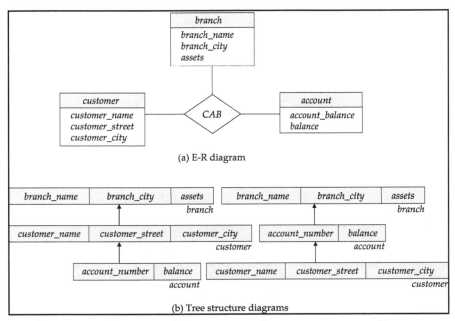

Figure: E-R diagram and its corresponding tree-structure diagrams.

Rather than present a general transformation algorithm, we present a single ex- ample to illustrate the overall strategy that you can apply to deal with such a transformation.

Consider the E-R diagram of Figure above, which consists of the three entity sets customer, account, and branch, related through the general relationship set CAB with no descriptive attribute.

There are many different ways to transform this E-R diagram into a tree- structure diagram. Again, all share the property that the underlying database tree (or trees) will have replicated records. The most straightforward transformation is to create two tree-structure diagrams, as shown in figure above.

An instance of the database corresponding to this schema is illustrated in figure below. It shows that Hayes has account A-102 in the Perry ridge branch; Johnson has accounts A-101 and A-201 in the Downtown and Perry ridge branches, respectively; and Smith has accounts A-201 and A-215 in the Perry ridge and Mianus branches, respectively.

We can extend the preceding transformation algorithm in a straightforward manner to deal with relationships that span more than three entity sets. We simply replicate the various record types, and generate as many tree-structure diagram as necessary.

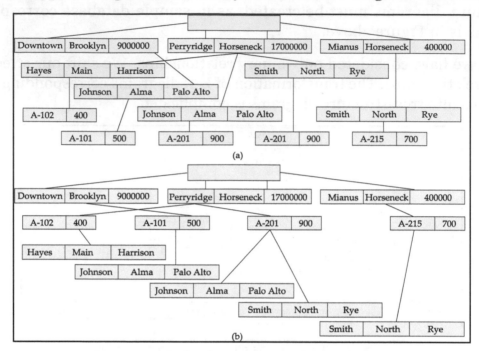

Figure: Sample database corresponding to diagram.

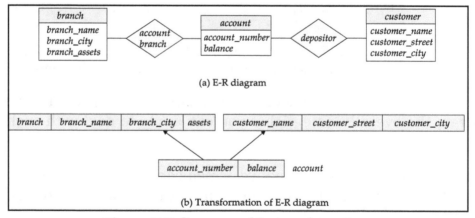

Figure: E-R diagram and its transformation.

We can extend this approach, in turn, to deal with a general relationship that has descriptive attributes. We need only to create a new record type with one field for each descriptive attribute, and then to insert that record type in the appropriate location in the tree-structure diagram.

Characteristics of a Hierarchical Data Model

Structure

The main characteristic of a hierarchical data model is the treelike structure. For example, a company database might organize using one branch for Staff, followed by Departments, Teams and then Team Members. This parent-child structure is consistent throughout the database, and each child segment can only have one parent segment. Each segment, or record, can have any number of field elements giving information on that record. For example, the team member record would have details like name, supervisor and contact details.

One-to-many and Redundancy

Because hierarchical models do not allow for composite records -- that is, for an entry to have more than one parent - the database has a one-to-many structure; one company can have many departments, and one department can have many team leaders. This can lead to redundancy in the model. For example, a branch below Team Members might be called Ongoing Projects. Since multiple staff members may work on one project, the project information must be duplicated, possibly leading to consistency issues.

Navigation

The hierarchical data model is a navigational data model; the access paths in the model are limited by predetermined structures. To obtain a specific file record, the query moves from the root segment in the database down through the branches. This is fine if you already know the location of the records you seek, but if you are making exploratory queries, this is slow, as the database must read all the records on a given level before moving to the next one.

Logical Parent Pointers

The limitations of the hierarchical structure are assuaged somewhat by using logical parent pointers. Developed by IBM in their Information Management System data model, this involves setting up a new database for entries that have many-to-many relationships and linking the two. For example, the Ongoing Projects branch would have pointers that link the user to a separate Projects database where project information is contained. This is similar to how the XML Extensible Markup Language IDREF function works.

Advantages

The model allows easy addition and deletion of new information. Data at the top of the Hierarchy is very fast to access. It was very easy to work with the model because it worked well with linear type data storage such as tapes. The model relates very well to natural hierarchies such as assembly plants and employee organization in corporations. It relates well to anything that works through a one to many relationship. For example; there is a president with many managers below them, and those managers have many employees below them, but each employee has only one manager.

Disadvantages

This model has many issues that hold it back now that we require more sophisticated relationships. It requires data to be repetitively stored in many different entities. The database can be very slow when searching for information on the lower entities. We no longer use linear data storage mediums such as tapes so that advantage is null. Searching for data requires the DBMS to run through the entire model from top to bottom until the required information is found, making queries very slow. Can only model one to many relationships, many to many relationships are not supported.

Network Model

A network model is a database model that is designed as a flexible approach to representing objects and their relationships. A unique feature of the network model is its schema, which is viewed as a graph where relationship types are arcs and object types are nodes.

The network model replaces the hierarchical tree with a graph thus allowing more general connections among the nodes. The main difference of the network model from the hierarchical model, is its ability to handle many to many (N:N) relations. In other words, it allows a record to have more than one parent. Suppose an employee works for two departments. The strict hierarchical arrangement is not possible here and the tree becomes a more generalized graph - a network. The network model was evolved to specifically handle non-hierarchical relationships. As shown below data can belong to more than one parent. Note that there are lateral connections as well as top-down connections. A network structure thus allows 1:1 (one: one), l: M (one: many), M: M (many: many) relationships among entities.

In network database terminology, a relationship is a set. Each set is made up of at least two types of records: an owner record (equivalent to parent in the hierarchical model) and a member record (similar to the child record in the hierarchical model).

The database of Customer-loan, is now represented for network model as shown in figure.

In can easily depict that now the information about the joint loan L1 appears single time, but in case of hierarchical model it appears for two times. Thus, it reduces the redundancy and is better as compared to hierarchical model.

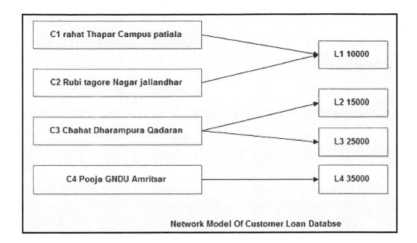

Network Model Of Customer Loan Databse

Network View of Sample Database

Considering again the sample supplier-part database, its network view is shown. In addition to the part and supplier record types, a third record type is introduced which we will call as the connector. A connector occurrence specifies the association (shipment) between one supplier and one part. It contains data (quantity of the parts supplied) describing the association between supplier and part records.

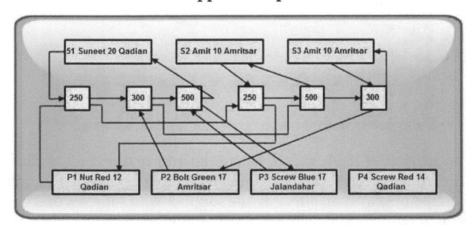

All connector occurrences for given supplier are placed on a chain .The chain starts from a supplier and finally returns to the supplier. Similarly, all connector occurrences for a given part are placed on a chain starting from the part and finally returning to the same part.

Operations on Network Model

Detailed description of all basic operations in network model is as under:

- Insert Operation: To insert a new record containing the details of a new supplier, we simply create a new record occurrence. Initially, there will be no connector. The new supplier's chain will simply consist of a single pointer starting from the supplier to itself.

For example, supplier S4 can be inserted in network model that does not supply any part as a new record occurrence with a single pointer from S4 to itself. This is not possible in case of hierarchical model. Similarly a new part can be inserted who does not supplied by any supplier.

Consider another case if supplier S1 now starts supplying P3 part with quantity 100, then a new connector containing the 100 as supplied quantity is added in to the model and the pointer of S1 and P3 are modified as shown in the below.

We can summarize that there is no insert anomalies in network model as in hierarchical model.

- Update Operation: Unlike hierarchical model, where updation was carried out by search and had many inconsistency problems, in a network model updating a record is a much easier process. We can change the city of SI from Qadian to Jalandhar without search or inconsistency problems because the city for S1 appears at just one place in the network model. Similarly, same operation is performed to change the any attribute of part.

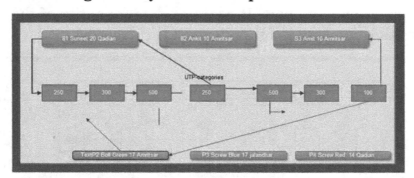

- Delete Operation: If we wish to delete the information of any part say PI, then that record occurrence can be deleted by removing the corresponding pointers and connectors, without affecting the supplier who supplies that part i.e. P1, the model is modified as shown. Similarly, same operation is performed to delete the information of supplier.

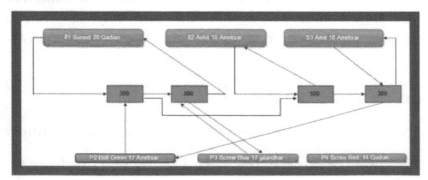

In order to delete the shipment information, the connector for that shipment and its corresponding pointers are removed without affecting supplier and part information.

For example, if supplier SI stops the supply of part PI with 250 quantity the model is modified as shown below without affecting P1 and S1 information.

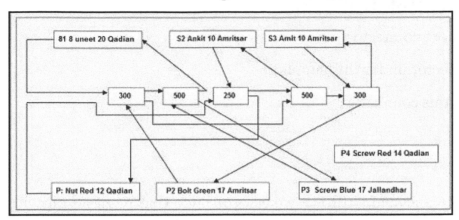

Retrieval Operation

Record retrieval methods for network model are symmetric but complex. In order to understand this considers the following example queries.

- Query 1: Find Supplier Number for Suppliers who Supply Part P2.

Solution: In order to retrieve the required information, first we search for the required part i.e. P2 we will get only one occurrence of P2 from the entire database, Then a loop is constructed to visit each connector under this part i.e. P2. Then for each connector we check the supplier over that connector and supplier number for the concerned supplier record occurrence is printed as shown in below algorithm.

Algorithm:

get [next] part where PNO=P2;

do until no more connectors under this part;

get next connector under this part;

get supplier over this connector;

print SNO;

- Query 2: Find Part Number for Parts Supplied by Supplier S2.

Solution: In order to retrieve the required information, same procedure is adopted. First we search for the required supplier i.e. S2 and we will get only one occurrence of S2 from the entire database. Then a loop is constructed to visit each connector under this supplier i.e. S2. Then for each connector we check the part over that connector and part number for the concerned part record occurrence is printed as shown in below algorithm.

Algorithm:

get [next] supplier where SNO=S2;

do until no more connectors under this supplier;

get next connector under this supplier;

get part over this connector;

print PNO;

end;

From both the above algorithms, we can conclude that retrieval algorithms are symmetric, but they are complex because they involved lot of pointers.

As explained earlier, we can conclude that network model does not suffers from the Insert anomalies, Update anomalies and Deletion anomalies, also the retrieve operation is symmetric, as compared to hierarchical model, but the main disadvantage is the complexity of the model. Since, each above operation involves the modification of pointers, which makes whole model complicated and complex.

Advantages of Network Model

The Network model retains almost all the advantages of the hierarchical model while eliminating some of its shortcomings.

The main advantages of the network model are:

- Conceptual simplicity: Just like the hierarchical model, the network model IS also conceptually simple and easy to design.

- Capability to handle more relationship types: The network model can handle the one to- many (l:N) and many to many (N:N) relationships, which is a real help in modeling the real life situations.

- Ease of data access: The data access is easier and flexible than the hierarchical model.

- Data Integrity: The network model does not allow a member to exist without an owner. Thus, a user must first define the owner record and then the member record. This ensures the data integrity.

- Data independence: The network model is better than the hierarchical model in isolating the programs from the complex physical storage details.

- Database Standards: One of the major drawbacks of the hierarchical model was the non-availability of universal standards for database design and modeling. The network model is based on the standards formulated by the DBTG and augmented by ANSI/SP ARC (American National Standards Institute/Standards Planning and Requirements Committee) in the 1970s. All the network database management systems conformed to these standards. These standards included a Data Definition Language (DDL) and the Data Manipulation Language (DML), thus greatly enhancing database administration and portability.

Disadvantages of Network Model

Even though the network database model was significantly better than the hierarchical database model, it also had many drawbacks. Some of them are:

- System complexity: All the records are maintained using pointers and hence the whole database structure becomes very complex.

- Operational Anomalies: As discussed earlier, network model's insertion, deletion and updating operations of any record require large number of pointer adjustments, which makes its implementation very complex and complicated.

- Absence of structural independence: Since the data access method in the network database model is a navigational system, making structural changes to the database is very difficult in most cases and impossible in some cases. If changes are made to the database structure then all the application programs need to be modified before they can access data. Thus, even though the network database model succeeds in achieving data independence, it still fails to achieve structural independence.

Because of the disadvantages mentioned and the implementation and administration complexities, the relational database model replaced both the hierarchical and network database models in the 1980s. The evolution of the relational database model is considered as one of the greatest events-a major breakthrough in the history of database management.

Entity–attribute–value Model

One problem many developers encounter while defining and analyzing data requirements is the situation where a number of different attributes can be used to describe an object, but only few attributes actually apply to each one. One option is to create a table with a column representing each attribute; this is suitable for objects with a fixed number of attributes, where all or most attributes have values for a most objects. However, in our case we would end up with records where majority of columns would be empty, because attributes may be unknown or inapplicable. To solve the above problem you can apply the EAV (Entity, Attribute, Value) model. This pattern is also known under several alternative names including "object-attribute-value" model and "open schema". In the EAV data model only non-empty values are stored in database, where each attribute-value (or key-value) pair describes one attribute of a given entity. EAV tables are often characterized as "long and skinny"; "long" refers to multiple rows describing entity, and "skinny" to the small number of columns used.

The entity-attribute-value model is useful for situations where attributes are dynamically added to or removed from an entity. It is normally composed of three tables.

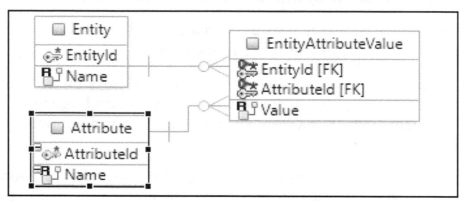

Here's an example of data in the model.

EntityId	Name
1	45 Shepherd
2	Laser Pistol
3	Apoca-Fist
4	D4TH Blossom
5	Rapid-Fire SMG
6	Black Hole Launcher
7	Dubstep Gun
8	Sniper Rifle
9	Genki Manapult

EntityId	AttributeId	Value
1	2	100
1	3	300
1	4	YES
2	1	40
2	2	100
2	3	90
2	5	YES
3	2	2
3	3	2000
6	7	It really, really sucks.
7	8	A Bass Renaissance

AttributeId	Name
1	Magazine Size
2	Range
3	Power
4	Dual Wieldable
5	Is DLC
6	Fire Mode
7	Slogan
8	Song

You'll notice in this example that each entity does not have all the attributes, or the same attributes as some other entities, or even any attributes at all. These are dynamic relationships, created on the fly by users in the front-end application. This is the scenario that the Entity-attribute-value model is meant for.

In the example above the primary key of Entity Attribute Value is {Entity Id, Entity Attribute Id}, which means that each entity can have a particular attribute 0 or 1 times. This may be undesirable for your business case, for example if your entities were people they could legitimately have 0 or 1 or many phone numbers. If this is the case, you can assign a surrogate key to Entity Attribute Value.

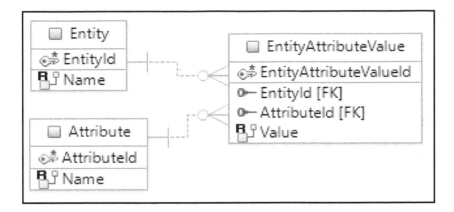

This will support a zero-to-many relationship for entities to attributes.

Because the attributes are dynamic, their value types are dynamic also. In this example Value column is set to varchar (128) so that a wide variety of values can be placed into in. Users can and will store text and numeric data in the Value column.

This can sometimes be a stumbling block if you have an application that needs to use values from the Entity Attribute Value table. There might be a "freight rate" attribute, for example, that your application needs to include in a calculation. But because it is a varchar field it could contain non-numeric data.

In this case you can create multiple value columns with different specific types. This way the attribute's value type can be specified as 'numeric', and your application will only check the appropriate value column.

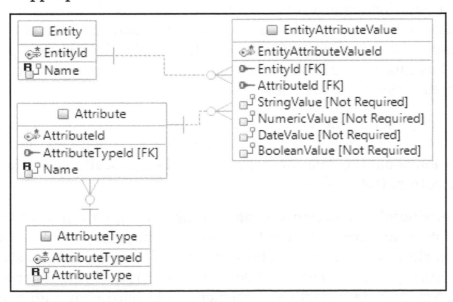

There is some criticism for this model. It can sometimes be tempting to run wild with it, thinking that this is generic enough that anything can fit, so why create a bunch of unnecessary tables. And so it sometimes becomes a one-size-fits-all model, ripe for the inner-platform effect.

EAV Databases

The term "EAV database" refers to a database design where a significant proportion of the data is modeled as EAV. However, even in a database described as "EAV-based", some tables in the system are traditional relational tables.

- EAV modeling makes sense for categories of data, such as clinical findings, where attributes are numerous and sparse. Where these conditions do not hold, standard relational modeling (i.e., one column per attribute) is preferable; using EAV does not mean abandoning common sense or principles of good relational design. In clinical record systems, the subschemas dealing with patient demographics and billing are typically modeled conventionally. (While most vendor database schemas are proprietary, VistA, the system used throughout the United States Department of Veterans Affairs (VA) medical system, known as the Veterans Health Administration (VHA), is open-source and its schema is readily inspectable, though it uses a MUMPS database engine rather than a relational database.).

- EAV database is essentially unmaintainable without numerous supporting tables that contain supporting metadata. The metadata tables, which typically outnumber the EAV tables by a factor of at least three or more, are typically standard relational tables. An example of a metadata table is the Attribute Definitions table mentioned above.

EAV versus Row Modeling

The EAV data described above is comparable to the contents of a supermarket sales receipt (which would be reflected in a Sales Line Items table in a database). The receipt lists only details of the items actually purchased, instead of listing every product in the shop that the customer might have purchased but didn't. Like the clinical findings for a given patient, the sales receipt is sparse:

- The "entity" is the sale/transaction id — a foreign key into a sales transactions table. This is used to tag each line item internally, though on the receipt the information about the Sale appears at the top (shop location, sale date/time) and at the bottom (total value of sale).

- The "attribute" is a foreign key into a products table, from where one looks up description, unit price, discounts and promotions, etc. (Products are just as volatile as clinical findings, possibly even more so: new products are introduced every month, while others are taken off the market if consumer acceptance is poor. No competent database designer would hard-code individual products such as Doritos or Diet Coke as columns in a table.).

- The "values" are the quantity purchased and total line item price.

Row modeling, where facts about something (in this case, a sales transaction) are recorded as multiple rows rather than multiple columns, is a standard data modeling technique. The differences between row modeling and EAV (which may be considered a generalization of row-modeling) are:

- A row-modeled table is homogeneous in the facts that it describes: a Line Items table describes only products sold. By contrast, an EAV table contains almost any type of fact.

- The data type of the value column/s in a row-modeled table is pre-determined by the nature of the facts it records. By contrast, in an EAV table, the conceptual data type of a value in a particular row depends on the attribute in that row. It follows that in production systems, allowing direct data entry into an EAV table would be a recipe for disaster, because the database engine itself would not be able to perform robust input validation.

In a clinical data repository, row modeling also finds numerous uses; the laboratory test subschema is typically modeled this way, because lab test results are typically numeric, or can be encoded numerically.

The circumstances where you would need to go beyond standard row-modeling to EAV are listed below:

- The data type of individual attributes varies (as seen with clinical findings).

- The categories of data are numerous, growing or fluctuating, but the number of instances (records/rows) within each category is very small. Here, with conventional modeling, the database's entity–relationship diagram might have hundreds of tables: the tables that contain thousands/ millions of rows/instances are emphasized visually to the same extent as those with very few rows. The latter are candidates for conversion to an EAV representation.

This situation arises in ontology-modeling environments, where categories ("classes") must often be created on the fly, and some classes are often eliminated in subsequent cycles of prototyping.

- Certain ("hybrid") classes have some attributes that are non-sparse (present in all or most instances), while other attributes are highly variable and sparse. The latter are suitable for EAV modeling. For example, descriptions of products made by a conglomerate corporation depend on the product category, e.g., the attributes necessary to describe a brand of light bulb are quite different from those required to describe a medical imaging device, but both have common attributes such as packaging unit and per-item cost.

Entity

In clinical data, the entity is typically a clinical event, as described above. In more general-purpose settings, the entity is a foreign key into an "objects" table that records common information about every "object" (thing) in the database – at the minimum, a preferred name and brief description, as well as the category/class of entity to which it belongs. Every record (object) in this table is assigned a machine-generated object ID.

The "objects table" approach was pioneered by Tom Slezak and colleagues at Lawrence Livermore Laboratories for the Chromosome 19 database, and is now standard in most large bioinformatics databases. The use of an objects table does not mandate the concurrent use of an EAV design: conventional tables can be used to store the category-specific details of each object.

The major benefit to a central objects table is that, by having a supporting table of object synonyms and keywords, one can provide a standard Google-like search mechanism across the entire system where the user can find information about any object of interest without having to first specify the category that it belongs to. (This is important in bioscience systems where a keyword like "acetylcholine" could refer either to the molecule itself, which is a neurotransmitter, or the biological receptor to which it binds.)

Attribute

In the EAV table itself, this is just an attribute ID, a foreign key into an Attribute Definitions table, as stated above. However, there are usually multiple metadata tables that contain attribute-related information, and these are discussed shortly.

Value

Coercing all values into strings, as in the EAV data example above, results in a simple, but non-scalable, structure: constant data type inter-conversions are required if one wants to do anything with the values, and an index on the value column of an EAV table is essentially useless. Also, it is not convenient to store large binary data, such as images, in Base64 encoded form in the same table as small integers or strings. Therefore, larger systems use separate EAV tables for each data type (including binary large objects, "BLOBS"), with the metadata for a given attribute identifying the EAV table in which its data will be stored. This approach is actually quite efficient because the modest amount of attribute metadata for a given class or form that a user chooses to work with can be cached readily in memory. However, it requires moving of data from one table to another if an attribute's data type is changed. (This does not happen often, but mistakes can be made in metadata definition just as in database schema design.).

Representing Substructure: EAV with Classes and Relationships (EAV/CR)

In a simple EAV design, the values of an attribute are simple or primitive data types as far as the database engine is concerned. However, in EAV systems used for representation of highly diverse data, it is possible that a given object (class instance) may have substructure: that is, some of its attributes may represent other kinds of objects, which in turn may have substructure, to an arbitrary level of complexity. A car, for example, has an engine, a transmission, etc., and the engine has components such as cylinders. (The permissible substructure for a given class is defined within the system's attribute metadata. Thus, for example, the attribute "random-access-memory" could apply to the class "computer" but not to the class "engine").

To represent substructure, one incorporates a special EAV table where the value column contains references to other entities in the system (i.e., foreign key values into the objects table). To get all the information on a given object requires a recursive traversal of the metadata, followed by a recursive traversal of the data that stops when every attribute retrieved is simple (atomic). Recursive traversal is necessary whether details of an individual class are represented in conventional or EAV form; such traversal is performed in standard object–relational systems, for example. In practice, the number of levels of recursion tends to be relatively modest for most classes, so the performance penalties due to recursion are modest, especially with indexing of object IDs.

EAV/CR (EAV with Classes and Relationships) refers to a framework that supports complex substructure. Its name is somewhat of a misnomer: while it was an outshoot of work on EAV systems, in practice, many or even most of the classes in such a system may be represented in standard relational form, based on whether the attributes are sparse or dense. EAV/CR is really characterized by its very detailed metadata, which is rich enough to support the automatic generation of browsing interfaces to individual classes without having to write class-by-class user-interface code. The basis of such browser interfaces is that it is possible to generate a batch of dynamic SQL queries that is independent of the class of the object, by first consulting its metadata and using metadata information to generate a sequence of queries against the data tables, and some of these queries may be arbitrarily recursive. This approach works well for object-at-a-time queries, as in Web-based browsing interfaces where clicking on the name of an object brings up all details of the object in a separate page: the metadata associated with that object's class also facilitates presentation of the object's details, because it includes captions of individual attributes, the order in which they are to be presented as well as how they are to be grouped.

One approach to EAV/CR is to allow columns to hold JSON structures, which thus provide the needed class structure. For example, PostgreSQL, as of version 9.4, offers JSON binary column (JSONB) support, allowing JSON attributes to be queried, indexed and joined.

Critical Role of Metadata in EAV Systems

In the words of Prof. Dr. Daniel Masys (formerly Chair of Vanderbilt University's Medical Informatics Department), the challenges of working with EAV stem from the fact that in an EAV database, the "physical schema" (the way data are stored) is radically different from the "logical schema" – the way users, and many software applications such as statistics packages, regard it, i.e., as conventional rows and columns for individual classes. (Because an EAV table conceptually mixes apples, oranges, grapefruit and chop suey, if you want to do any analysis of the data using standard off-the-shelf software, in most cases you have to convert subsets of it into columnar form. The process of doing this, called pivoting, is important enough to be discussed separately.)

Metadata helps perform the sleight of hand that lets users interact with the system in terms of the logical schema rather than the physical: the software continually consults the metadata for various operations such as data presentation, interactive validation, bulk data extraction and ad hoc query. The metadata can actually be used to customize the behavior of the system.

EAV systems trade off simplicity in the physical and logical structure of the data for complexity in their metadata, which, among other things, plays the role that database constraints and referential integrity do in standard database designs. Such a tradeoff is generally worthwhile, because in the typical mixed schema of production systems, the data in conventional relational tables can also benefit from functionality such as automatic interface generation. The structure of the metadata is complex enough that it comprises its own subschema within the database: various foreign keys in the data tables refer to tables within this subschema. This subschema is standard-relational, with features such as constraints and referential integrity being used to the hilt.

The correctness of the metadata contents, in terms of the intended system behavior, is critical and the task of ensuring correctness means that, when creating an EAV system, considerable design efforts must go into building user interfaces for metadata editing that can be used by people on the team who know the problem domain (e.g., clinical medicine) but are not necessarily programmers. (Historically, one of the main reasons why the pre-relational TMR system failed to be adopted at sites other than its home institution was that all metadata was stored in a single file with a non-intuitive structure. Customizing system behavior by altering the contents of this file, without causing the system to break, was such a delicate task that the system's authors only trusted themselves to do it.).

Where an EAV system is implemented through RDF, the RDF Schema language may conveniently be used to express such metadata. This Schema information may then be used by the EAV database engine to dynamically re-organize its internal table structure for best efficiency.

Some Final Caveats Regarding Metadata

- Because the business logic is in the metadata rather than explicit in the database schema (i.e., one level removed, compared with traditionally designed systems), it is less apparent to one who is unfamiliar with the system. Metadata-browsing and metadata-reporting tools are therefore important in ensuring the maintainability of an EAV system. In the common scenario where metadata is implemented as a relational sub-schema, these tools are nothing more than applications built using off-the-shelf reporting or querying tools that operate on the metadata tables.

- It is easy for an insufficiently knowledgeable user to corrupt (i.e., introduce inconsistencies and errors in) metadata. Therefore, access to metadata must be restricted, and an audit trail of accesses and changes put into place to deal with situations where multiple individuals have metadata access. Using an RDBMS for metadata will simplify the process of maintaining consistency during metadata creation and editing, by leveraging RDBMS features such as support for transactions. Also, if the metadata is part of the same database as the data itself, this ensures that it will be backed up at least as frequently as the data itself, so that it can be recovered to a point in time.

- The quality of the annotation and documentation within the metadata (i.e., the narrative/explanatory text in the descriptive columns of the metadata sub-schema) must be much higher, in order to facilitate understanding by various members of the development team. Ensuring metadata quality (and keeping it current as the system evolves) takes very high priority in the long-term management and maintenance of any design that uses an EAV component. Poorly-documented or out-of-date metadata can compromise the system's long-term viability.

Information Captured in Metadata

Attribute Metadata

- Validation metadata: include data type, range of permissible values or membership in a set of values, regular expression match, default value, and whether the value is permitted to be null. In EAV systems representing classes with substructure, the validation metadata will also record what class, if any, a given attribute belongs to.

- Presentation metadata: how the attribute is to be displayed to the user (e.g., as a text box or image of specified dimensions, a pull-down list or a set of radio buttons). When a compound object is composed of multiple attributes, as in the EAV/CR design, there is additional metadata on the order in which the attributes should be presented, and how these attributes should optionally be grouped (under descriptive headings).

- For attributes which happen to be laboratory parameters, ranges of normal values, which may vary by age, sex, physiological state and assay method, are recorded.

- Grouping metadata: Attributes are typically presented as part of a higher-order group, e.g., a specialty-specific form. Grouping metadata includes information such as the order in which attributes are presented. Certain presentation metadata, such as fonts/colors and the number of attributes displayed per row, apply to the group as a whole.

Advanced Validation Metadata

- Dependency metadata: in many user interfaces, entry of specific values into certain fields/attributes is required to either disable/hide certain other fields or enable/show other fields. (For example, if a user chooses the response "No" to a Boolean question "Does the patient have diabetes?", then subsequent questions about the duration of diabetes, medications for diabetes, etc. must be disabled.) To effect this in a generic framework involves storing of dependencies between the controlling attributes and the controlled attributes.

- Computations and complex validation: As in a spreadsheet, the value of certain attributes can be computed, and displayed, based on values entered into fields that are presented earlier in sequence. (For example, body surface area is a function of height and width). Similarly, there may be "constraints" that must be true for the data to be valid: for example, in a differential white cell count, the sum of the counts of the individual white cell types must always equal 100, because the individual counts represent percentages. Computed formulas and complex validation are generally effected by storing expressions in the metadata that are macro-substituted with the values that the user enters and can be evaluated. In Web browsers, both JavaScript and VBScript have an Eval() function that can be leveraged for this purpose.

Validation, presentation and grouping metadata make possible the creation of code frameworks that support automatic user interface generation for both data browsing as well as interactive editing. In a production system that is delivered over the Web, the task of validation of EAV data is essentially moved from the back-end/database tier (which is powerless with respect to this task) to the middle /Web server tier. While back-end validation is always ideal, because it is impossible to subvert by attempting direct data entry into a table, middle tier validation through a generic framework is quite workable, though a significant amount of software design effort must go into building the framework first. The availability of open-source frameworks that can be studied and modified for individual needs can go a long way in avoiding wheel reinvention.

Scenarios that are Appropriate for EAV Modeling

EAV modeling, under the alternative terms "generic data modeling" or "open schema", has long been a standard tool for advanced data modelers. Like any advanced technique, it can be double-edged, and should be used judiciously.

Also, the employment of EAV does not preclude the employment of traditional relational database modeling approaches within the same database schema. In EMRs that rely on an RDBMS, such as Cerner, which use an EAV approach for their clinical-data subschema, the vast majority of tables in the schema are in fact traditionally modeled, with attributes represented as individual columns rather than as rows.

The modeling of the metadata subschema of an EAV system, in fact, is a very good fit for traditional modeling, because of the inter-relationships between the various components of the metadata. In the Trial DB system, for example, the number of metadata tables in the schema outnumber the data tables by about ten to one. Because the correctness and consistency of metadata is critical to the correct operation of an EAV system, the system designer wants to take full advantages of all of the features that RDBMSs provide, such as referential integrity and programmable constraints, rather than having to reinvent the RDBMS-engine wheel. Consequently, the numerous metadata tables that support EAV designs are typically in third-normal relational form.

Commercial electronic health record Systems (EHRs) use row-modeling for classes of data such as diagnoses, surgical procedures performed on and laboratory test results, which are segregated into separate tables. In each table, the "entity" is a composite of the patient ID and the date/time the diagnosis was made (or the surgery or lab test performed); the attribute is a foreign key into a specially designated lookup table that contains a controlled vocabulary - e.g., ICD-10 for diagnoses, Current Procedural Terminology for surgical procedures, with a set of value attributes. (E.g., for laboratory-test results, one may record the value measured, whether it is in the normal, low or high range, the ID of the person responsible for performing the test, the date/time the test was performed, and so on. As stated earlier, this is not a full-fledged EAV approach because the domain of attributes for a given table is restricted, just as the domain of product IDs in a supermarket's Sales table would be restricted to the domain of Products in a Products table.

However, to capture data on parameters that are not always defined in standard vocabularies, EHRs also provide a "pure" EAV mechanism, where specially designated power-users can define new attributes, their data type, maximum and minimal permissible values (or permissible set of values/codes), and then allow others to capture data based on these attributes. In the Epic (TM) EHR, this mechanism is termed "Flow sheets", and is commonly used to capture inpatient nursing observation data.

Modeling Sparse Attributes

The typical case for using the EAV model is for highly sparse, heterogeneous attributes, such as clinical parameters in the electronic medical record (EMRs). Even here, however, it is accurate to state that the EAV modeling principle is applied to a sub-schema of the database rather than for all of its contents. (Patient demographics, for example, are most naturally modeled in one-column-per-attribute, traditional relational structure.)

Consequently, the arguments about EAV vs. "relational" design reflect incomplete understanding of the problem: An EAV design should be employed only for that sub-schema of a database where sparse attributes need to be modeled: even here, they need to be supported by third normal form metadata tables. There are relatively few database-design problems where sparse attributes are encountered: this is why the circumstances where EAV design is applicable are relatively rare. Even where they are encountered, a set of EAV tables is not the only way to address sparse data: an XML-based solution is applicable when the maximum number of attributes per entity is relatively modest, and the total volume of sparse data is also similarly modest. An example of this situation is the problems of capturing variable attributes for different product types.

Sparse attributes may also occur in E-commerce situations where an organization is purchasing or selling a vast and highly diverse set of commodities, with the details of individual categories of commodities being highly variable. The Magento E-commerce software employs an EAV approach to address this issue.

Modeling Numerous Classes with very few instances Per Class: Highly Dynamic Schemas

Another application of EAV is in modeling classes and attributes that, while not sparse, are dynamic, but where the number of data rows per class will be relatively modest – a couple of hundred rows at most, but typically a few dozen – and the system developer is also required to provide a Web-based end-user interface within a very short turnaround time. "Dynamic" means that new classes and attributes need to be continually defined and altered to represent an evolving data model. This scenario can occur in rapidly evolving scientific fields as well as in ontology development, especially during the prototyping and iterative refinement phases.

While creation of new tables and columns to represent a new category of data is not especially labor-intensive, the programming of Web-based interfaces that support browsing or basic editing with type- and range-based validation is. In such a case, a more maintainable long-term solution is to create a framework where the class and attribute definitions are stored in metadata, and the software generates a basic user interface from this metadata dynamically.

The EAV/CR framework, mentioned earlier, was created to address this very situation. Note that an EAV data model is not essential here, but the system designer may consider it an acceptable alternative to creating, say, sixty or more tables containing a total of not more than two thousand rows. Here, because the number of rows per class is so few, efficiency considerations are less important; with the standard indexing by class ID/attribute ID, DBMS optimizers can easily cache the data for a small class in memory when running a query involving that class or attribute.

In the dynamic-attribute scenario, it is worth noting that Resource Description

Framework (RDF) is being employed as the underpinning of Semantic-Web-related ontology work. RDF, intended to be a general method of representing information, is a form of EAV: an RDF triple comprises an object, a property, and a value.

At the end of Jon Bentley's book "Writing Efficient Programs", the author warns that making code more efficient generally also makes it harder to understand and maintain, and so one does not rush in and tweak code unless one has first determined that there is a performance problem, and measures such as code profiling have pinpointed the exact location of the bottleneck. Once you have done so, you modify only the specific code that needs to run faster. Similar considerations apply to EAV modeling: you apply it only to the sub-system where traditional relational modeling is known a priori to be unwieldy (as in the clinical data domain), or is discovered, during system evolution, to pose significant maintenance challenges. Database Guru (and currently a vice-president of Core Technologies at Oracle Corporation) Tom Kyte, for example, correctly points out drawbacks of employing EAV in traditional business scenarios, and makes the point that mere "flexibility" is not a sufficient criterion for employing EAV. (However, he makes the sweeping claim that EAV should be avoided in all circumstances, even though Oracle's Health Sciences division itself employs EAV to model clinical-data attributes in its commercial systems ClinTrial and Oracle Clinical.).

Working with EAV Data

The Achilles heel of EAV is the difficulty of working with large volumes of EAV data. It is often necessary to transiently or permanently inter-convert between columnar and row-or EAV-modeled representations of the same data; this can be both error-prone if done manually as well as CPU-intensive. Generic frameworks that utilize attribute and attribute-grouping metadata address the former but not the latter limitation; their use is more or less mandated in the case of mixed schemas that contain a mixture of conventional-relational and EAV data, where the error quotient can be very significant.

The conversion operation is called pivoting. Pivoting is not required only for EAV data but also for any form or row-modeled data. (For example, implementations of the Apriori algorithm for Association Analysis, widely used to process supermarket sales data to identify other products that purchasers of a given product are also likely to buy, pivot row-modeled data as a first step.) Many database engines have proprietary SQL extensions to facilitate pivoting, and packages such as Microsoft Excel also support it. The circumstances where pivoting is necessary are considered below:

- Browsing: of modest amounts of data for an individual entity, optionally followed by data editing based on inter-attribute dependencies. This operation is facilitated by caching the modest amounts of the requisite supporting metadata.

Some programs, such as Trial DB, access the metadata to generate semi-static Web pages that contain embedded programming code as well as data structures holding metadata.

- Bulk extraction: transforms large (but predictable) amounts of data (e.g., a clinical study's complete data) into a set of relational tables. While CPU-intensive, this task is infrequent and does not need to be done in real-time; i.e., the user can wait for a batched process to complete. The importance of bulk extraction cannot be overestimated, especially when the data is to be processed or analyzed with standard third-party tools that are completely unaware of EAV structure. Here, it is not advisable to try to reinvent entire sets of wheels through a generic framework, and it is best just to bulk-extract EAV data into relational tables and then work with it using standard tools.

- Ad hoc query: interfaces to row- or EAV-modeled data, when queried from the perspective of individual attributes, (e.g., "retrieve all patients with the presence of liver disease, with signs of liver failure and no history of alcohol abuse") must typically show the results of the query with individual attributes as separate columns. For most EAV database scenarios ad hoc query performance must be tolerable, but sub-second responses are not necessary, since the queries tend to be exploratory in nature.

Relational Division

However, the structure of EAV data model is a perfect candidate for Relational Division. With a good indexing strategy it's possible to get a response time in less than a few hundred milliseconds on a billion row EAV table. Microsoft SQL Server MVP Peter Larsson has proved this on a laptop and made the solution general available.

Optimizing Pivoting Performance

- One possible optimization is the use of a separate "warehouse" or query able schema whose contents are refreshed in batch mode from the production (transaction) schema. The tables in the warehouse are heavily indexed and optimized using de normalization, which combines multiple tables into one to minimize performance penalty due to table joins. This is the approach that Kalido uses to convert highly normalized EAV tables to standard reporting schemas.

- Certain EAV data in a warehouse may be converted into standard tables using "materialized views", but this is generally a last resort that must be used carefully, because the number of views of this kind tends to grow non-linearly with the number of attributes in a system.

- In-memory data structures one can use hash tables and two-dimensional arrays in memory in conjunction with attribute-grouping metadata to pivot data, one group at a time. This data is written to disk as a flat delimited file, with the internal names for each attribute in the first row: this format can be readily bulk-imported into a relational table. This "in-memory" technique significantly outperforms alternative approaches by keeping the queries on EAV tables as simple as possible and minimizing the number of I/O operations. Each statement retrieves a large amount of data, and the hash tables help carry out the pivoting operation, which involves placing a value for a given attribute instance into the appropriate row and column. Random Access Memory (RAM) is sufficiently abundant and affordable in modern hardware that the complete data set for a single attribute group in even large data sets will usually fit completely into memory, though the algorithm can be made smarter by working on slices of the data if this turns out not to be the case.

Obviously, no matter what approaches you take, querying EAV will not be as fast as querying standard column-modeled relational data for certain types of query, in much the same way that access of elements in sparse matrices are not as fast as those on non-sparse matrices if the latter fit entirely into main memory. (Sparse matrices, represented using structures such as linked lists, require list traversal to access an element at a given X-Y position, while access to elements in matrices represented as 2-D arrays can be performed using fast CPU register operations.) If, however, you chose the EAV approach correctly for the problem that you were trying to solve, this is the price that you pay; in this respect, EAV modeling is an example of a space (and schema maintenance) versus CPU-time tradeoff.

EAV vs. the Universal Data Model

Originally postulated by Maier, Ullman and Vardi, the "Universal Data Model" (UDM) seeks to simplify the query of a complex relational schema by naive users, by creating the illusion that everything is stored in a single giant "universal table". It does this by utilizing inter-table relationships, so that the user does not need to be concerned about what table contains what attribute. C.J. Date, however, pointed out that in circumstances where a table is multiply related to another (as in genealogy databases, where an individual's father and mother are also individuals, or in some business databases where all addresses are stored centrally, and an organization can have different office addresses and shipping addresses), there is insufficient metadata within the database schema to specify unambiguous joins. When UDM has been commercialized, as in SAP Business Objects, this limitation is worked around through the creation of "Universes", which are relational views with predefined joins between sets of tables: the "Universe" developer disambiguates ambiguous joins by including the multiply-related table in a view multiple times using different aliases.

Apart from the way in which data is explicitly modeled (UDM simply uses relational views to intercede between the user and the database schema), EAV differs from Universal Data Models in that it also applies to transactional systems, not only query oriented (read-only) systems as in UDM. Also, when used as the basis for clinical-data query systems, EAV implementations do not necessarily shield the user from having to specify the class of an object of interest. In the EAV-based i2b2 clinical data mart, for example, when the user searches for a term, she has the option of specifying the category of data that the user is interested in. For example, the phrase "lithium" can refer either to the medication (which is used to treat bipolar disorder), or a laboratory assay for lithium level in the patient's blood. (The blood level of lithium must be monitored carefully: too much of the drug causes severe side effects, while too little is ineffective).

Graph Databases

An alternative approach to managing the various problems encountered with EAV-structured data is to employ a graph database. These represent entities as the nodes of a graph or hyper graph, and attributes as links or edges of that graph. The issue of table joins are addressed by providing graph-specific query languages, such as Apache Tinker Pop, or the Open Cog atom space pattern matcher.

EAV and Cloud Computing

Many cloud computing vendors offer data stores based on the EAV model, where an arbitrary number of attributes can be associated with a given entity. Roger Jennings provides an in-depth comparison of these. In Amazon's offering, Simple DB, the data type is limited to strings, and data that is intrinsically non-string must be coerced to string (e.g., numbers must be padded with leading zeros) if you wish to perform operations such as sorting. Microsoft's offering, Windows Azure Table Storage, offers a limited set of data types: byte, bool, Date, time, double, Guid, int, long and string. The Google App Engine offers the greatest variety of data types: in addition to dividing numeric data into int, long, float. it also defines custom data types such as phone number, E-mail address, geocode and hyperlink. Google, but not Amazon or Microsoft, lets you define metadata that would prevent invalid attributes from being associated with a particular class of entity, by letting you create a metadata model.

Google lets you operate on the data using a subset of SQL; Microsoft offer a URL-based querying syntax that is abstracted via a LINQ provider; Amazon offer a more limited syntax. Of concern, built-in support for combining different entities through joins is currently (April 10) non-existent with all three engines. Such operations have to be performed by application code. This may not be a concern if the application servers are co-located with the data servers at the vendor's data center, but a lot of network traffic would be generated if the two were geographically separated.

An EAV approach is justified only when the attributes that are being modeled are numerous and sparse: if the data being captured does not meet this requirement, the cloud vendors' default EAV approach is often a mismatch for applications that require a true back-end database (as opposed to merely a means of persistent data storage). Retrofitting the vast majority of existing database applications, which use a traditional data-modeling approach, to an EAV-type cloud architecture, would require major surgery. Microsoft discovered, for example, that its database-application-developer base was largely reluctant to invest such effort. More recently, therefore, Microsoft has provided a premium offering – a cloud-accessible full-fledged relational engine, SQL Server Azure, which allows porting of existing database applications with modest changes.

One limitation of SQL Azure is that physical databases are limited to 500GB in size as of January 2015. Microsoft recommends that data sets larger than this be split into multiple physical databases and accessed with parallel queries.

Tree Structures and Relational Databases

There exist several other approaches for the representation of tree-structured data, be it XML, JSON or other formats, such as the nested set model, in a relational database. On the other hand, database vendors have begun to include JSON and XML support into their data structures and query features, like in IBM DB2, where XML data is stored as XML separate from the tables, using X-path queries as part of SQL statements, or in PostgreSQL, with a JSON data type that can be indexed and queried. These developments accomplish, improve or substitute the EAV model approach.

It should be noted, however, that the uses of JSON and XML are not necessarily the same as the use of an EAV model, though they can overlap. XML is preferable to EAV for arbitrarily hierarchical data that is relatively modest in volume for a single entity: it is not intended to scale up to the multi-gigabyte level with respect to data-manipulation performance. XML is not concerned per-se with the sparse-attribute problem, and when the data model underlying the information to be represented can be decomposed straightforwardly into a relational structure, XML is better suited as a means of data interchange than as a primary storage mechanism. EAV, as stated earlier, is specifically (and only) applicable to the sparse-attribute scenario. When such a scenario holds, the use of data type-specific attribute-value tables than can be indexed by entity, by attribute, and by value and manipulated through simple SQL statements is vastly more scalable than the use of an XML tree structure. The Google App Engine, mentioned above, uses strongly-typed-value tables for a good reason.

Associative Model

The associative data model is a model for databases. Unlike the relational model, which is record based and deals with entities and attributes, this model works with entities that have a discreet independent existence, and their relationships are modeled as associations.

The associative model was bases on a subject-verb-object syntax with bold parallels in sentences built from English and other languages. Some examples of phrases that are suitable for the Associative model could include:

- Cyan **is** a color;

- Marc **is** a musician;

- Musicians **play** instruments;

- Swings **are in** a park;

- A park **is in** a city (the bold text indicates the verbs).

By studying the example above it is easy to see that the verb is actually a way of association. The association's sole purpose is to identify the relationship between the subject and the object.

The associative database had two structures, there are a set of items and a set of links that are used to connected them together. With the item structure the entries must contain a unique indication, a type, and a name. Entries in the links structure must also have a unique indicator along with indicators for the related source, subject, object, and verb.

Associative Data Model is Different

The associative model structure is efficient with the storage room fore there is no need to put aside existing space for the data that is not yet available. This differs from the relational model structure. With the relational model the minimum of a single null byte is stored for missing data in any given row. Also some relational databases set aside the maximum room for a specified column in each row.

The associative database creates storage of custom data for each user, or other needs clear cut and economical when considering maintenance or network resources. When different data needs to be stored the Associative model is able to manage the task more effectively then the relational model.

With the associative model there are entities and associations. The entity is identified as discrete and has an independent existence, where-as the association depends on other things. Let's try to simplify this a little before moving on.

Let's say the entity is an organization, the associations would be the customer and the employees. It is possible for the entity to have many business roles at the same time, each role would be recorded as an association. When the circumstances change, one or more of the associations may no longer apply, but the entity will continue to endure.

The associative model is designed to store metadata in the same structures where the data itself is stored. This metadata describes the structure of the database and the how different kinds of data can interconnect. Simple data structures need more to transport a database competent of storing the varying of data that a modernized business requires along with the protection and managements that is important for internet implementation.

The associative model is built from chapters and the user's view the content of the database is controlled by their profile. The profile is a list of chapters. When some links between items in the chapters inside as well as outside of a specific profile exist, those links will not be visible to the user.

There is a combination of chapters and profiled that can simplify the making of the database to specific users or ever subject groups. The data that is related to one of the user groups would remain unseen to another, and would be replaced by a different data set.

Disadvantages of Associative Data Model

With the associative model there is not record. When assembling all of the current information on a complex order the data storage needs to be re-visited multiple times. This could pose as a disadvantage. Some calculations seem to suggest that Associative database would need as many as four times the data reads as the relational database.

All of the changes and deletions to the associative model are directly affected by adding links to the database. However we must not that a deleted association is not actually deleted itself. Rather it is linked to an assertion that has been deleted. Also when an entity is re-named it is not actually re-named but rather linked to its new name.

In order to reduce the complexity that is a direct result from the parameterization required by heftier software packages we can rely on the chapters, profiles and the continuation of database engines that expect data stored to be different between the individual entities or associations. To set or hold back program functions in a database the use of "Flags" has begun to be practiced.

The packages that are based on an associative model would use the structure of the database along with the metadata to control this process. This can ultimately lead to the generalization of what are often lengthy and costly implementation processes.

A generalization such as this would produce considerable cost reductions for users purchasing or implementing bigger software packages, this could reduce risks related with the changes of post implementation as well.

Associative Model does Suit the Demands of Data

Some ask if there is still an ongoing demand for a better database. Honestly, there will always be that demand. The weaker points of the current relational model are now apparent, due to the character of the data we still need to store changing. Binary structures that are supportive to multimedia have posed real challenged for relational databases in the same way that the object-oriented programming methods did.

When we look back on the object databases we can see that they have no conquered the market, and have their cousins the hybrid relational products with their object extensions. So will the Associative model solve some of the issues surrounding the relational model? The answer is not entirely clear, though it may resolve some issues it is not completely clear how efficiently the model will manage when set against the bigger binary blocks of data.

The security of data is crucial, as is the speed of transaction. User interfaces and database management facilities should but up to pace. When a database is designed to aid in the use of internet applications it should allow backups without needing to take the data off-line as well.

Programming interfaces need to be hearty and readily available to a range of development languages, the Associative database will need to show that it is good practice to store data using the subject-verb-object method in every case as well. There will always be questions about maintaining performance as the database grows, this should be expected.

In conclusion, areas of the associative database design do seem simpler then the relational models, still as we have pointed out there are also areas that call for careful attention. There are issues related to the creation of chapters that remain daunting at best.

Even so, if the concept of the associative model proves itself to be a genuinely feasible and is able to bring out a new and efficient database, then others could bring to life products that are built upon the base ideas that exist with this model.

There is definitely an undeniable demand for a faster operating database model that will scale up to bigger servers and down to the smaller devices.

References

- Nadkarni, Prakash (2011), Metadata-driven Software Systems in Biomedicine, Springer, ISBN 978-0-85729-509-5

- Network-model, what-is-a-database, fundamental: ecomputernotes.com, Retrieved 17, April 2020

- The-entity-attribute-value-model: sqlspellbook.com, Retrieved 11,June 2020

- Dinu, Valentin; Nadkarni, Prakash (2007), "Guidelines for the effective use of entity-attribute-value modeling for biomedical databases", International journal of medical informatics, 76 (11–12): 769–79, doi:10.1016/j.ijmedinf.2006.09.023, PMC 2110957, PMID 17098467

- Characteristics-of-a-hierarchical-data-model: techwalla.com, Retrieved 11, May 2020

- The-associative-model, data-modeling: learn.geekinterview.com, Retrieved 25, May 2020

- c Dinu, Valentin; Nadkarni, Prakash; Brandt, Cynthia (2006), "Pivoting approaches for bulk extraction of Entity–Attribute–Value data", Computer Methods and Programs in Biomedicine, 82 (1): 38–43, doi:10.1016/j.cmpb.2006.02.001, PMID 16556470

- Network-model-databases-30613: techopedia.com, Retrieved 31, March 2020

Designing a Database

Organizing data according to a database model is known as database design. Any change to a database schema which improves the design of the database while holding on to its behavioral and informational semantics is known as database refactoring. This chapter discusses in detail the theories and methodologies related to database design.

Database Design

Database design is the process of producing a detailed data model of database. This data model contains all the needed logical and physical design choices and physical storage parameters needed to generate a design in a data definition language, which can then be used to create a database. A fully attributed data model contains detailed attributes for each entity.

The term database design can be used to describe many different parts of the design of an overall database system. Principally, and most correctly, it can be thought of as the logical design of the base data structures used to store the data. In the relational model these are the tables and views. In an object database the entities and relationships map directly to object classes and named relationships. However, the term database design could also be used to apply to the overall process of designing, not just the base data structures, but also the forms and queries used as part of the overall database application within the database management system (DBMS).

The process of doing database design generally consists of a number of steps which will be carried out by the database designer. Usually, the designer must:

- Determine the data to be stored in the database.

- Determine the relationships between the different data elements.

- Superimpose a logical structure upon the data on the basis of these relationships.

Within the relational model the final step above can generally be broken down into two further steps, that of determining the grouping of information within the system, generally determining what are the basic objects about which information is being stored, and then determining the relationships between these groups of information, or objects. This step is not necessary with an Object database.

Determining Data to be Stored

In a majority of cases, a person who is doing the design of a database is a person with expertise in the area of database design, rather than expertise in the domain from which the data to be stored is drawn e.g. financial information, biological information etc. Therefore, the data to be stored in the database must be determined in cooperation with a person who does have expertise in that domain, and who is aware of what data must be stored within the system.

This process is one which is generally considered part of requirements analysis, and requires skill on the part of the database designer to elicit the needed information from those with the domain knowledge. This is because those with the necessary domain knowledge frequently cannot express clearly what their system requirements for the database are as they are unaccustomed to thinking in terms of the discrete data elements which must be stored. Data to be stored can be determined by Requirement Specification.

Determining Data Relationships

Once a database designer is aware of the data which is to be stored within the database, they must then determine where dependency is within the data. Sometimes when data is changed you can be changing other data that is not visible. For example, in a list of names and addresses, assuming a situation where multiple people can have the same address, but one person cannot have more than one address, the address is dependent upon the name. When provided a name and the list the address can be uniquely determined; however, the inverse does not hold - when given an address and the list, a name cannot be uniquely determined because multiple people can reside at an address. Because an address is determined by a name, an address is considered dependent on a name.

(NOTE: A common misconception is that the relational model is so called because of the stating of relationships between data elements therein. This is not true. The relational model is so named because it is based upon the mathematical structures known as relations.)

Logically Structuring Data

Once the relationships and dependencies amongst the various pieces of information have been determined, it is possible to arrange the data into a logical structure which can then be mapped into the storage objects supported by the database management system. In the case of relational databases the storage objects are tables which store data in rows and columns. In an Object database the storage objects correspond directly to the objects used by the Object-oriented programming language used to write the applications that will manage and access the data. The relationships may be defined as attributes of the object classes involved or as methods that operate on the object classes.

The way this mapping is generally performed is such that each set of related data which depends upon a single object, whether real or abstract, is placed in a table. Relationships between these dependent objects is then stored as links between the various objects.

Each table may represent an implementation of either a logical object or a relationship joining one or more instances of one or more logical objects. Relationships between tables may then be stored as links connecting child tables with parents. Since complex logical relationships are themselves tables they will probably have links to more than one parent.

ER Diagram (Entity-relationship Model)

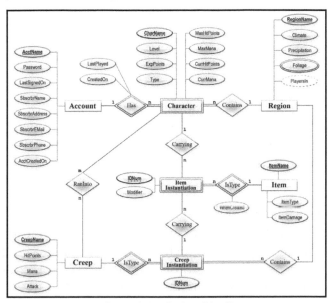

A sample Entity-relationship diagram.

Database designs also include ER (entity-relationship model) diagrams. An ER diagram is a diagram that helps to design databases in an efficient way.

Attributes in ER diagrams are usually modeled as an oval with the name of the attribute, linked to the entity or relationship that contains the attribute.

A Design Process Suggestion for Microsoft Access

1. Determine the purpose of the database - This helps prepare for the remaining steps.

2. Find and organize the information required - Gather all of the types of information to record in the database, such as product name and order number.

3. Divide the information into tables - Divide information items into major entities or subjects, such as Products or Orders. Each subject then becomes a table.

4. Turn information items into columns - Decide what information needs to be stored in each table. Each item becomes a field, and is displayed as a column in the table. For example, an Employees table might include fields such as Last Name and Hire Date.

5. Specify primary keys - Choose each table's primary key. The primary key is a column, or a set of columns, that is used to uniquely identify each row. An example might be Product ID or Order ID.

6. Set up the table relationships - Look at each table and decide how the data in one table is related to the data in other tables. Add fields to tables or create new tables to clarify the relationships, as necessary.

7. Refine the design - Analyze the design for errors. Create tables and add a few records of

sample data. Check if results come from the tables as expected. Make adjustments to the design, as needed.

8. Apply the normalization rules - Apply the data normalization rules to see if tables are structured correctly. Make adjustments to the tables.

Normalization

In the field of relational database design, *normalization* is a systematic way of ensuring that a database structure is suitable for general-purpose querying and free of certain undesirable characteristics—insertion, update, and deletion anomalies that could lead to loss of data integrity.

A standard piece of database design guidance is that the designer should create a fully normalized design; selective denormalization can subsequently be performed, but only for performance reasons. However, some modeling disciplines, such as the dimensional modeling approach to data warehouse design, explicitly recommend non-normalized designs, i.e. designs that in large part do not adhere to 3NF. Normalization consists of normal forms that are 1NF,2NF,3NF,BOYCE-CODD NF (3.5NF),4NF and 5NF.

Conceptual Schema

Schema Refinement

Schema refinement of the database specifies that the data is normalized to reduce data insufficiency and conflicts.

Physical Design

The physical design of the database specifies the physical configuration of the database on the storage media. This includes detailed specification of data elements, data types, indexing options and other parameters residing in the DBMS data dictionary. It is the detailed design of a system that includes modules & the database's hardware & software specifications of the system.

Database Refactoring

A database refactoring is a simple change to a database schema that improves its design while retaining both its behavioral and informational semantics. A database refactoring is conceptually more difficult than a code refactoring; code refactorings only need to maintain behavioral semantics while database refactorings also must maintain informational semantics.

The process of database refactoring is the act of applying database refactorings to evolve an existing database schema (database refactoring is a core practice of evolutionary database design). You refactor a database schema for one of two reasons: to develop the schema in an evolutionary manner in parallel with the evolutionary design of the rest of your system or to fix design problems with an existing legacy database schema.

Database refactoring does not change the way data is interpreted or used and does not fix bugs or add new functionality. Every refactoring to a database leaves the system in a working state, thus not causing maintenance lags, provided the meaningful data exists in the production environment.

An example of database refactoring would be splitting an aggregate table into two different tables in the process of database normalization.

Tools

- LiquiBase

Database Normalization

Database normalization, or simply normalization, is the process of organizing the columns (attributes) and tables (relations) of a relational database to reduce data redundancy and improve data integrity.

Normalization involves arranging attributes in tables based on dependencies between attributes, ensuring that the dependencies are properly enforced by database integrity constraints. Normalization is accomplished through applying some formal rules either by a process of synthesis or decomposition. Synthesis creates a normalized database design based on a known set of dependencies. Decomposition takes an existing (insufficiently normalized) database design and improves it based on the known set of dependencies.

Edgar F. Codd, the inventor of the relational model (RM), introduced the concept of normalization and what we now know as the First normal form (1NF) in 1970. Codd went on to define the Second normal form (2NF) and Third normal form (3NF) in 1971, and Codd and Raymond F. Boyce defined the Boyce-Codd Normal Form (BCNF) in 1974. Informally, a relational database table is often described as "normalized" if it meets Third Normal Form. Most 3NF tables are free of insertion, update, and deletion anomalies.

Objectives

A basic objective of the first normal form defined by Codd in 1970 was to permit data to be queried and manipulated using a "universal data sub-language" grounded in first-order logic. (SQL is an example of such a data sub-language, albeit one that Codd regarded as seriously flawed.)

The objectives of normalization beyond 1NF (First Normal Form) were stated as follows by Codd:

1. To free the collection of relations from undesirable insertion, update and deletion dependencies.

2. To reduce the need for restructuring the collection of relations, as new types of data are introduced, and thus increase the life span of application programs.

3. To make the relational model more informative to users.

4. To make the collection of relations neutral to the query statistics, where these statistics are liable to change as time goes by.

Free the Database of Modification Anomalies

Employees' Skills

Employee ID	Employee Address	Skill
426	87 Sycamore Grove	Typing
426	87 Sycamore Grove	Shorthand
519	94 Chestnut Street	Public Speaking
519	96 Walnut Avenue	Carpentry

An **update anomaly**. Employee 519 is shown as having different addresses on different records.

Faculty and Their Courses

Faculty ID	Faculty Name	Faculty Hire Date	Course Code
389	Dr. Giddens	10-Feb-1985	ENG-206
407	Dr. Saperstein	19-Apr-1999	CMP-101
407	Dr. Saperstein	19-Apr-1999	CMP-201
424	Dr. Newsome	29-Mar-2007	?

An **insertion anomaly**. Until the new faculty member, Dr. Newsome, is assigned to teach at least one course, his details cannot be recorded.

Faculty and Their Courses

Faculty ID	Faculty Name	Faculty Hire Date	Course Code
389	Dr. Giddens	10-Feb-1985	ENG-206
407	Dr. Saperstein	19-Apr-1999	CMP-101
407	Dr. Saperstein	19-Apr-1999	CMP-201

DELETE

A **deletion anomaly**. All information about Dr. Giddens is lost if he temporarily ceases to be assigned to any courses.

When an attempt is made to modify (update, insert into, or delete from) a table, undesired side-effects may arise in tables that have not been sufficiently normalized. An insufficiently normalized table might have one or more of the following characteristics:

*   The same information can be expressed on multiple rows; therefore updates to the table may result in logical inconsistencies. For example, each record in an "Employees' Skills" table might contain an Employee ID, Employee Address, and Skill; thus a change of address for a particular employee will potentially need to be applied to multiple records (one for each skill). If the update is not carried through successfully—if, that is, the employee's address is updated on some records but not others—then the table is left in an inconsistent

state. Specifically, the table provides conflicting answers to the question of what this particular employee's address is. This phenomenon is known as an update anomaly.

- There are circumstances in which certain facts cannot be recorded at all. For example, each record in a "Faculty and Their Courses" table might contain a Faculty ID, Faculty Name, Faculty Hire Date, and Course Code—thus we can record the details of any faculty member who teaches at least one course, but we cannot record the details of a newly hired faculty member who has not yet been assigned to teach any courses except by setting the Course Code to null. This phenomenon is known as an insertion anomaly.

- Under certain circumstances, deletion of data representing certain facts necessitates deletion of data representing completely different facts. The "Faculty and Their Courses" table described in the previous example suffers from this type of anomaly, for if a faculty member temporarily ceases to be assigned to any courses, we must delete the last of the records on which that faculty member appears, effectively also deleting the faculty member, unless we set the Course Code to null in the record itself. This phenomenon is known as a deletion anomaly.

Minimize Redesign When Extending the Database Structure

When a fully normalized database structure is extended to allow it to accommodate new types of data, the pre-existing aspects of the database structure can remain largely or entirely unchanged. As a result, applications interacting with the database are minimally affected.

Normalized tables, and the relationship between one normalized table and another, mirror real-world concepts and their interrelationships.

Example

Querying and manipulating the data within a data structure that is not normalized, such as the following non-1NF representation of customers, credit card transactions, involves more complexity than is really necessary:

Customer	Cust. ID	Transactions		
Jones	1	**Tr. ID**	**Date**	**Amount**
		12890	14-Oct-2003	−87
		12904	15-Oct-2003	−50
Wilkins	2	**Tr. ID**	**Date**	**Amount**
		12898	14-Oct-2003	−21
Stevens	3	**Tr. ID**	**Date**	**Amount**
		12907	15-Oct-2003	−18
		14920	20-Nov-2003	−70
		15003	27-Nov-2003	−60

To each customer corresponds a *repeating group* of transactions. The automated evaluation of any query relating to customers' transactions therefore would broadly involve two stages:

1. Unpacking one or more customers' groups of transactions allowing the individual transactions in a group to be examined.

2. Deriving a query result based on the results of the first stage.

For example, in order to find out the monetary sum of all transactions that occurred in October 2003 for all customers, the system would have to know that it must first unpack the *Transactions* group of each customer, then sum the *Amounts* of all transactions thus obtained where the *Date* of the transaction falls in October 2003.

One of Codd's important insights was that this structural complexity could always be removed completely, leading to much greater power and flexibility in the way queries could be formulated (by users and applications) and evaluated (by the DBMS). The normalized equivalent of the structure above would look like this:

Customer	Cust. ID
Jones	1
Wilkins	2
Stevens	3

Cust. ID	Tr. ID	Date	Amount
1	12890	14-Oct-2003	−87
1	12904	15-Oct-2003	−50
2	12898	14-Oct-2003	−21
3	12907	15-Oct-2003	−18
3	14920	20-Nov-2003	−70
3	15003	27-Nov-2003	−60

In the modified structure, the keys are {Customer} and {Cust. ID} in the first table, {Cust. ID, Tr ID} in the second table.

Now each row represents an individual credit card transaction, and the DBMS can obtain the answer of interest, simply by finding all rows with a Date falling in October, and summing their Amounts. The data structure places all of the values on an equal footing, exposing each to the DBMS directly, so each can potentially participate directly in queries; whereas in the previous situation some values were embedded in lower-level structures that had to be handled specially. Accordingly, the normalized design lends itself to general-purpose query processing, whereas the unnormalized design does not. The normalized version also allows the user to change the customer name in one place and guards against errors that arise if the customer name is misspelled on some records.

List of Normal Forms

*   UNF - "Unnormalized Form".

*   1NF - First Normal Form.

- 2NF - Second Normal Form.

- 3NF - Third Normal Form.

- EKNF - Elementary Key Normal Form.

- BCNF - Boyce–Codd Normal Form.

- 4NF - Fourth Normal Form.

- ETNF - Essential Tuple Normal Form.

- 5NF - Fifth Normal Form.

- 6NF - Sixth Normal Form.

- DKNF - Domain/Key Normal Form.

Data Structure

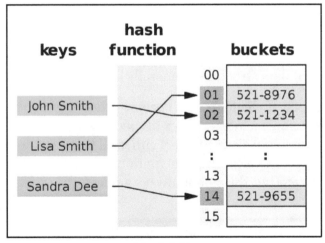

A hash table.

In computer science, a data structure is a particular way of organizing data in a computer so that it can be used efficiently. Data structures can implement one or more particular abstract data types (ADT), which specify the operations that can be performed on a data structure and the computational complexity of those operations. In comparison, a data structure is a concrete implementation of the specification provided by an ADT.

Different kinds of data structures are suited to different kinds of applications, and some are highly specialized to specific tasks. For example, relational databases commonly use B-tree indexes for data retrieval, while compiler implementations usually use hash tables to look up identifiers.

Data structures provide a means to manage large amounts of data efficiently for uses such as large databases and internet indexing services. Usually, efficient data structures are key to designing efficient algorithms. Some formal design methods and programming languages emphasize data structures, rather than algorithms, as the key organizing factor in software design. Data structures can be used to organize the storage and retrieval of information stored in both main memory and secondary memory.

Overview

Data structures are generally based on the ability of a computer to fetch and store data at any place in its memory, specified by a pointer—a bit string, representing a memory address, that can be itself stored in memory and manipulated by the program. Thus, the array and record data structures are based on computing the addresses of data items with arithmetic operations; while the linked data structures are based on storing addresses of data items within the structure itself. Many data structures use both principles, sometimes combined in non-trivial ways (as in XOR linking).

The implementation of a data structure usually requires writing a set of procedures that create and manipulate instances of that structure. The efficiency of a data structure cannot be analyzed separately from those operations. This observation motivates the theoretical concept of an abstract data type, a data structure that is defined indirectly by the operations that may be performed on it, and the mathematical properties of those operations (including their space and time cost).

Examples

There are numerous types of data structures, generally built upon simpler primitive data types:

- An *array* is a number of elements in a specific order, typically all of the same type. Elements are accessed using an integer index to specify which element is required (Depending on the language, individual elements may either all be forced to be the same type, or may be of almost any type). Typical implementations allocate contiguous memory words for the elements of arrays (but this is not always a necessity). Arrays may be fixed-length or resizable.

- A *linked list* (also just called *list*) is a linear collection of data elements of any type, called nodes, where each node has itself a value, and points to the next node in the linked list. The principal advantage of a linked list over an array, is that values can always be efficiently inserted and removed without relocating the rest of the list. Certain other operations, such as random access to a certain element, are however slower on lists than on arrays.

- A *record* (also called *tuple* or *struct*) is an aggregate data structure. A record is a value that contains other values, typically in fixed number and sequence and typically indexed by names. The elements of records are usually called *fields* or *members*.

- A *union* is a data structure that specifies which of a number of permitted primitive types may be stored in its instances, e.g. *float* or *long integer*. Contrast with a record, which could be defined to contain a float *and* an integer; whereas in a union, there is only one value at a time. Enough space is allocated to contain the widest member datatype.

- A *tagged union* (also called *variant, variant record, discriminated union,* or *disjoint union*) contains an additional field indicating its current type, for enhanced type safety.

- A *class* is a data structure that contains data fields, like a record, as well as various methods which operate on the contents of the record. In the context of object-oriented programming, records are known as plain old data structures to distinguish them from classes.

Language Support

Most assembly languages and some low-level languages, such as BCPL (Basic Combined Programming Language), lack built-in support for data structures. On the other hand, many high-level programming languages and some higher-level assembly languages, such as MASM, have special syntax or other built-in support for certain data structures, such as records and arrays. For example, the C and Pascal languages support structs and records, respectively, in addition to vectors (one-dimensional arrays) and multi-dimensional arrays.

Most programming languages feature some sort of library mechanism that allows data structure implementations to be reused by different programs. Modern languages usually come with standard libraries that implement the most common data structures. Examples are the C++ Standard Template Library, the Java Collections Framework, and Microsoft's .NET Framework.

Modern languages also generally support modular programming, the separation between the interface of a library module and its implementation. Some provide opaque data types that allow clients to hide implementation details. Object-oriented programming languages, such as C++, Java and Smalltalk may use classes for this purpose.

Many known data structures have concurrent versions that allow multiple computing threads to access the data structure simultaneously.

Database Engine

A database engine (or storage engine) is the underlying software component that a database management system (DBMS) uses to create, read, update and delete (CRUD) data from a database. Most database management systems include their own application programming interface (API) that allows the user to interact with their underlying engine without going through the user interface of the DBMS.

The term "database engine" is frequently used interchangeably with "database server" or "database management system". A 'database instance' refers to the processes and memory structures of the running database engine.

Storage Engines

Many of the modern DBMS support multiple storage engines within the same database. For example, MySQL supports InnoDB as well as MyISAM.

Some storage engines are transactional.

Name	License	Transactional
Aria	GPL	No
BlitzDB	GPL	No
Falcon	GPL	Yes
InnoDB	GPL	Yes
MyISAM	GPL	No
InfiniDB	CPL	No
TokuDB	GPL	Yes
WiredTiger	GPL	Yes
XtraDB	GPL	Yes

Additional engine types include:

- Embedded database engines.

- In-memory database engines.

Design Considerations

Database bits are laid out in storage in data structures and groupings that can take advantage of both known effective algorithms to retrieve and manipulate them and the storage own properties. Typically the storage itself is designed to meet requirements of various areas that extensively utilize storage, including databases. A DBMS in operation always simultaneously utilizes several storage types (e.g., memory, and external storage), with respective layout methods.

In principle the database storage can be viewed as a linear address space, where every bit of data has its unique address in this address space. In practice, only a very small percentage of addresses are kept as initial reference points (which also requires storage); most data is accessed by indirection using displacement calculations (distance in bits from the reference points) and data structures which define access paths (using pointers) to all needed data in an effective manner, optimized for the needed data access operations.

Database Storage Hierarchy

A database, while in operation, resides simultaneously in several types of storage, forming a storage hierarchy. By the nature of contemporary computers most of the database part inside a computer that hosts the DBMS resides (partially replicated) in volatile storage. Data (pieces of the database) that are being processed/manipulated reside inside a processor, possibly in processor's caches. These data are being read from/written to memory, typically through a computer bus (so far typically volatile storage components). Computer memory is communicating data (transferred to/from) external storage, typically through standard storage interfaces or networks (e.g., fibre channel, iSCSI). A storage array, a common external storage unit, typically has storage hierarchy of its own, from a fast cache, typically consisting of (volatile and fast) DRAM, which is connected (again via standard interfaces) to drives, possibly with different speeds, like flash drives and magnetic disk drives (non-volatile). The drives may be connected to magnetic tapes, on which typically the least active parts of a large database may reside, or database backup generations.

Typically a correlation exists currently between storage speed and price, while the faster storage is typically volatile.

Data Structures

A data structure is an abstract construct that embeds data in a well defined manner. An efficient data structure allows to manipulate the data in efficient ways. The data manipulation may include data insertion, deletion, updating and retrieval in various modes. A certain data structure type may be very effective in certain operations, and very ineffective in others. A data structure type is selected upon DBMS development to best meet the operations needed for the types of data it contains. Type of data structure selected for a certain task typically also takes into consideration the type of storage it resides in (e.g., speed of access, minimal size of storage chunk accessed, etc.). In some DBMSs database administrators have the flexibility to select among options of data structures to contain user data for performance reasons. Sometimes the data structures have selectable parameters to tune the database performance.

Databases may store data in many data structure types. Common examples are the following:

- Ordered/unordered flat files.

- Hash tables.

- B+ trees.

- ISAM.

- Heaps.

Data Orientation and Clustering

In contrast to conventional row-orientation, relational databases can also be column-oriented or correlational in the way they store data in any particular structure.

In general, substantial performance improvement is gained if different types of database objects that are usually utilized together are laid in storage in proximity, being "clustered". This usually allows to retrieve needed related objects from storage in minimum number of input operations (each sometimes substantially time consuming). Even for in-memory databases clustering provides performance advantage due to common utilization of large caches for input-output operations in memory, with similar resulting behavior.

For example, it may be beneficial to cluster a record of an "item" in stock with all its respective "order" records. The decision of whether to cluster certain objects or not depends on the objects' utilization statistics, object sizes, caches sizes, storage types, etc.

Database Indexing

Indexing is a technique some storage engines use for improving database performance. The many types of indexes share the common property that they reduce the need to examine every entry when running a query. In large databases, this can reduce query time/cost by orders of magnitude. The simplest form of index is a sorted list of values that can be searched using a binary search with an adjacent reference to the location of the entry, analogous to the index in the back of a book. The same data can have multiple indexes (an employee database could be indexed by last name and hire date).

Indexes affect performance, but not results. Database designers can add or remove indexes without changing application logic, reducing maintenance costs as the database grows and database usage evolves. Indexes can speed up data access, but they consume space in the database, and must be updated each time the data is altered. Indexes therefore can speed data access but slow data maintenance. These two properties determine whether a given index is worth the cost.

Database Server

A database server is a computer program that provides database services to other computer programs or computers, as defined by the client–server model. The term may also refer to a computer dedicated to running such a program. Database management systems frequently provide database server functionality, and some DBMSs (e.g., MySQL) rely exclusively on the client–server model for database access.

Such a server is accessed either through a "front end" running on the user's computer which displays requested data or the "back end" which runs on the server and handles tasks such as data analysis and storage.

In a master-slave model, database master servers are central and primary locations of data while database slave servers are synchronized backups of the master acting as proxies.

Most of the Database servers works with the base of Query language. Each Database understands its query language and converts it to Server readable form and executes it to retrieve the results.

Some examples of proprietary database servers are Oracle, DB2, Informix, and Microsoft SQL Server. Examples of GNU General Public Licence database servers are Ingres and MySQL. Every server uses its own query logic and structure. The SQL query language is more or less the same in all relational database servers. DB-Engines lists over 200 DBMSs in its ranking.

History

The foundations for modeling large sets of data were first introduced by Charles Bachman in 1969. Bachman introduced Data Structure Diagrams (DSDs) as a means to graphically represent data. DSDs provided a means to represent the relationships between different data entities. In 1970, Codd introduced the concept that users of a database should be ignorant of the "inner workings" of the database. Codd proposed the "relational view" of data which later evolved into the Relational Model which most databases use today. In 1971, the Database Task Report Group of CODASYL (the driving force behind the development of the programming language COBOL) first proposed a "data description language for describing a database, a data description language for describing that part of the data base known to a program, and a data manipulation language." Most of the research and development of databases focused on the relational model during the 1970s.

In 1975 Bachman demonstrated how the relational model and the data structure set were similar and "congruent" ways of structuring data while working for the Honeywell. The Entity-relationship model was first proposed in its current form by Peter Chen in 1976 while he was conducting research at MIT. This model became the most frequently used model to describe relational databases. Chen was able to propose a model that was superior to the navigational model and was more applicable to the "real world" than the relational model proposed by Codd.

Database Schema

A database schema of a database system is its structure described in a formal language supported by the database management system (DBMS). The term "schema" refers to the organization of data as a blueprint of how the database is constructed (divided into database tables in the case of relational databases). The formal definition of a database schema is a set of formulas (sentences) called integrity constraints imposed on a database. These integrity constraints ensure compatibility between parts of the schema. All constraints are expressible in the same language. A database can be considered a structure in realization of the database language. The states of a created conceptual schema are transformed into an explicit mapping, the database schema. This describes how real-world entities are modeled in the database.

"A database schema specifies, based on the database administrator's knowledge of possible applications, the facts that can enter the database, or those of interest to the possible end-users." The notion of a database schema plays the same role as the notion of theory in predicate calculus. A model of this "theory" closely corresponds to a database, which can be seen at any instant of time as a mathematical object. Thus a schema can contain formulas representing integrity constraints specifically for an application and the constraints specifically for a type of database, all expressed in the same database language. In a relational database, the schema defines the tables, fields, relationships, views, indexes, packages, procedures, functions, queues, triggers, types, sequences, materialized views, synonyms, database links, directories, XML schemas, and other elements.

A database generally stores its schema in a data dictionary. Although a schema is defined in text database language, the term is often used to refer to a graphical depiction of the database structure. In other words, schema is the structure of the database that defines the objects in the database.

In an Oracle Database system, the term "schema" has a slightly different connotation.

Ideal Requirements for Schema Integration

The requirements listed below influence the detailed structure of schemas that are produced. Certain applications will not require that all of these conditions are met, but these four requirements are the most ideal.

Overlap preservation

> Each of the overlapping elements specified in the input mapping is also in a database schema relation.

Extended overlap preservation

> Source-specific elements that are associated with a source's overlapping elements are passed through to the database schema.

Normalization

> Independent entities and relationships in the source data should not be grouped together in the same relation in the database schema. In particular, source specific schema elements should not be grouped with overlapping schema elements, if the grouping co-locates independent entities or relationships.

Minimality

> If any elements of the database schema are dropped then the database schema is not ideal.

Example of two Schema Integrations

Suppose we want a mediated (database) schema to integrate two travel databases, Go-travel and Ok-travel.

Go-travel has two relations:

Go-flight(f-num, time, meal(yes/no))

Go-price(f-num, date, price)

(f-num being the flight number)

Ok-travel has just one relation:

Ok-flight(f-num, date, time, price, nonstop(yes/no))

The overlapping information in Ok-travel's and Go-travel's schemas could be represented in a mediated schema:

Flight(f-num, date, time, price)

Oracle Database Specificity

In the context of Oracle databases, a schema object is a logical data storage structure.

An Oracle database associates a separate schema with each database user. A schema comprises a collection of schema objects. Examples of schema objects include:

- Tables
- Views

- Sequences

- Synonyms

- Indexes

- Clusters

- Database links

- Snapshots

- Procedures

- Functions

- Packages

On the other hand, non-schema objects may include:

- Users

- Roles

- Contexts

- Directory objects

Schema objects do not have a one-to-one correspondence to physical files on disk that store their information. However, Oracle databases store schema objects logically within a tablespace of the database. The data of each object is physically contained in one or more of the tablespace's datafiles. For some objects (such as tables, indexes, and clusters) a database administrator can specify how much disk space the Oracle RDBMS allocates for the object within the tablespace's datafiles.

There is no necessary relationship between schemas and tablespaces: a tablespace can contain objects from different schemas, and the objects for a single schema can reside in different tablespaces.

Reversible Changes in Database Schema

Schema Migration

In software engineering, schema migration (also database migration, database change management) refers to the management of incremental, reversible changes to relational database schemas. A schema migration is performed on a database whenever it is necessary to update or revert that database's schema to some newer or older version.

Migrations are performed programmatically by using a *schema migration tool*. When invoked with a specified desired schema version, the tool automates the successive application or reversal of an appropriate sequence of schema changes until it is brought to the desired state.

Most schema migration tools aim to minimise the impact of schema changes on any existing data in the database. Despite this, preservation of data in general is not guaranteed because schema changes such as the deletion of a database column can destroy data (i.e. all values stored under that column for all rows in that table are deleted). Instead, the tools help to preserve the meaning of the data or to reorganize existing data to meet new requirements. Since meaning of the data often cannot be encoded, the configuration of the tools usually needs manual intervention.

Risks and Benefits

Schema migration allows for fixing mistakes and adapting the data as requirements change. They are an essential part of software evolution, especially in agile environments.

Applying a schema migration to a production database is always a risk. Development and test databases tend to be smaller and cleaner. The data in them is better understood or, if everything else fails, the amount of data is small enough for a human to process. Production databases are usually huge, old and full of surprises. The surprises can come from many sources:

- Corrupt data that was written by old versions of the software and not cleaned properly.

- Implied dependencies in the data which no one knows about anymore.

- People directly changing the database without using the designated tools.

- Bugs in the schema migration tools.

- Mistakes in assumptions how data should be migrated.

For these reasons, the migration process needs a high level of discipline, thorough testing and a sound backup strategy.

Schema Migration in Agile Software Development

When developing software applications backed by a database, developers typically develop the application source code in tandem with an evolving database schema. The code typically has rigid expectations of what columns, tables and constraints are present in the database schema whenever it needs to interact with one, so only the version of database schema against which the code was developed is considered fully compatible with that version of source code.

In software testing, while developers may mock the presence of a compatible database system for unit testing, any level of testing higher than this (e.g. integration testing or system testing) it is common for developers to test their application against a local or remote test database schematically compatible with the version of source code under test. In advanced applications, the migration itself can be subject to migration testing.

With schema migration technology, data models no longer need to be fully designed up-front, and are more capable of being adapted with changing project requirements throughout the software development lifecycle.

Relation to Revision Control Systems

Teams of software developers usually use version control systems to manage and collaborate on changes made to versions of source code. Different developers can develop on divergent, relatively older or newer branches of the same source code to make changes and additions during development.

Supposing that the software under development interacts with a database, every version of the source code can be associated with at least one database schema with which it is compatible.

Under good software testing practise, schema migrations can be performed on test databases to ensure that their schema is compatible to the source code. To streamline this process, a schema migration tool is usually invoked as a part of an automated software build as a prerequisite of the automated testing phase.

Schema migration tools can be said to solve versioning problems for database schemas just as version control systems solve versioning problems for source code. In practice, many schema migration tools actually rely on a textual representation of schema changes (such as files containing SQL statements) such that the version history of schema changes can effectively be stored alongside program source code within VCS. This approach ensures that the information necessary to recover a compatible database schema for a particular code branch is recoverable from the source tree itself. Another benefit of this approach is the handling of concurrent conflicting schema changes; developers may simply use their usual text-based conflict resolution tools to reconcile differences.

Relation to Schema Evolution

Schema migration tooling could be seen as a facility to track the history of an evolving schema.

Advantages

Developers no longer need to remove the entire test database in order to create a new test database from scratch (e.g. using schema creation scripts from DDL generation tools). Further, if generation of test data costs a lot of time, developers can avoid regenerating test data for small, non-destructive changes to the schema.

Available Tools

- ESF Database Migration Toolkit A toolkit migrate data between various database formats. Supports Oracle, MS-SQL, MySQL, PostgreSQL, DB2, MS-Access, SQLite and so on.

- Flyway - database migration tool (for Windows, OSX, Linux, Android and the JVM) where migrations are written in SQL or Java.

- LiquiBase - cross platform tool where migrations are written in XML, YAML, JSON or SQL.

- Datical - Enterprise commercial version of Liquibase.

- Redgate SQL Compare - a schema comparison and deployment tool for SQL Server and Oracle.

- ReadyRoll - a migrations-based Visual Studio extension for SQL Server development and deployment.

- Active Record (Migrations) - schema migration tool for Ruby on Rails projects based on Active Record.

- Ruckusing-migrations - schema migration tool for PHP projects.

- Phinx - another framework-independent PHP migration tool.

- MyBatis Migrations - seeks to be the best migration tool of its kind.

- Ragtime - a SQL database schema migration library written in Clojure.

- Lobos - a SQL database schema manipulation and migration library written in Clojure.

- Alembic - a lightweight database migration tool for usage with the SQLAlchemy Database Toolkit for Python.

- RoundhousE - a SQL database versioning and change management tool written in C#.

- XMigra - a SQL database evolution management tool written in Ruby that generates scripts without communicating with the database.

- DBmaestro - a database version control and schema migration solution for SQL Server and Oracle.

- DB Change Manager - Commercial Change Management Software by Embarcadero.

- Sqitch - Sqitch by Theory.

- Goose - database migration tool where migrations are written in SQL or Go.

- knexjs - schema and data migration tool built on top of a query builder tool written in javascript.

Flyway (Software)

Flyway is an open source database migration tool. It strongly favors simplicity and convention over configuration.

It is based around 6 basic commands: Migrate, Clean, Info, Validate, Baseline and Repair.

Migrations can be written in SQL (database-specific syntax (such as PL/SQL, T-SQL, ...) is supported) or Java (for advanced data transformations or dealing with LOBs).

It has a Command-line client, a Java API (also works on Android) for migrating the database on application startup, a Maven plugin, Gradle plugin, SBT plugin and Ant tasks.

Plugins are available for Spring Boot, Dropwizard, Grails, Play, Griffon, Grunt, Ninja and more.

Supported databases are Oracle, SQL Server, SQL Azure, DB2, DB2 z/OS, MySQL (including Amazon RDS), MariaDB, Google Cloud SQL, PostgreSQL (including Amazon RDS and Heroku), Redshift, Vertica, H2, Hsql, Derby, SQLite, SAP HANA, solidDB, Sybase ASE and Phoenix.

Adoption

Flyway has been widely adopted in the industry, with over 850,000 downloads in 2015 alone.

In January 2015, Flyway was placed in the "Adopt" section of the Thoughtworks Technology Radar.

Liquibase

Liquibase is an open source database-independent library for tracking, managing and applying database schema changes. It was started in 2006 to allow easier tracking of database changes, especially in an agile software development environment.

Overview

All changes to the database are stored in text files (XML, YAML, JSON or SQL) and identified by a combination of an "id" and "author" tag as well as the name of the file itself. A list of all applied changes is stored in each database which is consulted on all database updates to determine what new changes need to be applied. As a result, there is no database version number but this approach allows it to work in environments with multiple developers and code branches.

Automatically creates DatabaseChangeLog Table and DatabaseChangeLogLock Table when you first execute a changeLog File.

Major Functionality

- Over 30 built-in database refactorings.

- Extensibility to create custom changes.

- Update database to current version.

- Rollback last X changes to database.

- Rollback database changes to particular date/time.

- Rollback database to "tag".

- SQL for Database Updates and Rollbacks can be saved for manual review.

- Stand-alone IDE and Eclipse plug-in.

- "Contexts" for including/excluding change sets to execute.

- Database diff report.

- Database diff changelog generation.

- Ability to create changelog to generate an existing database.

- Database change documentation generation.

- DBMS Check, user check, and SQL check preconditions.

- Ability to split change log into multiple files for easier management.

- Executable via command line, Apache Ant, Apache Maven, servlet container, or Spring Framework.

- Support for 10 database systems.

Commercial Version

Datical is both the largest contributor to the Liquibase project and the developer of Datical DB – a commercial product which provides the core Liquibase functionality plus additional features to remove complexity, simplify deployment and bridge the gap between development and operations. Datical DB was created to satisfy the Application Schema management requirements of large enterprises as they move from Continuous Integration to Continuous Delivery.

- Change Forecasting: Forecast upcoming changes to be executed before they are run to determine how those changes will impact your data.

- Rules Engine to enforce Corporate Standards and Policies.

- Supports database Stored Logic: functions, stored procedures, packages, table spaces, triggers, sequences, user defined types, synonyms, etc.

- Compare Databases enables you to compare two database schemas to identify change and easily move it to your change log.

- Change Set Wizard to easily define and capture database changes in a database neutral manner.

- Deployment Plan Wizard for modeling and managing your logical deployment workflow.

- Plug-ins to Jenkins, Bamboo, UrbanCode, CA Release Automation (Nolio), Serena Release Automation, BMC Bladelogic, Puppet, Chef, as well all popular source control systems like SVN, Git, TFS, CVS, etc.

Datical DB is used by DBAs, Release Managers, DevOps teams, Application Owners, Architects, and Developers involved in the Application Release process. It manages Database Schema changes together with application code in a programmatic fashion that eliminates errors and delays and enables rapid Agile releases. Datical DB builds upon the Liquibase Data Model Approach for managing data structure specific content across application versions as they advance from Development to Test to Production environments. Datical previews the impact of Schema changes in any environment before deployment thus mitigating risk and resulting in smoother and faster application changes.

Liquibase developer, Nathan Voxland, is an executive at Datical.

Sample Liquibase ChangeLog file

```xml
<?xml version="1.0" encoding="UTF-8"?>


<databaseChangeLog

    xmlns="http://www.liquibase.org/xml/ns/dbchangelog/1.3"

    xmlns:xsi="http://www.w3.org/2001/XMLSchema-instance"

    xsi:schemaLocation="http://www.liquibase.org/xml/ns/dbchangelog/1.3

    http://www.liquibase.org/xml/ns/dbchangelog/dbchangelog-1.3.xsd">

  <preConditions>

      <dbms type="oracle"/>

  </preConditions>


  <changeSet id="1" author="alice">

    <createTable tableName="news">

      <column name="id" type="int">

        <constraints primaryKey="true" nullable="false"/>

      </column>

      <column name="title" type="varchar(50)"/>

    </createTable>

  </changeSet>


  <changeSet id="12" author="bob">

    <createSequence sequenceName="seq_news"/>

  </changeSet>


  <changeSet id="2" author="cpa" context="test">

    <insert tableName="news">

      <column name="id" value="1"/>
```

```
    <column name="title" value="Liquibase 0.8 Released"/>

  </insert>

  <insert tableName="news">

    <column name="id" value="2"/>

    <column name="title" value="Liquibase 0.9 Released"/>

  </insert>

 </changeSet>

</databaseChangeLog>
```

References

- Teorey, T.; Lightstone, S. and Nadeau, T.(2005) Database Modeling & Design: Logical Design, 4th edition, Morgan Kaufmann Press. ISBN 0-12-685352-5

- Gavin Powell (2006). "Chapter : Building Fast-Performing Database Models". Beginning Database Design ISBN 978-0-7645-7490-0

Common Database Designing Languages

The computer languages which are used to make queries in information systems and databases are known as query languages. A data control language is a computer programming language which is used to control access to data stored in a database. This chapter closely examines the key concepts of database designing languages to provide an extensive understanding of the subject.

Query Language

A query is a question, often expressed in a formal way. A database query can be either a select query or an action query. A select query is a data retrieval query, while an action query asks for additional operations on the data, such as insertion, updating or deletion.

Query language is a computer programming language used to retrieve information from a database.

The uses of databases are manifold. They provide a means of retrieving records or parts of records and performing various calculations before displaying the results. The interface by which such manipulations are specified is called the query language. Whereas early query languages were originally so complex that interacting with electronic databases could be done only by specially trained individuals, modern interfaces are more user-friendly, allowing casual users to access database information.

The main types of popular query modes are the menu, the "fill-in-the-blank" technique, and the structured query. Particularly suited for novices, the menu requires a person to choose from several alternatives displayed on a monitor. The fill-in-the-blank technique is one in which the user is prompted to enter key words as search statements. The structured query approach is effective with relational databases. It has a formal, powerful syntax that is in fact a programming language, and it is able to accommodate logical operators. One implementation of this approach, the Structured Query Language (SQL), has the form:

select [field Fa, Fb, . . ., Fn]

from [database Da, Db, . . ., Dn]

where, [field Fa = abc] *and* [field Fb = def].

Structured query languages support database searching and other operations by using commands such as "find", "delete", "print", "sum" and so forth. The sentence like structure of a SQL query resembles natural language except that its syntax is limited and fixed. Instead of using a SQL statement, it is possible to represent queries in tabular form. The technique, referred to as query-by-example (or QBE), displays an empty tabular form and expects the searcher to enter the search specifications into appropriate columns. The program then constructs a SQL-type query from the table and executes it.

The most flexible query language is of course natural language. The use of natural-language sentences in a constrained form to search databases is allowed by some commercial database management software. These programs parse the syntax of the query; recognize its action words and their synonyms; identify the names of files, records, and fields; and perform the logical operations required. Experimental systems that accept such natural-language queries in spoken voice have been developed; however, the ability to employ unrestricted natural language to query unstructured information will require further advances in machine understanding of natural language, particularly in techniques of representing the semantic and pragmatic context of ideas.

In a relational database, which contains records or rows of information, the SQL SELECT statement query allows the user to choose data and return it from the database to an application. The resulting query is stored in a result-table, which is called the result-set. The SELECT statement can be broken down into other categories, such as FROM, WHERE and ORDER BY. The SQL SELECT query also can group and aggregate data, such as summarize or analyze.

Search a Query

The text typed into search engines, such as Bing, Google or Yahoo, is called a query. Search-engine queries provide information that is much different from SQL languages because they don't require keyword or positional parameters. A search-engine query is a request for information on a particular topic, and the request is made once a user selects 'Enter.'

Once the request is made, the search engine uses an algorithm to determine the best results, which are sorted based on significance according to the search engine details of which are not revealed publicly.

Types of search queries include navigational, informational and transactional. Navigational searches are intended to find a particular website, such as ESPN.com; informational searches are designed to cover a broad topic, such a comparison between a new iPhone and Android device; and transactional searches seek to complete a transaction.

Data Control Language

The Data Control Language (DCL) is a subset of the Structured Query Language (SQL) and allows database administrators to configure security access to relational databases. It complements the Data Definition Language (DDL), which is used to add and delete database objects, and the Data Manipulation Language (DML) used to retrieve, insert, and modify the contents of a database.

DCL is the simplest of the SQL subsets, as it consists of only three commands: GRANT, REVOKE, and DENY. Combined, these three commands provide administrators with the flexibility to set and remove database permissions in an extremely granular fashion.

Adding Permissions with the GRANT Command

The GRANT command is used by administrators to add new permissions to a database user. It has a very simple syntax, defined as follows:

```
GRANT [privilege]

ON [object]

TO [user]

[WITH GRANT OPTION]
```

Here's the rundown on each of the parameters you can supply with this command:

- Privilege: can be either the keyword ALL (to grant a wide variety of permissions) or a specific database permission or set of permissions. Examples include CREATE DATABASE, SELECT, INSERT, UPDATE, DELETE, EXECUTE and CREATE VIEW.

- Object: can be any database object. The valid privilege options vary based on the type of database object you include in this clause. Typically, the object will be either a database, function, stored procedure, table or view.

- User: can be any database user. You can also substitute a role for the user in this clause if you wish to make use of role-based database security.

- If you include the optional With Grant Option clause at the end of the GRANT command, you not only grant the specified user the permissions defined in the SQL statement but also give the user the ability to grant those same permissions to *other* database users. For this reason, use this clause with care.

For example, assume you wish to grant the user Joe the ability to retrieve information from the employees table in a database called HR. You might use the following SQL command:

```
GRANT SELECT
```

```
ON HR.employees

TO Joe
```

Joe will now have the ability to retrieve information from the employees table. He will not, however, be able to grant other users permission to retrieve information from that table because you did not include the WITH GRANT OPTION clause in the GRANT statement.

Revoking Database Access

The REVOKE command is used to remove database access from a user previously granted such access. The syntax for this command is defined as follows:

```
REVOKE [GRANT OPTION FOR] [permission]

ON [object]

FROM [user]

[CASCADE]
```

Here's the rundown on the parameters for the REVOKE command:

- Permission: specifies the database permissions to remove from the identified user. The command revokes both GRANT and DENY assertions previously made for the identified permission.

- Object: can be any database object. The valid privilege options vary based on the type of database object you include in this clause. Typically, the object will be either a database, function, stored procedure, table or view.

- User: can be any database user. You can also substitute a role for the user in this clause if you wish to make use of role-based database security.

- The GRANT OPTION FOR clause removes the specified user's ability to grant the specified permission to other users. Note: *If you include the GRANT OPTION FOR clause in a REVOKE statement, the primary permission is not revoked.* This clause revokes *only* the granting ability.

- The CASCADE option also revokes the specified permission from any users that the specified user granted the permission.

For example, the following command revokes the permission granted to Joe in the previous:

```
REVOKE SELECT

ON HR.employees

FROM Joe
```

Explicitly Denying Database Access

The DENY command is used to explicitly prevent a user from receiving a particular permission. This is helpful when a user is a member of a role or group that is granted permission and you want to prevent that individual user from inheriting the permission by creating an exception. The syntax for this command is as follows:

```
DENY [permission]

ON [object]

TO [user]
```

The parameters for the DENY command are identical to those used for the GRANT command. For example, if you wished to ensure that Matthew would never receive the ability to delete information from the employees table, issue the following command:

```
DENY DELETE

ON HR.employees

TO Matthew
```

Data Definition Language

- DDL stands for Data Definition Language.

- It is a language used for defining and modifying the data and its structure.

- It is used to build and modify the structure of your tables and other objects in the database.

DDL commands are as follows:

- CREATE.

- DROP.

- ALTER.

- RENAME.

- TRUNCATE.

- These commands can be used to add, remove or modify tables within a database.

- DDL has pre-defined syntax for describing the data.

CREATE Command

- CREATE command is used for creating objects in the database.

- It creates a new table.

Syntax:

CREATE TABLE <table_name>

(column_name1 datatype,column_name2 datatype,

...column_name_n datatype);

Example: CREATE command

CREATE TABLE employee

(empid INT, ename CHAR,age INT, city CHAR(25), phone_no VARCHAR(20));

DROP Command

- DROP command allows to remove entire database objects from the database.

- It removes entire data structure from the database.

- It deletes a table, index or view.

Syntax:

DROP TABLE <table_name>;

or

DROP DATABASE <database_name>;

Example: DROP Command

DROP TABLE employee;

or

DROP DATABASE employees;

- If you want to remove individual records, then use DELETE command of the DML statement.

ALTER Command

- An ALTER command allows to Alter or modify the structure of the database.

- It modifies an existing database object.

- Using this command, you can add additional column, drop existing column and even change the data type of columns.

Syntax:

ALTER TABLE <table_name>

ADD <column_name datatype>;

or

ALTER TABLE <table_name>

CHANGE <old_column_name> <new_column_name>;

or

ALTER TABLE <table_name>

DROP COLUMN <column_name>;

Example: ALTER Command

ALTER TABLE employee

ADD (address varchar2(50));

or

ALTER TABLE employee

CHANGE (phone_no) (contact_no);

or

ALTER TABLE employee

DROP COLUMN age;

To view the changed structure of table, use 'DESCRIBE' command.

For example:

DESCRIBE TABLE employee;

RENAME Command

- RENAME command is used to rename an object.

- It renames a database table.

Syntax:

RENAME TABLE <old_name> TO <new_name>.

Example:

RENAME TABLE emp TO employee.

TRUNCATE Command

- TRUNCATE command is used to delete all the rows from the table permanently.

- It removes all the records from a table, including all spaces allocated for the records.

- This command is same as DELETE command, but TRUNCATE command does not generate any rollback data.

Syntax:

TRUNCATE TABLE <table_name>.

Example:

TRUNCATE TABLE employee.

Data Manipulation Language

A data manipulation language (DML) is a family of computer languages including commands permitting users to manipulate data in a database. This manipulation involves inserting data into database tables, retrieving existing data, deleting data from existing tables and modifying existing data. DML is mostly incorporated in SQL databases.

Data manipulation language is of two types:

- Procedural – The type of data needed and the mechanism to get it is specified by the user.

- Non Procedural – Only the type of data needed is specified by the user.

The basic DML commands are:

- SELECT

- INSERT

- UPDATE

- DELETE

DML performs read-only queries of data.

SELECT Command

- SELECT command is used to retrieve data from the database.

- This command allows database users to retrieve the specific information they desire from an operational database.

- It returns a result set of records from one or more tables.

SELECT Command has many Optional Clauses are as Stated Below:

Clause	Description
WHERE	It specifies which rows to retrieve.
GROUP BY	It is used to arrange the data into groups.
HAVING	It selects among the groups defined by the GROUP BY clause.
ORDER BY	It specifies an order in which to return the rows.
AS	It provides an alias which can be used to temporarily rename tables or columns.

Syntax:

SELECT * FROM <table_name>;

Example:

SELECT Command

SELECT * FROM employee;

or

SELECT * FROM employee

where salary >=10,000;

INSERT Command

- INSERT command is used for inserting a data into a table.

- Using this command, you can add one or more records to any single table in a database.

- It is also used to add records to an existing code.

Syntax:

INSERT INTO <table_name> (`column_name1` <datatype>, `column_name2` <data-type>, ..., `column_name_n` <database>) VALUES (`value1`, `value2`, ..., `value n`);

Example:

INSERT INTO employee (`eid` int, `ename` varchar(20), `city` varchar(20))

VALUES (`1`, `ABC`, `PUNE`);

UPDATE Command

- UPDATE command is used to modify the records present in existing table.

- This command updates existing data within a table.

- It changes the data of one or more records in a table.

Syntax:

UPDATE <table_name>

SET <column_name = value>

WHERE condition;

Example: UPDATE Command

UPDATE EMPLOYEE

SET SALARY=20000

WHERE ENAME='ABC';

DELETE Command

- DELETE command is used to delete some or all records from the existing table.

- It deletes all the records from a table.

Syntax:

DELETE FROM <table_name> WHERE <condition>;

Example:

DELETE Command

DELETE FROM employee

WHERE emp_id = '001';

If we does not write the WHERE condition, then all rows will get deleted.

References

- Automate-database-administration-tasks: dbmaestro.com, Retrieved 11, May 2020

- Query-language, technology: britannica.com, Retrieved 21, April 2020

- Data-manipulation-language-1179: techopedia.com, Retrieved 27, May 2020

- Data-control-language-dcl-1019477: lifewire.com, Retrieved 18, June 2020

- Get-ready-to-learn-sql-database-normalization-explained-in-simple-english: essentialsql.com, Retrieved 29, May 2020

Database Management Techniques

ACID is atomicity, consistency, isolation, durability. It is a set of properties of database transactions that can ensure database transactions can be processed reliably. There are four basic functions of persistent storage; create, read, update and delete. The diverse tools and techniques of database management in the current scenario have been thoroughly discussed in this chapter.

ACID

In computer science, ACID (*Atomicity, Consistency, Isolation, Durability*) is a set of properties of database transactions. In the context of databases, a single logical operation on the data is called a transaction. For example, a transfer of funds from one bank account to another, even involving multiple changes such as debiting one account and crediting another, is a single transaction.

Jim Gray defined these properties of a reliable transaction system in the late 1970s and developed technologies to achieve them automatically.

In 1983, Andreas Reuter and Theo Härder coined the acronym *ACID* to describe them.

Characteristics

The characteristics of these four properties as defined by Reuter and Härder:

Atomicity

Atomicity requires that each transaction be "all or nothing": if one part of the transaction fails, then the entire transaction fails, and the database state is left unchanged. An atomic system must guarantee atomicity in each and every situation, including power failures, errors, and crashes. To the outside world, a committed transaction appears (by its effects on the database) to be indivisible ("atomic"), and an aborted transaction does not happen.

Consistency

The consistency property ensures that any transaction will bring the database from one valid state to another. Any data written to the database must be valid according to all defined rules, including constraints, cascades, triggers, and any combination thereof. This does not guarantee correctness of the transaction in all ways the application programmer might have wanted (that is the responsibility of application-level code) but merely that any programming errors cannot result in the violation of any defined rules.

Isolation

The isolation property ensures that the concurrent execution of transactions results in a system state that would be obtained if transactions were executed serially, i.e., one after the other. Providing isolation is the main goal of concurrency control. Depending on the concurrency control method (i.e., if it uses strict - as opposed to relaxed - serializability), the effects of an incomplete transaction might not even be visible to another transaction.

Durability

The durability property ensures that once a transaction has been committed, it will remain so, even in the event of power loss, crashes, or errors. In a relational database, for instance, once a group of SQL statements execute, the results need to be stored permanently (even if the database crashes immediately thereafter). To defend against power loss, transactions (or their effects) must be recorded in a non-volatile memory.

Examples

The following examples further illustrate the ACID properties. In these examples, the database table has two columns, A and B. An integrity constraint requires that the value in A and the value in B must sum to 100. The following SQL code creates a table as described above:

CREATE TABLE acidtest (A INTEGER, B INTEGER, CHECK (A + B = 100));

Atomicity Failure

In database systems, atomicity (or atomicness; from Greek a-tomos, undividable) is one of the ACID transaction properties. In an atomic transaction, a series of database operations either all occur, or nothing occurs. The series of operations cannot be divided apart and executed partially from each other, which makes the series of operations "indivisible", hence the name. A guarantee of atomicity prevents updates to the database occurring only partially, which can cause greater problems than rejecting the whole series outright. In other words, atomicity means indivisibility and irreducibility.

Consistency Failure

Consistency is a very general term, which demands that the data must meet all validation rules. In the previous example, the validation is a requirement that A + B = 100. Also, it may be inferred that both A and B must be integers. A valid range for A and B may also be inferred. All validation rules must be checked to ensure consistency. Assume that a transaction attempts to subtract 10 from A without altering B. Because consistency is checked after each transaction, it is known that A + B = 100 before the transaction begins. If the transaction removes 10 from A successfully, atomicity will be achieved. However, a validation check will show that A + B = 90, which is inconsistent with the rules of the database. The entire transaction must be cancelled and the affected rows rolled back to their pre-transaction state. If there had been other constraints, triggers, or cascades, every single change operation would have been checked in the same way as above before the transaction was committed.

Isolation Failure

To demonstrate isolation, we assume two transactions execute at the same time, each attempting to modify the same data. One of the two must wait until the other completes in order to maintain isolation.

Consider two transactions. T_1 transfers 10 from A to B. T_2 transfers 10 from B to A. Combined, there are four actions:

- T_1 subtracts 10 from A.

- T_1 adds 10 to B.

- T_2 subtracts 10 from B.

- T_2 adds 10 to A.

If these operations are performed in order, isolation is maintained, although T_2 must wait. Consider what happens if T_1 fails halfway through. The database eliminates T_1's effects, and T_2 sees only valid data.

By interleaving the transactions, the actual order of actions might be:

- T_1 subtracts 10 from A.

- T_2 subtracts 10 from B.

- T_2 adds 10 to A.

- T_1 adds 10 to B.

Again, consider what happens if T_1 fails halfway through. By the time T_1 fails, T_2 has already modified A; it cannot be restored to the value it had before T_1 without leaving an invalid database. This is known as a write-write failure, because two transactions attempted to write to the same data field. In a typical system, the problem would be resolved by reverting to the last known good state, canceling the failed transaction T_1, and restarting the interrupted transaction T_2 from the good state.

Durability Failure

Consider a transaction that transfers 10 from A to B. First it removes 10 from A, then it adds 10 to B. At this point, the user is told the transaction was a success, however the changes are still queued in the disk buffer waiting to be committed to disk. Power fails and the changes are lost. The user assumes (understandably) that the changes have been persisted.

Implementation

Processing a transaction often requires a sequence of operations that is subject to failure for a number of reasons. For instance, the system may have no room left on its disk drives, or it may have used up its allocated CPU time. There are two popular families of techniques: write-ahead logging and shadow paging. In both cases, locks must be acquired on all information to be updated, and depending on the level of isolation, possibly on all data that be read as well. In write ahead logging, atomicity is guaranteed by copying the original (unchanged) data to a log before changing the database. That allows the database to return to a consistent state in the event of a crash. In shadowing, updates are applied to a partial copy of the database, and the new copy is activated when the transaction commits.

Locking vs Multiversioning

Many databases rely upon locking to provide ACID capabilities. Locking means that the transaction marks the data that it accesses so that the DBMS knows not to allow other transactions to modify it until the first transaction succeeds or fails. The lock must always be acquired before processing data, including data that is read but not modified. Non-trivial transactions typically require a large number of locks, resulting in substantial overhead as well as blocking other transactions. For example, if user A is running a transaction that has to read a row of data that user B wants to modify, user B must wait until user A's transaction completes. Two phase locking is often applied to guarantee full isolation.

An alternative to locking is multiversion concurrency control, in which the database provides each reading transaction the prior, unmodified version of data that is being modified by another active transaction. This allows readers to operate without acquiring locks, i.e. writing transactions do not block reading transactions, and readers do not block writers. Going back to the example, when user A's transaction requests data that user B is modifying, the database provides A with the version of that data that existed when user B started his transaction. User A gets a consistent view of the database even if other users are changing data. One implementation, namely snapshot isolation, relaxes the isolation property.

Distributed Transactions

Guaranteeing ACID properties in a distributed transaction across a distributed database, where no single node is responsible for all data affecting a transaction, presents additional complications. Network connections might fail, or one node might successfully complete its part of the transaction and then be required to roll back its changes because of a failure on another node. The two-phase commit protocol provides atomicity for distributed transactions to ensure that each participant in the transaction agrees on whether the transaction should be committed or not. Briefly, in the first phase, one node (the coordinator) interrogates the other nodes (the participants) and only when all reply that they are prepared does the coordinator, in the second phase, formalize the transaction.

Create, Read, Update and Delete

In computer programming, create, read, update and delete (as an acronym CRUD) are the four basic functions of persistent storage. Alternate words are sometimes used when defining the four basic functions of *CRUD*, *retrieve* instead of *read*, *modify* instead of *update*, or *destroy* instead of *delete*. *CRUD* is also sometimes used to describe user interface conventions that facilitate viewing, searching, and changing information; often using computer-based forms and reports. The term was likely first popularized by James Martin in his 1983 book *Managing the Data-base Environment*. The acronym may be extended to CRUDL to cover *listing* of large data sets which bring additional complexity such as pagination when the data sets are too large to hold easily in memory.

Another variation of CRUD is BREAD, an acronym for "Browse, Read, Edit, Add, Delete".This extension is mostly used in context with data protection concepts, when it is legally not allowed to delete data directly. Locking the data prevents the access for users without destroying still needed data. Yet another variation, used before CRUD became more common, is MADS, an acronym for "Modify, Add, Delete, Show."

Database Applications

The acronym CRUD refers to all of the major functions that are implemented in relational database applications. Each letter in the acronym can map to a standard SQL statement, HTTP method (this is typically used to build RESTful APIs) or DDS operation:

Operation	SQL	HTTP	DDS
Create	INSERT	PUT / POST	write
Read (Retrieve)	SELECT	GET	read / take
Update (Modify)	UPDATE	POST / PUT / PATCH	write
Delete (Destroy)	DELETE	DELETE	dispose

The comparison of the database oriented CRUD operations to HTTP methods has some flaws. Strictly speaking, both PUT and POST can create resources; the key difference is that POST leaves it for the server to decide at what URI to make the new resource available, whilst PUT dictates what URI to use; URIs are of course a concept that doesn't really line up with CRUD. The significant point about PUT is that it will replace whatever resource the URI was previously referring to with a brand new version, hence the PUT method being listed for Update as well. PUT is a 'replace' operation, which one could argue is not 'update'.

Although a relational database provides a common persistence layer in software applications, numerous other persistence layers exist. CRUD functionality can be implemented with an object database, an XML database, flat text files, custom file formats, tape, or card, for example.

User Interface

CRUD is also relevant at the user interface level of most applications. For example, in address book software, the basic storage unit is an individual *contact entry*. As a bare minimum, the software must allow the user to:

- Create or add new entries.

- Read, retrieve, search, or view existing entries.

- Update or edit existing entries.

- Delete/deactivate/remove existing entries.

Without at least these four operations, the software cannot be considered complete. Because these operations are so fundamental, they are often documented and described under one comprehensive heading, such as "contact management", "content management" or "contact maintenance" (or "document management" in general, depending on the basic storage unit for the particular application).

Null

The Greek lowercase omega (ω) character is used to represent Null in database theory.

Null (or NULL) is a special marker used in Structured Query Language (SQL) to indicate that a data value does not exist in the database. Introduced by the creator of the relational database model, E. F. Codd, SQL Null serves to fulfil the requirement that all *true relational database management systems (RDBMS)* support a representation of "missing information and inapplicable information". Codd also introduced the use of the lowercase Greek omega (ω) symbol to represent Null in database theory. In SQL, NULL is a reserved word used to identify this marker.

This should not be confused with a value of 0. A null value indicates a lack of a value - a lack of a value is not the same thing as a value of zero in the same way that a lack of an answer is not the same thing as an answer of "no". For example, consider the question "How many books does Juan own?" The answer may be "zero" (we *know* that he owns *none*) or "null" (we *do not know* how many he owns). In a database table, the column reporting this answer would start out with no value (marked by Null), and it would not be updated with the value "zero" until we have ascertained that Juan owns no books.

SQL null is a state, not a value. This usage is quite different from most programming languages, where null means not assigned to a particular instance.

History

E. F. Codd mentioned nulls as a method of representing missing data in the relational model in a 1975 paper in the *FDT Bulletin of ACM-SIGMOD*. Codd's paper that is most commonly cited in relation with the semantics of Null (as adopted in SQL) is his 1979 paper in the *ACM Transactions on Database Systems*, in which he also introduced his Relational Model/Tasmania, although much of the other proposals from the latter paper have remained obscure. Section 2.3 of his 1979 paper details the semantics of Null propagation in arithmetic operations as well as comparisons employing a ternary (three-valued) logic when comparing to nulls; it also details the treatment of Nulls on other set operations (the latter issue still controversial today). In database theory circles, the original proposal of Codd (1975, 1979) is now referred to as "Krokk tables". Codd later reinforced his requirement that all RDBMSs support Null to indicate missing data in a 1985 two-part article published in *ComputerWorld* magazine.

The 1986 SQL standard basically adopted Codd's proposal after an implementation prototype in IBM System R. Although Don Chamberlin recognized nulls (alongside duplicate rows) as one of the most controversial features of SQL, he defended the design of Nulls in SQL invoking the pragmatic arguments that it was the least expensive form of system support for missing information, saving the programmer from many duplicative application-level checks while at the same time providing the database designer with the option not to use Nulls if he so desires; for example, in order to avoid well known anomalies. Chamberlin also argued that besides providing some missing-value functionality, practical experience with Nulls also led to other language features which rely on Nulls, like certain grouping constructs and outer joins. Finally, he argued that in practice Nulls also end up being used as a quick way to patch an existing schema when it needs to evolve beyond its original intent, coding not for missing but rather for inapplicable information; for example, a database that quickly needs to support electric cars while having a miles-per-gallon column.

Codd indicated in his 1990 book *The Relational Model for Database Management, Version 2* that the single Null mandated by the SQL standard was inadequate, and should be replaced by two separate Null-type markers to indicate the reason why data is missing. In Codd's book, these two Null-type markers are referred to as 'A-Values' and 'I-Values', representing 'Missing But Applicable' and 'Missing But Inapplicable', respectively. Codd's recommendation would have required SQL's logic system be expanded to accommodate a four-valued logic system. Because of this additional complexity, the idea of multiple Nulls with different definitions has not gained widespread acceptance in the database practitioners' domain. It remains an active field of research though, with numerous papers still being published.

Challenges

Null has been the focus of controversy and a source of debate because of its associated three-valued logic (3VL), special requirements for its use in SQL joins, and the special handling required by aggregate functions and SQL grouping operators. Computer science professor Ron van der Meyden summarized the various issues as: "The inconsistencies in the SQL standard mean that it is not possible to ascribe any intuitive logical semantics to the treatment of nulls in SQL." Although various proposals have been made for resolving these issues, the complexity of the alternatives has prevented their widespread adoption.

Null Propagation

Arithmetic Operations

Because Null is not a data value, but a marker for an absent value, using mathematical operators on Null gives an unknown result, which is represented by Null. In the following example, multiplying 10 by Null results in Null:

```
10 * NULL        -- Result is NULL
```

This can lead to unanticipated results. For instance, when an attempt is made to divide Null by zero, platforms may return Null instead of throwing an expected "data exception - division by zero". Though this behavior is not defined by the ISO SQL standard many DBMS vendors treat this operation similarly. For instance, the Oracle, PostgreSQL, MySQL Server, and Microsoft SQL Server platforms all return a Null result for the following:

NULL / 0

String Concatenation

String concatenation operations, which are common in SQL, also result in Null when one of the operands is Null. The following example demonstrates the Null result returned by using Null with the SQL || string concatenation operator.

'Fish ' || NULL || 'Chips'   -- Result is NULL

This is not true for all database implementations. In an Oracle RDBMS for example NULL and the empty string are considered the same thing and therefore 'Fish ' || NULL || 'Chips' results in 'Fish Chips'.

Comparisons with NULL and the Three-valued Logic (3VL)

Since Null is not a member of any data domain, it is not considered a "value", but rather a marker (or placeholder) indicating the absence of value. Because of this, comparisons with Null can never result in either True or False, but always in a third logical result, Unknown. The logical result of the expression below, which compares the value 10 to Null, is Unknown:

SELECT 10 = NULL   -- Results in Unknown

However, certain operations on Null can return values if the absent value is not relevant to the outcome of the operation. Consider the following example:

SELECT NULL OR TRUE   -- Results in True

In this case, the fact that the value on the left of OR is unknowable is irrelevant, because the outcome of the OR operation would be True regardless of the value on the left.

SQL implements three logical results, so SQL implementations must provide for a specialized three-valued logic (3VL). The rules governing SQL three-valued logic are shown in the tables below (p and q represent logical states)" The truth tables SQL uses for AND, OR, and NOT correspond to a common fragment of the Kleene and Łukasiewicz three-valued logic (which differ in their definition of implication, however SQL defines no such operation).

p	q	p OR q	p AND q	$p = q$
True	True	True	True	True
True	False	True	False	False
True	Unknown	True	Unknown	Unknown
False	True	True	False	False

False	False	False	False	True
False	Unknown	Unknown	False	Unknown
Unknown	True	True	Unknown	Unknown
Unknown	False	Unknown	False	Unknown
Unknown	Unknown	Unknown	Unknown	Unknown

p	NOT p
True	False
False	True
Unknown	Unknown

Effect of Unknown in WHERE Clauses

SQL three-valued logic is encountered in Data Manipulation Language (DML) in comparison predicates of DML statements and queries. The WHERE clause causes the DML statement to act on only those rows for which the predicate evaluates to True. Rows for which the predicate evaluates to either False or Unknown are not acted on by INSERT, UPDATE, or DELETE DML statements, and are discarded by SELECT queries. Interpreting Unknown and False as the same logical result is a common error encountered while dealing with Nulls. The following simple example demonstrates this fallacy:

SELECT *

FROM t

WHERE i = NULL;

The example query above logically always returns zero rows because the comparison of the i column with Null always returns Unknown, even for those rows where i is Null. The Unknown result causes the SELECT statement to summarily discard each and every row. (However, in practice, some SQL tools will retrieve rows using a comparison with Null.)

Null-specific and 3VL-specific Comparison Predicates

Basic SQL comparison operators always return Unknown when comparing anything with Null, so the SQL standard provides for two special Null-specific comparison predicates. The IS NULL and IS NOT NULL predicates (which use a postfix syntax) test whether data is, or is not, Null.

The SQL standard contains an extension F571 "Truth value tests" that introduces three additional logical unary operators (six in fact, if we count their negation, which is part of their syntax), also using postfix notation. They have the following truth tables:

p	true	false	unknown
p IS TRUE	true	false	false
p IS NOT TRUE	false	true	true
p IS FALSE	false	true	false
p IS NOT FALSE	true	false	true

p IS UNKNOWN	false	false	true
p IS NOT UNKNOWN	true	true	false

The F571 extension is orthogonal to the presence of the boolean datatype in SQL and, despite syntactic similarities, F571 does not introduce boolean or three-valued literals in the language. The F571 extension was actually present in SQL92, well before the boolean datatype was introduced to the standard in 1999. The F571 extension is implemented by few systems however; PostgreSQL is one of those implementing it.

The addition of IS UNKNOWN to the other operators of SQL's three-valued logic makes the SQL three-valued logic functionally complete, meaning its logical operators can express (in combination) any conceivable three-valued logical function.

On systems which don't support the F571 extension, it is possible to emulate IS UNKNOWN p by going over every argument that could make the expression p Unknown and test those arguments with IS NULL or other NULL-specific functions, although this may be more cumbersome.

Law of the Excluded Fourth (in WHERE Clauses)

In SQL's three-valued logic the law of the excluded middle, p OR NOT p, no longer evaluates to true for all p. More precisely, in SQL's three-valued logic p OR NOT p is unknown precisely when p is unknown and true otherwise. Because direct comparisons with Null result in the unknown logical value, the following query.

SELECT * FROM stuff WHERE (x = 10) OR NOT (x = 10);

is not equivalent in SQL with

SELECT * FROM stuff;

if the column x contains any Nulls; in that case the second query would return some rows the first one does not return, namely all those in which x is Null. In classical two-valued logic, the law of the excluded middle would allow the simplification of the WHERE clause predicate, in fact its elimination. Attempting to apply the law of the excluded middle to SQL's 3VL is effectively a false dichotomy. The second query is actually equivalent with:

SELECT * FROM stuff;

-- is (because of 3VL) equivalent to:

SELECT * FROM stuff WHERE (x = 10) OR NOT (x = 10) OR x IS NULL;

Thus, to correctly simplify the first statement in SQL requires that we return all rows in which x is not null.

SELECT * FROM stuff WHERE x IS NOT NULL;

In view of the above, observe that for SQL's WHERE clause a tautology similar to the law of excluded middle can be written. Assuming the IS UNKNOWN operator is present, p OR (NOT p) OR (p IS UNKNOWN) is true for every predicate p. Among logicians, this is called law of excluded fourth.

There are some SQL expressions in which it is less obvious where the false dilemma occurs, for example:

SELECT 'ok' WHERE 1 NOT IN (SELECT CAST (NULL AS INTEGER))

UNION

SELECT 'ok' WHERE 1 IN (SELECT CAST (NULL AS INTEGER));

produces no rows because IN is translates to an iterated version of equality over the argument set and 1<>NULL is Unknown, just as a 1=NULL is Unknown. (The CAST in this example is needed only in some SQL implementations like PostgreSQL, which would reject it with a type checking error otherwise. In many systems plain SELECT NULL works in the subquery.) The missing case above is of course:

SELECT 'ok' WHERE (1 IN (SELECT CAST (NULL AS INTEGER))) IS UNKNOWN;

Effect of Null and Unknown in Other Constructs

Joins

Joins evaluate using the same comparison rules as for WHERE clauses. Therefore, care must be taken when using nullable columns in SQL join criteria. In particular a table containing any nulls is *not equal* with a natural self-join of itself, meaning that whereas $R \setminus R = R$ is true for any relation R in relational algebra, a SQL self-join will exclude all rows having a Null anywhere. An example of this behavior is given in the section analyzing the missing-value semantics of Nulls.

The SQL COALESCE function or CASE expressions can be used to "simulate" Null equality in join criteria, and the IS NULL and IS NOT NULL predicates can be used in the join criteria as well. The following predicate tests for equality of the values A and B and treats Nulls as being equal.

(A = B) OR (A IS NULL AND B IS NULL)

CASE Expressions

SQL provides two flavours of conditional expressions. One is called "simple CASE" and operates like a switch statement. The other is called a "searched CASE" in the standard, and operates like an if...elseif.

The simple CASE expressions use implicit equality comparisons which operate under the same rules as the DML WHERE clause rules for Null. Thus, a *simple CASE expression* cannot check for the existence of Null directly. A check for Null in a simple CASE expression always results in Unknown, as in the following:

SELECT CASE i WHEN NULL THEN 'Is Null' -- This will never be returned

      WHEN   0 THEN 'Is Zero' -- This will be returned when i = 0

      WHEN   1 THEN 'Is One' -- This will be returned when i = 1

      END

FROM t;

Because the expression i = NULL evaluates to Unknown no matter what value column *i* contains (even if it contains Null), the string 'Is Null' will never be returned.

On the other hand, a "searched" CASE expression can use predicates like IS NULL and IS NOT NULL in its conditions. The following example shows how to use a searched CASE expression to properly check for Null:

SELECT CASE WHEN i IS NULL THEN 'Null Result' -- This will be returned when i is NULL

     WHEN   i = 0 THEN 'Zero'   -- This will be returned when i = 0

     WHEN   i = 1 THEN 'One'   -- This will be returned when i = 1

     END

FROM t;

In the searched CASE expression, the string 'Null Result' is returned for all rows in which *i* is Null.

Oracle's dialect of SQL provides a built-in function DECODE which can be used instead of the simple CASE expressions and considers two nulls equal.

SELECT DECODE(i, NULL, 'Null Result', 0, 'Zero', 1, 'One') FROM t;

Finally, all these constructs return a NULL if no match is found; they have a default ELSE NULL clause.

IF Statements in Procedural Extensions

SQL/PSM (SQL Persistent Stored Modules) defines procedural extensions for SQL, such as the IF statement. However, the major SQL vendors have historically included their own proprietary procedural extensions. Procedural extensions for looping and comparisons operate under Null comparison rules similar to those for DML statements and queries. The following code fragment, in ISO SQL standard format, demonstrates the use of Null 3VL in an IF statement.

IF i = NULL THEN

    SELECT 'Result is True'

ELSEIF NOT(i = NULL) THEN

    SELECT 'Result is False'

ELSE

    SELECT 'Result is Unknown';

The IF statement performs actions only for those comparisons that evaluate to True. For statements that evaluate to False or Unknown, the IF statement passes control to the ELSEIF clause, and finally to the ELSE clause. The result of the code above will always be the message 'Result is Unknown' since the comparisons with Null always evaluate to Unknown.

Analysis of SQL Null Missing-value Semantics

The groundbreaking work of T. Imielinski and W. Lipski (1984) provided a framework in which to evaluate the intended semantics of various proposals to implement missing-value semantics. This section roughly follows chapter 19 the "Alice" textbook. A similar presentation appears in the review of Ron van der Meyden, §10.4.

In Selections and Projections: Weak Representation

Constructs representing missing information, such as Codd tables, are actually intended to represent a set of relations, one for each possible instantiation of their parameters; in the case of Codd tables, this means replacement of Nulls with some concrete value. For example,

This Codd table	may represent	this relation	or equally well	this relation

Emp	
Name	**Age**
George	43
Harriet	NULL
Charles	56

EmpH22	
Name	**Age**
George	43
Harriet	22
Charles	56

EmpH37	
Name	**Age**
George	43
Harriet	37
Charles	56

A construct (such as a Codd table) is said to be a *strong representation* system (of missing information) if any answer to a query made on the construct can be particularized to obtain an answer for *any* corresponding query on the relations it represents, which are seen as models of the construct. More precisely, if q is a query formula in the relational algebra (of "pure" relations) and if $\overline{q}$ is its lifting to a construct intended to represent missing information, a strong representation has the property that for any query q and (table) construct T, $\overline{q}$ lifts *all* the answers to the construct, i.e.:

$$\text{Models}(\overline{q}(T)) = \{q(R)|\ R \in \text{Models}(T)\}$$

(The above has to hold for queries taking any number of tables as arguments, but the restriction to one table suffices for this discussion.) Clearly Codd tables do not have this strong property if selections and projections are considered as part of the query language. For example, *all* the answers to

SELECT * FROM Emp WHERE Age = 22;

should include the possibility that a relation like EmpH22 may exist. However Codd tables cannot represent the disjunction "result with possibly 0 or 1 rows". A device, mostly of theoretical interest, called conditional table (or c-table) can however represent such an answer:

Result		
Name	**Age**	**condition**
Harriet	ω_1	$\omega_1 = 22$

where the condition column is interpreted as the row doesn't exist if the condition is false. It turns out that because the formulas in the condition column of a c-table can be arbitrary propositional logic formulas, an algorithm for the problem whether a c-table represents some concrete relation has a co-NP-complete complexity, thus is of little practical worth.

A weaker notion of representation is therefore desirable. Imielinski and Lipski introduced the notion of *weak representation*, which essentially allows (lifted) queries over a construct to return a representation only for *sure* information, i.e. if it's valid for all "possible world" instantiations (models) of the construct. Concretely, a construct is a weak representation system if,

$$\bigcap \text{Models}(\overline{q}(T)) = \bigcap \{q(R)|\ R \in \text{Models}(T)\}$$

The right-hand side of the above equation is the *sure* information, i.e. information which can be certainly extracted from the database regardless of what values are used to replace Nulls in the database. In the example we considered above, it's easy to see that the intersection of all possible models (i.e. the sure information) of the query selecting WHERE Age = 22 is actually empty because, for instance, the (unlifted) query returns no rows for the relation EmpH37. More generally, it was shown by Imielinski and Lipski that Codd tables are a weak representation system if the query language is restricted to projections, selections (and renaming of columns). However, as soon as we add either joins or unions to the query language, even this weak property is lost, as evidenced in the next section.

If Joins or Unions are Considered: Not Even Weak Representation

Let us consider the following query over the same Codd table Emp from the previous section:

SELECT Name FROM Emp WHERE Age = 22;

UNION

SELECT Name FROM Emp WHERE Age <> 22;

Whatever concrete value one would choose for the NULL age of Harriet, the above query will return the full column of names of any model of Emp, but when the (lifted) query is run on Emp itself, Harriet will always be missing, i.e. we have:

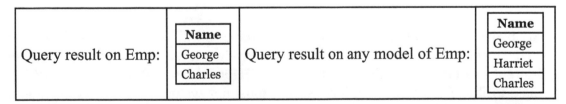

Thus when unions are added to the query language, Codd tables are not even a weak representation system of missing information, meaning that queries over them don't even report all *sure* information. It's important to note here that semantics of UNION on Nulls, which are discussed in a later section, did not even come into play in this query. The "forgetful" nature of the two sub-queries was all that it took to guarantee that some sure information went unreported when the above query was run on the Codd table Emp.

For natural joins, the example needed to show that sure information may be unreported by some query is slightly more complicated.

J

F1	F2	F3
11	NULL	13
21	NULL	23
31	32	33

Consider the table and the query

SELECT F1, F3 FROM

(SELECT F1, F2 FROM J) AS F12

NATURAL JOIN

(SELECT F2, F3 FROM J) AS F23;

Query result on J:			Query result on any model of J:	

	F1	F3
	31	33

F1	F3
11	13
21	23
31	33

The intuition for what happens above is that the Codd tables representing the projections in the sub-queries lose track of the fact that the Nulls in the columns F12.F2 and F23.F2 are actually copies of the originals in the table J. This observation suggests that a relatively simple improvement of Codd tables (which works correctly for this example) would be to use *Skolem constants* (meaning Skolem functions which are also constant functions), say ω_{12} and ω_{22} instead of a single NULL symbol. Such an approach, called v-tables or Naive tables, is computationally less expensive that the c-tables discussed above. However it is still not a complete solution for incomplete information in the sense that v-tables are only a weak representation for queries not using any negations in selection (and not using any set difference either). The first example considered in this section is using a negative selection clause, WHERE Age <> 22, so it is also an example where v-tables queries would not report sure information.

Check Constraints and Foreign Keys

The primary place in which SQL three-valued logic intersects with SQL Data Definition Language (DDL) is in the form of check constraints. A check constraint placed on a column operates under a slightly different set of rules than those for the DML WHERE clause. While a DML WHERE clause must evaluate to True for a row, a check constraint must not evaluate to False. (From a logic perspective, the designated values are True and Unknown.) This means that a check constraint will succeed if the result of the check is either True or Unknown. The following example table with a check constraint will prohibit any integer values from being inserted into column i, but will allow Null to be inserted since the result of the check will always evaluate to Unknown for Nulls.

CREATE TABLE t (

 i INTEGER,

 CONSTRAINT ck_i CHECK (i < 0 AND i = 0 AND i > 0));

Because of the change in designated values relative to the WHERE clause, from a logic perspective the law of excluded middle is a tautology for CHECK constraints, meaning CHECK (p OR NOT p) always succeeds. Furthermore, assuming Nulls are to be interpreted as existing but unknown values, some pathological CHECKs like the one above allow insertion of Nulls that could never be replaced by any non-null value.

In order to constrain a column to reject Nulls, the NOT NULL constraint can be applied, as shown in the example below. The NOT NULL constraint is semantically equivalent to a check constraint with an IS NOT NULL predicate.

CREATE TABLE t (i INTEGER NOT NULL);

By default check constraints against foreign keys succeed if any of the fields in such keys are Null. For example, the table

CREATE TABLE Books

(title VARCHAR(100),

  author_last VARCHAR(20),

  author_first VARCHAR(20),

FOREIGN KEY (author_last, author_first)

  REFERENCES Authors(last_name, first_name));

would allow insertion of rows where author_last or author_first are NULL irrespective of how the table Authors is defined or what it contains. More precisely, a null in any of these fields would allow any value in the other one, even on that is not found in Authors table. For example, if Authors contained only ('Doe', 'John'), then ('Smith', NULL) would satisfy the foreign key constraint. SQL-92 added two extra options for narrowing down the matches in such cases. If MATCH PARTIAL is added after the REFERENCES declaration then any non-null must match the foreign key, e. g. ('Doe', NULL) would still match, but ('Smith', NULL) would not. Finally, if MATCH FULL is added then ('Smith', NULL) would not match the constraint either, but (NULL, NULL) would still match it.

Outer Joins

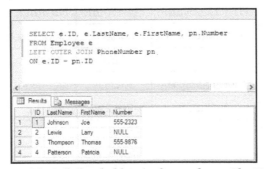

Example SQL outer join query with Null placeholders in the result set. The Null markers are represented by the word NULL in place of data in the results. Results are from Microsoft SQL Server, as shown in SQL Server Management Studio.

SQL outer joins, including left outer joins, right outer joins, and full outer joins, automatically produce Nulls as placeholders for missing values in related tables. For left outer joins, for instance, Nulls are produced in place of rows missing from the table appearing on the right-hand side of the LEFT OUTER JOIN operator. The following simple example uses two tables to demonstrate Null placeholder production in a left outer join.

The first table (Employee) contains employee ID numbers and names, while the second table (PhoneNumber) contains related employee ID numbers and phone numbers, as shown below.

Employee		
ID	**LastName**	**FirstName**
1	Johnson	Joe
2	Lewis	Larry
3	Thompson	Thomas
4	Patterson	Patricia

PhoneNumber	
ID	**Number**
1	555-2323
3	555-9876

The following sample SQL query performs a left outer join on these two tables.

SELECT e.ID, e.LastName, e.FirstName, pn.Number

FROM Employee e

LEFT OUTER JOIN PhoneNumber pn

ON e.ID = pn.ID;

The result set generated by this query demonstrates how SQL uses Null as a placeholder for values missing from the right-hand (PhoneNumber) table, as shown below.

Query result			
ID	**LastName**	**FirstName**	**Number**
1	Johnson	Joe	555-2323
2	Lewis	Larry	**NULL**
3	Thompson	Thomas	555-9876
4	Patterson	Patricia	**NULL**

Aggregate Functions

SQL defines aggregate functions to simplify server-side aggregate calculations on data. Except for the COUNT(*) function, all aggregate functions perform a Null-elimination step, so that Nulls are not included in the final result of the calculation.

Note that the elimination of Null is not equivalent to replacing Null with zero. For example, in the following table, AVG(i) (the average of the values of i) will give a different result from that of AVG(j):

Table	
i	**j**
150	150
200	200
250	250
NULL	0

Here AVG(i) is 200 (the average of 150, 200, and 250), while AVG(j) is 150 (the average of 150, 200, 250, and 0). A well-known side effect of this is that in SQL AVG(z) is not equivalent with SUM(z)/COUNT(*).

When two Nulls are Equal: Grouping, Sorting, and Some Set Operations

Because SQL:2003 defines all Null markers as being unequal to one another, a special definition was required in order to group Nulls together when performing certain operations. SQL defines "any two values that are equal to one another, or any two Nulls", as "not distinct". This definition of *not distinct* allows SQL to group and sort Nulls when the GROUP BY clause (and other keywords that perform grouping) are used.

Other SQL operations, clauses, and keywords use "not distinct" in their treatment of Nulls. These include the following:

- PARTITION BY clause of ranking and windowing functions like ROW_NUMBER.

- UNION, INTERSECT, and EXCEPT operator, which treat NULLs as the same for row comparison/elimination purposes.

- DISTINCT keyword used in SELECT queries.

The principle that Nulls aren't equal to each other (but rather that the result is Unknown) is effectively violated in the SQL specification for the UNION operator, which does identify nulls with each other. Consequently, some set operations in SQL, like union or difference, may produce results not representing sure information, unlike operations involving explicit comparisons with NULL (e.g. those in a WHERE clause discussed above). In Codd's 1979 proposal (which was basically adopted by SQL92) this semantic inconsistency is rationalized by arguing that removal of duplicates in set operations happens "at a lower level of detail than equality testing in the evaluation of retrieval operations."

The SQL standard does not explicitly define a default sort order for Nulls. Instead, on conforming systems, Nulls can be sorted before or after all data values by using the NULLS FIRST or NULLS LAST clauses of the ORDER BY list, respectively. Not all DBMS vendors implement this functionality, however. Vendors who do not implement this functionality may specify different treatments for Null sorting in the DBMS.

Effect on Index Operation

Some SQL products do not index keys containing NULLs. For instance, PostgreSQL versions prior to 8.3 did not, with the documentation for a B-tree index stating that.

B-trees can handle equality and range queries on data that can be sorted into some ordering. In particular, the PostgreSQL query planner will consider using a B-tree index whenever an indexed column is involved in a comparison using one of these operators: $<$ $\leq$ $=$ $\geq$ $>$

Constructs equivalent to combinations of these operators, such as BETWEEN and IN, can also be implemented with a B-tree index search. (But note that IS NULL is not equivalent to = and is not indexable.)

In cases where the index enforces uniqueness, NULLs are excluded from the index and uniqueness is not enforced between NULLs. Again, quoting from the PostgreSQL documentation:

When an index is declared unique, multiple table rows with equal indexed values will not be allowed. Nulls are not considered equal. A multicolumn unique index will only reject cases where all of the indexed columns are equal in two rows.

This is consistent with the SQL:2003-defined behavior of scalar Null comparisons.

Another method of indexing Nulls involves handling them as *not distinct* in accordance with the SQL:2003-defined behavior. For example, Microsoft SQL Server documentation states the following:

For indexing purposes, NULLs compare as equal. Therefore, a unique index, or UNIQUE constraint, cannot be created if the keys are NULL in more than one row. Select columns that are defined as NOT NULL when columns for a unique index or unique constraint are chosen.

Both of these indexing strategies are consistent with the SQL:2003-defined behavior of Nulls. Because indexing methodologies are not explicitly defined by the SQL:2003 standard, indexing strategies for Nulls are left entirely to the vendors to design and implement.

Null-handling Functions

SQL defines two functions to explicitly handle Nulls: NULLIF and COALESCE. Both functions are abbreviations for searched CASE expressions.

NULLIF

The NULLIF function accepts two parameters. If the first parameter is equal to the second parameter, NULLIF returns Null. Otherwise, the value of the first parameter is returned.

NULLIF(value1, value2)

Thus, NULLIF is an abbreviation for the following CASE expression:

CASE WHEN value1 = value2 THEN NULL ELSE value1 END

COALESCE

The COALESCE function accepts a list of parameters, returning the first non-Null value from the list:

COALESCE(value1, value2, value3, ...)

COALESCE is defined as shorthand for the following SQL CASE expression:

CASE WHEN value1 IS NOT NULL THEN value1

WHEN value2 IS NOT NULL THEN value2

WHEN value3 IS NOT NULL THEN value3

...

END

Some SQL DBMSs implement vendor-specific functions similar to COALESCE. Some systems (e.g. Transact-SQL) implement an ISNULL function, or other similar functions that are functionally similar to COALESCE.

NVL

The Oracle NVL function accepts two parameters. It returns the first non-NULL parameter or NULL if all parameters are NULL.

A COALESCE expression can be converted into an equivalent NVL expression thus:

COALESCE (val1, ... , val{n})

turns into:

NVL(val1 , NVL(val2 , NVL(val3 , ... , NVL (val{n-1} , val{n}) ...)))

A use case of this function is to replace in an expression a NULL by a value like in NVL(SALARY, 0) which says, 'if SALARY is NULL, replace it with the value 0'.

There is, however, one notable exception. In most implementations, COALESCE evaluates its parameters until it reaches the first non-NULL one, while NVL evaluates all of its parameters. This is important for several reasons. A parameter *after* the first non-NULL parameter could be a function, which could either be computationally expensive, invalid, or could create unexpected side effects.

Data Typing of Null and Unknown

The NULL literal is untyped in SQL, meaning that it is not designated as an integer, character, or any other specific data type. Because of this, it is sometimes mandatory (or desirable) to explicitly convert Nulls to a specific data type. For instance, if overloaded functions are supported by the RDBMS, SQL might not be able to automatically resolve to the correct function without knowing the data types of all parameters, including those for which Null is passed.

Conversion from the NULL literal to a Null of a specific type is possible using the CAST introduced in SQL-92. For example:

CAST (NULL AS INTEGER)

represents an absent value of type INTEGER.

The actual typing of Unknown (distinct or not from NULL itself) varies between SQL implementations. For example, the following:

SELECT 'ok' WHERE (NULL <> 1) IS NULL;

parses and executes successfully in some environments (e.g. SQLite or PostgreSQL) which unify a NULL boolean with Unknown but fails to parse in others (e.g. in SQL Server Compact). MySQL behaves similarly to PostgreSQL in this regard (with the minor exception that MySQL regards TRUE and FALSE as no different from the ordinary integers 1 and 0). PostgreSQL additionally implements a IS UNKNOWN predicate, which can be used to test whether a three-value logical outcome is Unknown, although this is merely syntactic sugar.

BOOLEAN Data Type

The ISO SQL:1999 standard introduced the BOOLEAN data type to SQL, however it's still just an optional, non-core feature, coded T031.

When restricted by a NOT NULL constraint, the SQL BOOLEAN works like the Boolean type from other languages. Unrestricted however, the BOOLEAN datatype, despite its name, can hold the truth values TRUE, FALSE, and UNKNOWN, all of which are defined as boolean literals according to the standard. The standard also asserts that NULL and UNKNOWN "may be used interchangeably to mean exactly the same thing".

The Boolean type has been subject of criticism, particularly because of the mandated behavior of the UNKNOWN literal, which is never equal to itself because of the identification with NULL.

As discussed above, in the PostgreSQL implementation of SQL, Null is used to represent all UNKNOWN results, including the UNKNOWN BOOLEAN. PostgreSQL does not implement the UNKNOWN literal (although it does implement the IS UNKNOWN operator, which is an orthogonal feature.) Most other major vendors do not support the Boolean type (as defined in T031) as of 2012. The procedural part of Oracle's PL/SQL supports BOOLEAN however variables; these can also be assigned NULL and the value is considered the same as UNKNOWN.

Controversy

Common Mistakes

Misunderstanding of how Null works is the cause of a great number of errors in SQL code, both in ISO standard SQL statements and in the specific SQL dialects supported by real-world database management systems. These mistakes are usually the result of confusion between Null and either 0 (zero) or an empty string (a string value with a length of zero, represented in SQL as ''). Null is defined by the ISO SQL standard as different from both an empty string and the numerical value 0, however. While Null indicates the absence of any value, the empty string and numerical zero both represent actual values.

A classic error is attempting to use the equality operator to find NULLs. Most SQL implementations will execute the following query as syntactically correct (therefore give no error message) but it never returns any rows, regardless of whether NULLs do exist in the table.

SELECT *

FROM sometable

WHERE num = NULL; -- Should be "WHERE num IS NULL"

In a related, but more subtle example, a WHERE clause or conditional statement might compare a column's value with a constant. It is often incorrectly assumed that a missing value would be "less than" or "not equal to" a constant if that field contains Null, but, in fact, such expressions return Unknown. An example is below:

SELECT *

FROM sometable

WHERE num <> 1; -- Rows where num is NULL will not be returned,

        -- contrary to many users' expectations.

Similarly, Nulls are often confused with empty strings. Consider the LENGTH function, which returns the number of characters in a string. When a Null is passed into this function, the function returns Null. This can lead to unexpected results, if users are not well versed in 3-value logic. An example is below:

SELECT *

FROM sometable

WHERE LENGTH(string) < 20; -- Rows where string is NULL will not be returned.

This is complicated by the fact that in some database interface programs (or even database implementations like Oracle's), NULL is reported as an empty string, and empty strings may be incorrectly stored as NULL.

Criticisms

The ISO SQL implementation of Null is the subject of criticism, debate and calls for change. In *The Relational Model for Database Management: Version 2*, Codd suggested that the SQL implementation of Null was flawed and should be replaced by two distinct Null-type markers. The markers he proposed were to stand for *"Missing but Applicable"* and *"Missing but Inapplicable"*, known as *A-values* and *I-values*, respectively. Codd's recommendation, if accepted, would have required the implementation of a four-valued logic in SQL. Others have suggested adding additional Null-type markers to Codd's recommendation to indicate even more reasons that a data value might be

"Missing", increasing the complexity of SQL's logic system. At various times, proposals have also been put forth to implement multiple user-defined Null markers in SQL. Because of the complexity of the Null-handling and logic systems required to support multiple Null markers, none of these proposals have gained widespread acceptance.

Chris Date and Hugh Darwen, authors of *The Third Manifesto*, have suggested that the SQL Null implementation is inherently flawed and should be eliminated altogether, pointing to inconsistencies and flaws in the implementation of SQL Null-handling (particularly in aggregate functions) as proof that the entire concept of Null is flawed and should be removed from the relational model. Others, like author Fabian Pascal, have stated a belief that "how the function calculation should treat missing values is not governed by the relational model."

Closed World Assumption

Another point of conflict concerning Nulls is that they violate the closed world assumption model of relational databases by introducing an open world assumption into it. The closed world assumption, as it pertains to databases, states that "Everything stated by the database, either explicitly or implicitly, is true; everything else is false." This view assumes that the knowledge of the world stored within a database is complete. Nulls, however, operate under the open world assumption, in which some items stored in the database are considered unknown, making the database's stored knowledge of the world incomplete.

Candidate Key

In the relational model of databases, a candidate key of a relation is a minimal superkey for that relation; that is, a set of attributes such that:

1. The relation does not have two distinct tuples (i.e. rows or records in common database language) with the same values for these attributes (which means that the set of attributes is a superkey).

2. There is no proper subset of these attributes for which (1) holds (which means that the set is minimal).

The constituent attributes are called prime attributes. Conversely, an attribute that does not occur in ANY candidate key is called a non-prime attribute.

Since a relation contains no duplicate tuples, the set of all its attributes is a superkey if NULL values are not used. It follows that every relation will have at least one candidate key.

The candidate keys of a relation tell us all the possible ways we can identify its tuples. As such they are an important concept for the design of database schema.

Example

The definition of candidate keys can be illustrated with the following (abstract) example. Consider a relation variable (relvar) R with attributes (A, B, C, D) that has only the following two legal values $r1$ and $r2$:

r1			
A	**B**	**C**	**D**
a1	b1	c1	d1
a1	b2	c2	d1
a2	b1	c2	d1

r2			
A	**B**	**C**	**D**
a1	b1	c1	d1
a1	b2	c2	d1
a1	b1	c2	d2

Here $r2$ differs from $r1$ only in the A and D values of the last tuple.

For $r1$ the following sets have the uniqueness property, i.e., there are no two distinct tuples in the instance with the same values for the attributes in the set:

{A,B}, {A,C}, {B,C}, {A,B,C}, {A,B,D}, {A,C,D}, {B,C,D}, {A,B,C,D}

For $r2$ the uniqueness property holds for the following sets:

{B,C}, {B,D}, {C,D}, {A,B,C}, {A,B,D}, {A,C,D}, {B,C,D}, {A,B,C,D}

Since superkeys of a relvar are those sets of attributes that have the uniqueness property for *all* legal values of that relvar and because we assume that $r1$ and $r2$ are all the legal values that R can take, we can determine the set of superkeys of R by taking the intersection of the two lists:

{B,C}, {A,B,C}, {A,B,D}, {A,C,D}, {B,C,D}, {A,B,C,D}

Finally we need to select those sets for which there is no proper subset in the list, which are in this case:

{B,C}, {A,B,D}, {A,C,D}

These are indeed the candidate keys of relvar R.

We have to consider *all* the relations that might be assigned to a relvar to determine whether a certain set of attributes is a candidate key. For example, if we had considered only $r1$ then we would have concluded that {A,B} is a candidate key, which is incorrect. However, we *might* be able to conclude from such a relation that a certain set is *not* a candidate key, because that set does not have the uniqueness property (example {A,D} for $r1$). Note that the existence of a proper subset of a set that has the uniqueness property *cannot* in general be used as evidence that the superset is not a candidate key. In particular, note that in the case of an empty relation, every subset of the heading has the uniqueness property, including the empty set.

Determining Candidate Keys

The set of all candidate keys can be computed e.g. from the set of functional dependencies. To this end we need to define the attribute closure for an attribute set . The set contains all attributes that are functionally implied by .

It is quite simple to find a single candidate key. We start with a set of attributes and try to remove successively each attribute. If after removing an attribute the attribute closure stays the same, then this attribute is not necessary and we can remove it permanently. We call the result . If is the set of all attributes, then is a candidate key.

Actually we can detect every candidate key with this procedure by simply trying every possible order of removing attributes. However there are many more permutations of attributes than sub-sets. That is, many attribute orders will lead to the same candidate key.

There is a fundamental difficulty for efficient algorithms for candidate key computation: Certain sets of functional dependencies lead to exponentially many candidate keys. Consider the functional dependencies which yields candidate keys: . That is, the best we can expect is an algorithm that is efficient with respect to the number of candidate keys.

The following algorithm actually runs in polynomial time in the number of candidate keys and functional dependencies:

```
function find_candidate_keys(A, F)

  /* A is the set of all attributes and F is the set of functional dependencies */

  K := minimize(A);

  n := 1; /* Number of Keys known so far */

  i := 0; /* Currently processed key */

  while i < n do

   foreach α → β ∈ F do

     /* Build a new potential key from the previous known key and the current FD */

     S := α ∪ (K[i] – β);

     /* Search whether the new potential key is part of the already known keys */

     found := false;

     for j := 0 to n-1 do

      if K[j] ⊇ S then found := true;

     /* If not, add if

     if not found then
```

K[n] := minimize(S);

n := n + 1;

i := i + 1

return K

The idea behind the algorithm is that given a candidate key and a functional dependency , the reverse application of the functional dependency yields the set , which is a key, too. It may however be covered by other already known candidate keys. (The algorithm checks this case using the 'found' variable.) If not, then minimizing the new key yields a new candidate key. The key insight is that all candidate keys can be created this way.

Foreign Key

In the context of relational databases, a foreign key is a field (or collection of fields) in one table that uniquely identifies a row of another table or the same table. In simpler words, the foreign key is defined in a second table, but it refers to the primary key in the first table. For example, a table called Employee has a primary key called employee_id. Another table called Employee Details has a foreign key which references employee_id in order to uniquely identify the relationship between both the tables.

The table containing the foreign key is called the child table, and the table containing the candidate key is called the referenced or parent table. In database relational modeling and implementation, a unique key is a set of zero or more attributes, the value(s) of which are guaranteed to be unique for each tuple (row) in a relation. The value or combination of values of unique key attributes for any tuple cannot be duplicated for any other tuple in that relation.

When more than one column is combined to form a unique key, their combined value is used to access each row and maintain uniqueness. Values are not combined, they are compared using their data types.

Since the purpose of the foreign key is to identify a particular row of the referenced table, it is generally required that the foreign key is equal to the candidate key in some row of the primary table, or else have no value (the NULL value.). This rule is called a referential integrity constraint between the two tables. Because violations of these constraints can be the source of many database problems, most database management systems provide mechanisms to ensure that every non-null foreign key corresponds to a row of the referenced table.

For example, consider a database with two tables: a CUSTOMER table that includes all customer data and an ORDER table that includes all customer orders. Suppose the business requires that each order must refer to a single customer. To reflect this in the database, a foreign key column is added to the ORDER table (e.g., CUSTOMERID), which references the primary key of CUSTOMER (e.g. ID). Because the primary key of a table must be unique, and because CUSTOMERID only contains values from that primary key field, we may assume that, when it has a value, CUSTOME-RID will identify the particular customer which placed the order. However, this can no longer be assumed if the ORDER table is not kept up to date when rows of the CUSTOMER table are deleted or the ID column altered, and working with these tables may become more difficult. Many real world databases work around this problem by 'inactivating' rather than physically deleting master table foreign keys, or by complex update programs that modify all references to a foreign key when a change is needed.

Foreign keys play an essential role in database design. One important part of database design is making sure that relationships between real-world entities are reflected in the database by references, using foreign keys to refer from one table to another. Another important part of database design is database normalization, in which tables are broken apart and foreign keys make it possible for them to be reconstructed.

Multiple rows in the referencing (or child) table may refer to the same row in the referenced (or parent) table. In this case, the relationship between the two tables is called a one to many relationship between the referenced table and the referencing table.

In addition, the child and parent table may, in fact, be the same table, i.e. the foreign key refers back to the same table. Such a foreign key is known in SQL:2003 as a self-referencing or recursive foreign key. In database management systems, this is often accomplished by linking a first and second reference to the same table.

A table may have multiple foreign keys, and each foreign key can have a different parent table. Each foreign key is enforced independently by the database system. Therefore, cascading relationships between tables can be established using foreign keys.

Defining Foreign Keys

Foreign keys are defined in the ISO SQL Standard, through a FOREIGN KEY constraint. The syntax to add such a constraint to an existing table is defined in SQL:2003 as shown below. Omitting the column list in the REFERENCES clause implies that the foreign key shall reference the primary key of the referenced table.

ALTER TABLE <table identifier>

  ADD [CONSTRAINT <constraint identifier>]

    FOREIGN KEY (<column expression> {, <column expression>}...)

    REFERENCES <table identifier> [(<column expression> {, <column expression>}...)]

    [ON UPDATE <referential action>]

    [ON DELETE <referential action>]

Likewise, foreign keys can be defined as part of the CREATE TABLE SQL statement.

CREATE TABLE table_name (

  id   INTEGER PRIMARY KEY,

col2 CHARACTER VARYING(20),

col3 INTEGER,

...

FOREIGN KEY(col3)

  REFERENCES other_table(key_col) ON DELETE CASCADE,

...)

If the foreign key is a single column only, the column can be marked as such using the following syntax:

CREATE TABLE table_name (

  id   INTEGER PRIMARY KEY,

  col2 CHARACTER VARYING(20),

  col3 INTEGER REFERENCES other_table(column_name),

  ...)

Foreign keys can be defined with a stored procedure statement.

sp_foreignkey tabname, pktabname, col1 [, col2] ... [, col8]

- Tabname: the name of the table or view that contains the foreign key to be defined.

- Pktabname: the name of the table or view that has the primary key to which the foreign key applies. The primary key must already be defined.

- Col1: the name of the first column that makes up the foreign key. The foreign key must have at least one column and can have a maximum of eight columns.

Referential Actions

Because the database management system enforces referential constraints, it must ensure data integrity if rows in a referenced table are to be deleted (or updated). If dependent rows in referencing tables still exist, those references have to be considered. SQL:2003 specifies 5 different referential actions that shall take place in such occurrences:

- CASCADE

- RESTRICT

- NO ACTION

- SET NULL

- SET DEFAULT

CASCADE

Whenever rows in the master (referenced) table are deleted (or updated), the respective rows of the child (referencing) table with a matching foreign key column will be deleted (or updated) as well. This is called a cascade delete (or update).

RESTRICT

A value cannot be updated or deleted when a row exists in a referencing or child table that references the value in the referenced table.

Similarly, a row cannot be deleted as long as there is a reference to it from a referencing or child table.

To understand RESTRICT (and CASCADE) better, it may be helpful to notice the following difference, which might not be immediately clear. The referential action CASCADE modifies the "behavior" of the (child) table itself where the word CASCADE is used. For example, ON DELETE CASCADE effectively says "When the referenced row is deleted from the other table (master table), then delete *also from me*". However, the referential action RESTRICT modifies the "behavior" of the master table, *not* the child table, although the word RESTRICT appears in the child table and not in the master table! So, ON DELETE RESTRICT effectively says: "When someone tries to delete the row from the other table (master table), prevent deletion *from that other table* (and of course, also don't delete from me, but that's not the main point here)."

RESTRICT is not supported by Microsoft SQL 2012 and earlier.

NO ACTION

NO ACTION and RESTRICT are very much alike. The main difference between NO ACTION and RESTRICT is that with NO ACTION the referential integrity check is done after trying to alter the table. RESTRICT does the check before trying to execute the UPDATE or DELETE statement. Both referential actions act the same if the referential integrity check fails: the UPDATE or DELETE statement will result in an error.

In other words, when an UPDATE or DELETE statement is executed on the referenced table using the referential action NO ACTION, the DBMS verifies at the end of the statement execution that none of the referential relationships are violated. This is different from RESTRICT, which assumes at the outset that the operation will violate the constraint. Using NO ACTION, the triggers or the semantics of the statement itself may yield an end state in which no foreign key relationships are violated by the time the constraint is finally checked, thus allowing the statement to complete successfully.

SET DEFAULT , SET NULL

In general, the action taken by the DBMS for SET NULL or SET DEFAULT is the same for both ON DELETE or ON UPDATE: The value of the affected referencing attributes is changed to NULL for SET NULL, and to the specified default value for SET DEFAULT.

Triggers

Referential actions are generally implemented as implied triggers (i.e. triggers with system-generated names, often hidden.) As such, they are subject to the same limitations as user-defined triggers, and their order of execution relative to other triggers may need to be considered; in some cases it may become necessary to replace the referential action with its equivalent user-defined trigger to ensure proper execution order, or to work around mutating-table limitations.

Another important limitation appears with transaction isolation: your changes to a row may not be able to fully cascade because the row is referenced by data your transaction cannot "see", and therefore cannot cascade onto. An example: while your transaction is attempting to renumber a customer account, a simultaneous transaction is attempting to create a new invoice for that same customer; while a CASCADE rule may fix all the invoice rows your transaction can see to keep them consistent with the renumbered customer row, it won't reach into another transaction to fix the data there; because the database cannot guarantee consistent data when the two transactions commit, one of them will be forced to roll back (often on a first-come-first-served basis.)

CREATE TABLE account (acct_num INT, amount DECIMAL(10,2));

CREATE TRIGGER ins_sum BEFORE INSERT ON account

FOR EACH ROW SET @sum = @sum + NEW.amount;

Example

As a first example to illustrate foreign keys, suppose an accounts database has a table with invoices and each invoice is associated with a particular supplier. Supplier details (such as name and address) are kept in a separate table; each supplier is given a 'supplier number' to identify it. Each invoice record has an attribute containing the supplier number for that invoice. Then, the 'supplier number' is the primary key in the Supplier table. The foreign key in the Invoices table points to that primary key. The relational schema is the following. Primary keys are marked in bold, and foreign keys are marked in italics.

Supplier (**SupplierNumber**, Name, Address, Type)

Invoices (**InvoiceNumber**, *SupplierNumber*, Text)

The corresponding Data Definition Language statement is as follows.

CREATE TABLE Supplier (

SupplierNumber INTEGER NOT NULL,

Name   VARCHAR(20) NOT NULL,

Address   VARCHAR(50) NOT NULL,

Type   VARCHAR(10),

```
     CONSTRAINT supplier_pk PRIMARY KEY(SupplierNumber),

     CONSTRAINT number_value CHECK (SupplierNumber > 0) )

   CREATE TABLE Invoices (

   InvoiceNumber   INTEGER NOT NULL,

   SupplierNumber  INTEGER NOT NULL,

   Text         VARCHAR(4096),

   CONSTRAINT invoice_pk PRIMARY KEY(InvoiceNumber),

   CONSTRAINT inumber_value CHECK (InvoiceNumber > 0),

   CONSTRAINT supplier_fk FOREIGN KEY(SupplierNumber)

     REFERENCES Supplier(SupplierNumber)

     ON UPDATE CASCADE ON DELETE RESTRICT )
```

Unique Key

In database relational modeling and implementation, a unique key is a superkey--that is, in the relational model of database organization, a set of attributes of a relation variable for which it holds that in all relations assigned to that variable, there are no two distinct tuples (rows) that have the same values for the attributes in this set.

When more than one column is combined to form a unique key, their combined value is used to access each row and maintain uniqueness. These keys are referred to as aggregate or compound keys. Values are not combined, they are compared using their data types.

When a column or set of columns is defined as unique to the database management system, the system verifies that each set of values is unique before assigning the constraint. After the column(s) is(are) defined as unique, an error will occur if an insertion is attempted with values that already exist. Some systems will not allow key values to be updated, all systems will not allow duplicates. This ensures that uniqueness is maintained in both the primary table and any relations that are later bound to it.

Summary

Keys provide the means for database users and application software to identify, access and update information in a database table. There may be several keys in any given table. For example, two distinct keys in a table of employees might be employee number and login name. The enforcement of a key constraint (i.e. a uniqueness constraint) in a table is also a data integrity feature of the database. The DBMS prevents updates that would cause duplicate key values and thereby ensures that tables always comply with the desired rules for uniqueness.

Proper selection of keys when designing a database is therefore an important aspect of database integrity.

A relational database table may have one or more available keys (formally called candidate keys). One of those keys per table may be designated the "primary" key, alternatively another key ("surrogate key") may be used. Any remaining keys are called alternate, or secondary, keys. Although mainly used today in the relational database context, the terms primary key and secondary key pre-date the relational model and are also used in other database models.

In relational database terms, a primary key need not differ in form or function from a key that isn't primary and in practice various different motivations may determine the choice of any one key as primary over another. The designation of a primary key may indicate the "preferred" identifier for data in the table, or that the primary key is to be used for foreign key references from other tables or it may indicate some other technical rather than semantic feature of the table. Some languages and software have special syntax features that can be used to identify a primary key as such (e.g. the PRIMARY KEY constraint in SQL).

Any key may consist of one or more attributes. For example, a Social Security Number might be a single attribute key for an employee; a combination of flight number and date might be a key consisting of two attributes for a scheduled flight.

There are several types of unique keys used in database modeling and implementations.

Key Name	Definition
Simple	A key made from only one attribute.
Concatenated	A key made from more than one attribute joined together as a single key, such as part or whole name with a system generated number appended as often used for E-mail addresses.
Compound	A key made from at least two attributes or simple keys, only simple keys exist in a compound key.
Composite	A key containing at least one compound key with at least one other attribute or simple key (this is an extension of a compound key).
Natural	A key made from data that exists outside the current database. In other words, the data is not system generated, such as a social security number imported from another system.
Surrogate	An artificial key made from data that is system assigned or generated when another candidate key exists. Surrogate keys are usually numeric ID values and often used for performance reasons.
Candidate	A key that may become the primary key.
Primary	The key that is selected as the primary key. Only one key within an entity is selected to be the primary key. This is the key that is allowed to migrate to other entities to define the relationships that exist among the entities. When the data model is instantiated into a physical database, it is the key that the system uses the most when accessing the table, or joining the tables together when selecting data.
Alternate	A non-primary key that can be used to identify only one row in a table. Alternate keys may be used like a primary key in a single-table select.
Foreign	A unique key that has migrated to another entity.

At the most basic definition, "a key is a unique identifier", so *unique* key is a pleonasm. Keys that are within their originating entity are unique within that entity. Keys that migrate to another entity may or may not be unique, depending on the design and how they are used in the other table. Foreign keys may be the primary key in another table; for example a PersonID may become the EmployeeID in the Employee table. In this case, the EmployeeID is both a foreign key and the unique primary key, meaning that the tables have a 1:1 relationship. In the case where the person entity contained the biological father ID, the father ID would not be expected to be unique because a father may have more than one child.

Here is an example of a primary key becoming a foreign key on a related table. ID migrates from the Author table to the Book table.

Author Table Schema:

Author(ID, Name, Address, Born)

Book Table Schema:

Book(ISBN, AuthorID, Title, Publisher, Price)

Here ID serves as the primary key in the table 'Author', but also as AuthorID serves as a Foreign Key in the table 'Book'. The Foreign Key serves as the link, and therefore the connection, between the two related tables in this sample database.

In a relational database, a candidate key uniquely identifies each row of data values in a database table. A candidate key comprises a single column or a set of columns in a single database table. No two distinct rows or data records in a database table can have the same data value (or combination of data values) in those candidate key columns since NULL values are not used. Depending on its design, a database table may have many candidate keys but at most one candidate key may be distinguished as the primary key.

A key constraint applies to the set of tuples in a table at any given point in time. A key is not necessarily a unique identifier across the population of all *possible* instances of tuples that could be stored in a table but it does imply a data integrity rule that duplicates should not be allowed in the database table. Some possible examples of unique keys are Social Security Numbers, ISBNs, vehicle registration numbers or user login names.

The relational model, as expressed through relational calculus and relational algebra, does not distinguish between primary keys and other kinds of keys. Primary keys were added to the SQL standard mainly as a convenience to the application programmer.

Unique keys as well as primary keys may be logically referenced by foreign keys, but most RDBMS only allow a foreign key constraint against a primary key.

Defining Primary Keys in SQL

Primary keys are defined in the ANSI SQL Standard, through the PRIMARY KEY constraint. The syntax to add such a constraint to an existing table is defined in SQL:2003 like this:

```
ALTER TABLE <table identifier>

    ADD [ CONSTRAINT <constraint identifier> ]

    PRIMARY KEY ( <column expression> {, <column expression>}... )
```

The primary key can also be specified directly during table creation. In the SQL Standard, primary keys may consist of one or multiple columns. Each column participating in the primary key is implicitly defined as NOT NULL. Note that some RDBMS require explicitly marking primary key columns as NOT NULL.

```
CREATE TABLE table_name (



    ...

)
```

If the primary key consists only of a single column, the column can be marked as such using the following syntax:

```
CREATE TABLE table_name (

    id_col  INT  PRIMARY KEY,

    col2    CHARACTER VARYING(20),

    ...

)
```

Differences between Primary Key Constraint and Unique Constraint:

Primary Key constraint

1. A primary key *cannot* allow null (a primary key cannot be defined on columns that allow nulls).
2. Each table cannot have more than one primary key.
3. On some RDBMS a primary key generates a clustered index by default.

Unique constraint

1. A unique constraint can be defined on columns that allow nulls.
2. Each table can have multiple unique keys.
3. On some RDBMS a unique key generates a nonclustered index by default.

Defining Other Keys in SQL

The definition of other unique keys is syntactically very similar to primary keys.

```
ALTER TABLE <table identifier>
  ADD [ CONSTRAINT <constraint identifier> ]
  UNIQUE ( <column expression> {, <column expression>}... )
```

Likewise, unique keys can be defined as part of the CREATE TABLE SQL statement.

```
CREATE TABLE table_name (
  id_col  INT,
  col2    CHARACTER VARYING(20),
  key_col SMALLINT NOT NULL,
  ...
  CONSTRAINT key_unique UNIQUE(key_col),
  ...
)

CREATE TABLE table_name (
  id_col  INT  PRIMARY KEY,
  col2    CHARACTER VARYING(20),
  ...
  key_col SMALLINT NOT NULL UNIQUE,
  ...
)
```

Note that unlike the PRIMARY KEY constraint a UNIQUE constraint does not imply NOT NULL for the columns participating in the constraint. NOT NULL must be specified to make the column(s) a key. It is possible to put UNIQUE constraints on nullable columns but the SQL standard states that the constraint does not guarantee uniqueness of nullable columns (uniqueness is not enforced for rows where any of the columns contains a null).

According to the SQL standard a unique constraint does not enforce uniqueness in the presence of nulls and can therefore contain several rows with identical combinations of nulls and non-null values — however not all RDBMS implement this feature according to the SQL standard.

Surrogate Keys

In some circumstances the natural key that uniquely identifies a tuple in a relation may be cumbersome to use for software development. For example, it may involve multiple columns or large text fields. In such cases, a surrogate key can be used instead as the primary key. In other situations there may be more than one candidate key for a relation, and no candidate key is obviously preferred. A surrogate key may be used as the primary key to avoid giving one candidate key artificial primacy over the others.

Since primary keys exist primarily as a convenience to the programmer, surrogate primary keys are often used, in many cases exclusively, in database application design.

Due to the popularity of surrogate primary keys, many developers and in some cases even theoreticians have come to regard surrogate primary keys as an inalienable part of the relational data model. This is largely due to a migration of principles from the Object-Oriented Programming model to the relational model, creating the hybrid object-relational model. In the ORM, these additional restrictions are placed on primary keys:

- Primary keys should be immutable, that is, never changed or re-used; they should be deleted along with the associated record.

- Primary keys should be anonymous integer or numeric identifiers.

However, neither of these restrictions is part of the relational model or any SQL standard. Due diligence should be applied when deciding on the immutability of primary key values during database and application design. Some database systems even imply that values in primary key columns cannot be changed using the UPDATE SQL statement.

Alternate Key

Typically, one candidate key is chosen as the primary key. Other candidate keys become alternate keys, each of which may have a unique index assigned to it in order to prevent duplicates (a duplicate entry is not valid in a unique column).

Alternate keys may be used like the primary key when doing a single-table select or when filtering in a *where* clause, but are not typically used to join multiple tables.

Surrogate Key

A surrogate key (or synthetic key, entity identifier, system-generated key, database sequence number, factless key, technical key, or arbitrary unique identifier) in a database is a unique identifier for either an *entity* in the modeled world or an *object* in the database. The surrogate key is *not* derived from application data, unlike a *natural* (or *business*) key which is derived from application data.

Definition

There are at least two definitions of a surrogate:

Surrogate (1) – Hall, Owlett and Todd (1976)

A surrogate represents an *entity* in the outside world. The surrogate is internally generated by the system but is nevertheless visible to the user or application.

Surrogate (2) – Wieringa and De Jonge (1991)

A surrogate represents an *object* in the database itself. The surrogate is internally generated by the system and is invisible to the user or application.

The *Surrogate (1)* definition relates to a data model rather than a storage model and is used throughout this article.

An important distinction between a surrogate and a primary key depends on whether the database is a current database or a temporal database. Since a *current database* stores only *currently* valid data, there is a one-to-one correspondence between a surrogate in the modeled world and the primary key of the database. In this case the surrogate may be used as a primary key, resulting in the term *surrogate key*. In a temporal database, however, there is a many-to-one relationship between primary keys and the surrogate. Since there may be several objects in the database corresponding to a single surrogate, we cannot use the surrogate as a primary key; another attribute is required, in addition to the surrogate, to uniquely identify each object.

Although Hall *et al.* (1976) say nothing about this, others have argued that a surrogate should have the following characteristics:

- The value is unique system-wide, hence never reused.

- The value is system generated.

- The value is not manipulable by the user or application.

- The value contains no semantic meaning.

- The value is not visible to the user or application.

- The value is not composed of several values from different domains.

Surrogates in Practice

In a current database, the surrogate key can be the primary key, generated by the database management system and *not* derived from any application data in the database. The only significance of the surrogate key is to act as the primary key. It is also possible that the surrogate key exists in addition to the database-generated UUID (for example, an HR number for each employee other than the UUID of each employee).

A surrogate key is frequently a sequential number (e.g. a Sybase or SQL Server "identity column", a PostgreSQL or Informix serial, an Oracle or SQL Server SEQUENCE or a column defined with AUTO_INCREMENT in MySQL). Some databases provide UUID/GUID as a possible data type for surrogate keys (e.g. PostgreSQL UUID or SQL Server UNIQUEIDENTIFIER).

Having the key independent of all other columns insulates the database relationships from changes in data values or database design (making the database more agile) and guarantees uniqueness.

In a temporal database, it is necessary to distinguish between the surrogate key and the business key. Every row would have both a business key and a surrogate key. The surrogate key identifies one unique row in the database, the business key identifies one unique entity of the modeled world. One table row represents a slice of time holding all the entity's attributes for a defined timespan. Those slices depict the whole lifespan of one business entity. For example, a table *EmployeeContracts* may hold temporal information to keep track of contracted working hours. The business key for one contract will be identical (non-unique) in both rows however the surrogate key for each row is unique.

Surrogate-Key	Business-Key	EmployeeName	WorkingHour-sPerWeek	RowValidFrom	RowValidTo
1	BOS0120	John Smith	40	2000-01-01	2000-12-31
56	P0000123	Bob Brown	25	1999-01-01	2011-12-31
234	BOS0120	John Smith	35	2001-01-01	2009-12-31

Some database designers use surrogate keys systematically regardless of the suitability of other candidate keys, while others will use a key already present in the data, if there is one.

Some of the alternate names ("system-generated key") describe the way of *generating* new surrogate values rather than the *nature* of the surrogate concept.

Approaches to generating surrogates include:

- Universally Unique Identifiers (UUIDs).

- Globally Unique Identifiers (GUIDs).

- Object Identifiers (OIDs).

- Sybase or SQL Server identity column IDENTITY OR IDENTITY(n,n).

- Oracle SEQUENCE, or GENERATED AS IDENTITY (starting from version 12.1).

- SQL Server SEQUENCE (starting from SQL Server 2012).

- PostgreSQL or IBM Informix serial.

- MySQL AUTO_INCREMENT.

- SQLite AUTOINCREMENT.

- AutoNumber data type in Microsoft Access.

- AS IDENTITY GENERATED BY DEFAULT in IBM DB2.

- Identity column (implemented in DDL) in Teradata.

- Table Sequence when the sequence is calculated by a procedure and a sequence table with fields: id, sequenceName, sequenceValue and incrementValue.

Advantages

Immutability

Surrogate keys do not change while the row exists. This has the following advantages:

- Applications cannot lose their reference to a row in the database (since the identifier never changes).

- The primary or natural key data can always be modified, even with databases that do not support cascading updates across related foreign keys.

Requirement Changes

Attributes that uniquely identify an entity might change, which might invalidate the suitability of natural keys. Consider the following example:

> An employee's network user name is chosen as a natural key. Upon merging with another company, new employees must be inserted. Some of the new network user names create conflicts because their user names were generated independently (when the companies were separate).

In these cases, generally a new attribute must be added to the natural key (for example, an *original_company* column). With a surrogate key, only the table that defines the surrogate key must be changed. With natural keys, all tables (and possibly other, related software) that use the natural key will have to change.

Some problem domains do not clearly identify a suitable natural key. Surrogate keys avoid choosing a natural key that might be incorrect.

Performance

Surrogate keys tend to be a compact data type, such as a four-byte integer. This allows the database to query the single key column faster than it could multiple columns. Furthermore, a non-redundant distribution of keys causes the resulting b-tree index to be completely balanced. Surrogate keys are also less expensive to join (fewer columns to compare) than compound keys.

Compatibility

While using several database application development systems, drivers, and object-relational mapping systems, such as Ruby on Rails or Hibernate, it is much easier to use an integer or GUID surrogate keys for every table instead of natural keys in order to support database-system-agnostic operations and object-to-row mapping.

Uniformity

When every table has a uniform surrogate key, some tasks can be easily automated by writing the code in a table-independent way.

Validation

It is possible to design key-values that follow a well-known pattern or structure which can be automatically verified. For instance, the keys that are intended to be used in some column of some table might be designed to "look differently from" those that are intended to be used in another column or table, thereby simplifying the detection of application errors in which the keys have been misplaced. However, this characteristic of the surrogate keys should never be used to drive any of the logic of the applications themselves, as this would violate the principles of Database normalization.

Disadvantages

Disassociation

The values of generated surrogate keys have no relationship to the real-world *meaning* of the data held in a row. When inspecting a row holding a foreign key reference to another table using a surrogate key, the meaning of the surrogate key's row cannot be discerned from the key itself. Every foreign key must be joined to see the related data item. This can also make auditing more difficult, as incorrect data is not obvious.

Surrogate keys are unnatural for data that is exported and shared. A particular difficulty is that tables from two otherwise identical schemas (for example, a test schema and a development schema) can hold records that are equivalent in a business sense, but have different keys. This can be mitigated by not exporting surrogate keys, except as transient data (most obviously, in executing applications that have a "live" connection to the database).

Query Optimization

Relational databases assume a unique index is applied to a table's primary key. The unique index serves two purposes: (i) to enforce entity integrity, since primary key data must be unique across rows and (ii) to quickly search for rows when queried. Since surrogate keys replace a table's identifying attributes—the natural key—and since the identifying attributes are likely to be those queried, then the query optimizer is forced to perform a full table scan when fulfilling likely queries. The remedy to the full table scan is to apply indexes on the identifying attributes, or sets of them. Where such sets are themselves a candidate key, the index can be a unique index.

These additional indexes, however, will take up disk space and slow down inserts and deletes.

Normalization

Surrogate keys can result in duplicate values in any natural keys. It is part of the implementation to ensure that such duplicates should not be possible.

Business Process Modeling

Because surrogate keys are unnatural, flaws can appear when modeling the business requirements. Business requirements, relying on the natural key, then need to be translated to the surrogate key. A strategy is to draw a clear distinction between the logical model (in which surrogate keys do not appear) and the physical implementation of that model, to ensure that the logical model is correct and reasonably well normalised, and to ensure that the physical model is a correct implementation of the logical model.

Inadvertent Disclosure

Proprietary information can be leaked if sequential key generators are used. By subtracting a previously generated sequential key from a recently generated sequential key, one could learn the number of rows inserted during that time period. This could expose, for example, the number of transactions or new accounts per period. There are a few ways to overcome this problem:

- Increase the sequential number by a random amount.

- Generate a random key such as a uuid.

Inadvertent Assumptions

Sequentially generated surrogate keys can imply that events with a higher key value occurred after events with a lower value. This is not necessarily true, because such values do not guarantee time sequence as it is possible for inserts to fail and leave gaps which may be filled at a later time. If chronology is important then date and time must be separately recorded.

References

- "RDBMS dominate the database market, but NoSQL systems are catching up". DB-Engines.com. 21 Nov 2013. Retrieved 24, August 2020

01

- Grolinger, K.; Higashino, W. A.; Tiwari, A.; Capretz, M. A. M. (2013). "Data management in cloud environments: NoSQL and NewSQL data stores" (PDF). Aira, Springer. Retrieved 8, January 2020

- Don Chamberlin (1998). A Complete Guide to DB2 Universal Database. Morgan Kaufmann. pp. 28–32. ISBN 978-1-55860-482-7

- MySQL AB (2006). MySQL Administrator's Guide and Language Reference. Sams Publishing. p. 40. ISBN 0-672-32870-4

- Martyn Prigmore (2007). Introduction to Databases With Web Applications. Pearson Education Canada. p. 197. ISBN 978-0-321-26359-9

- Jim Melton; Alan R. Simon (2002). SQL:1999: Understanding Relational Language Components. Morgan Kaufmann. p. 53. ISBN 978-1-55860-456-8

- C. Date (2011). SQL and Relational Theory: How to Write Accurate SQL Code. O'Reilly Media, Inc. p. 83. ISBN 978-1-4493-1640-2

- Jim Melton; Jim Melton Alan R. Simon (1993). Understanding The New SQL: A Complete Guide. Morgan Kaufmann pp 145–147 ISBN 978-1-55860-245-8

- Coronel, Carlos (2010). Database Systems: Design, Implementation, and Management. Independence KY: South-Western/Cengage Learning. p. 65. ISBN 978-0-538-74884-1

- Date, Christopher (2003). "5: Integrity". An Introduction to Database Systems. Addison-Wesley. pp. 268–276. ISBN 978-0-321-18956-1

- Steven Feuerstein; Bill Pribyl (2009). Oracle PL/SQL Programming. O'Reilly Media, Inc. pp. 74, 91. ISBN 978-0-596-51446-4

Permissions

All chapters in this book are published with permission under the Creative Commons Attribution Share Alike License or equivalent. Every chapter published in this book has been scrutinized by our experts. Their significance has been extensively debated. The topics covered herein carry significant information for a comprehensive understanding. They may even be implemented as practical applications or may be referred to as a beginning point for further studies.

We would like to thank the editorial team for lending their expertise to make the book truly unique. They have played a crucial role in the development of this book. Without their invaluable contributions this book wouldn't have been possible. They have made vital efforts to compile up to date information on the varied aspects of this subject to make this book a valuable addition to the collection of many professionals and students.

This book was conceptualized with the vision of imparting up-to-date and integrated information in this field. To ensure the same, a matchless editorial board was set up. Every individual on the board went through rigorous rounds of assessment to prove their worth. After which they invested a large part of their time researching and compiling the most relevant data for our readers.

The editorial board has been involved in producing this book since its inception. They have spent rigorous hours researching and exploring the diverse topics which have resulted in the successful publishing of this book. They have passed on their knowledge of decades through this book. To expedite this challenging task, the publisher supported the team at every step. A small team of assistant editors was also appointed to further simplify the editing procedure and attain best results for the readers.

Apart from the editorial board, the designing team has also invested a significant amount of their time in understanding the subject and creating the most relevant covers. They scrutinized every image to scout for the most suitable representation of the subject and create an appropriate cover for the book.

The publishing team has been an ardent support to the editorial, designing and production team. Their endless efforts to recruit the best for this project, has resulted in the accomplishment of this book. They are a veteran in the field of academics and their pool of knowledge is as vast as their experience in printing. Their expertise and guidance has proved useful at every step. Their uncompromising quality standards have made this book an exceptional effort. Their encouragement from time to time has been an inspiration for everyone.

The publisher and the editorial board hope that this book will prove to be a valuable piece of knowledge for students, practitioners and scholars across the globe.

Index